UNDER DARK STARS

RECENT BOOKS BY SATSVARŪPA DĀSA GOSWAMI

- VAISNAVA COMPASSION
- SPLASHES AND SACRED TEXT
- FROM MATTER TO SPIRIT
- EVERY DAY, JUST WRITE, VOLS. 1-19
- CAN A WHITE MAN BE A HARIBOL?
- WRITE & DIE
- WHEN THE SAINTS GO MARCHING IN
- VISITORS
- HUMAN AT BEST
- A POOR MAN READS THE BHAGAVATAM VOL. 4

RECENT ONLINE WRITINGS BY SATSVARŪPA DĀSA GOSWAMI

- VRINDAVANA JOURNAL 2009
- TACHYCARDIA
- THE YELLOW SUBMARINE, MY BHAJANA KUTIR

WWW.SDGONLINE.ORG

Cover artwork paintings by Satsvarūpa dāsa Goswami
Cover design and photo collage by Caitanya Candrodaya dāsa

UNDER DARK STARS

A NOVEL

BY SATSVARŪPA DĀSA GOSWAMI

GN PRESS

Persons interested in the subject matter are invited
to correspond with our Secretary, c/o GN Press, Inc.,
134 Glade Circle West, Rehoboth Beach, DE 19971

ISBN-10: 0-911233-11-3
ISBN-13: 978-0-911233-11-7

GN Press gratefully acknowledges the BBT
for the use of verses and purports
from Srila Prabhupada's books.

For more information about the author and latest publications
please visit:

www.sdgonline.org

Library of Congress Cataloguing-in-Publication Data
Gosvāmī, Satsvarūpa Dāsa, 1939-
Under dark stars/ Satsvarupa dasa Goswami
xii, 308 p. 23 cm. Novel.

1. Spiritual life--International Society for
Krishna Consciousness.--Spiritual Healing I. Title.
BL1285.852 .G667 2004
294.5/512 22
2003023769

CONTENTS

PREFACE

I'm tired of people at book tables picking up one of my books and saying, "This is Satsvarūpa Mahārāja's diary, isn't it?" I ask the booksellers to tell them it's not a diary, but they really don't know what to answer because to them, also, it seems to be a diary. Of course, there's nothing wrong with diaries as a genre, but I want my writing to be clearly a "genre bender," and I think it's becoming more and more so, especially with the addition of more poems and a freeing up of the prose. So let the persona who lives right now in Stuyvesant Falls, New York, remain, but I will try to continue smashing his pretensions, and all pretentiousness. Let us see what Kṛṣṇa and the Muses allow.

ACKNOWLEDGMENTS

The following people helped produce this book:

Dattātreya dāsa — Editor
Caitanya-candrodaya dāsa — Designer
Rādhā-ramaṇa dāsa — Proofreader
Nandarāṇī devī dāsī — Proofreader
Guru dāsa — Proofreader
Śāstra dāsa — Sponsor

I would like to especially thank Śāstra dāsa, who has generously funded the production and printing of this book.

INTRODUCTION

This novel, written in the late winter and spring of 2003, is without a plot. That's all right—plenty of new novels are plotless. But it has plenty of characters. The characters are close to me—like Tim, like Johannes, the organ player, Charlie Chaplin, Father Ted, Giovanni, and Fred. "I" appear also, but not solely. Not even mainly. Don't take it that all this talk is autobiographical. I'm mostly making it up, and that's why it's a novel. But like any novelist, my writing is built on experiences I've been through or something I heard someone else went through.

Someone said I should recommend that my disciples read my "siddhānta books." But all my books are Kṛṣṇa conscious siddhānta. The ones that directly present remembrances of Śrīla Prabhupāda, the ones teaching japa, books like Vaiṣṇava Compassion, and the wilder ones.

Why write the wilder ones? I contend that they are not less potent or less direct in Kṛṣṇa consciousness. They contain my free spirit, the attainment and failure to attain the theological goal—my own soul in my words—I have a right to that. Some people like it very much, but not everyone. I'm writing for those who like the freer expression of an individual groping for his own self-realization. To admit who you are is a most honest form of preaching.

I avoided profanities and explicit sexuality, but there is some down-to-earth rough stuff in these pages. This is the grit we find in the actual world and in the mind of an aspiring devotee. I did not indulge in it but just bore witness to its reality. I trust it won't be frowned upon by gentle yet truth-seeking persons, but there are some hard knocks, ups and downs, "the slings and arrows of outrageous fortune" we're all heir to as long as we're not yet perfect.

And it has art. We need art. Art is good for us. The creative urge. We need Kṛṣṇa conscious artists—thus, the many characters, fictional vignettes and subpersons in this book written under dark stars.

— Satsvarūpa dāsa Goswāmī

CHAPTER ONE

Welcome back. All personae, fall in! I want everyone to be happy. The critics cut your throat. But John is above, inured to it. Great.

Astrology, astronomy. Tim wanted to know what "stars" he was under, what "phase" he was going through. He had never consulted such figures before, but now he wanted to. His friend Bimla, who never did anything without consulting an astrologer, said, "Youse should go to a guy I know on 4th St., he's a paisan. Bigga moustache. He's gotta his own way. Don'na use computers or nothin like dhat. He communes (commutes even) directly with da stars."

"How can I believe?" asked Tim.

"Ain't dhat what the nondevotees and you yourself are always askin?"

"Yeah, but then we say, 'I believe because it's in the śāstra and Swami told me.'"

"Dhat's okay, we astrologers, we gotta our own *paramparā*. Youse gotta nothin to lose. It's pure vegetarian and plenny of Kṛṣṇas go dhare."

"Well, that's hardly a recommendation. Kṛṣṇa people nowadays often get into loony things."

"So why not you, Tim? You is loony, right?"

"Yeah, I'm okay. Where is that? 33rd and 4th St.?" He slapped hands with his buddy and headed downtown thinking, "What the hell? I've got nothing to lose and something to gain."

He met the man Giovanni, who was just as his friend described. "You do astrology?"

"Yeah, how mucha you wanna pay?"

"Five bucks. My grandfather was from Naples. My name" (shows passport) "is Tim Dimaggio."

"You don'na look Italian at all."

"Not even my nose?"

Giovanni was a cafī owner, but vegetarian—yeah, an Italian vegetarian cafe—but some anisette and spumoni ice cream. Great bread. And pasta! Mama mia!

"No meat, huh?"

"No meat. Okay, five-a bucks. Now tell me, whaddis your birthdate, time of birth, and year?"

Tim told him. "I want to know what to expect for the next few years in my life. I seem to be running into trouble and as close to it as I ever did in my life. I always seem to be under the influence of dark inauspicious stars. People used to say, 'Dimaggio is a good guy. Oh, you're lucky if you know him.'"

Giovanni stroked his beard. He sat down. He frowned. He looked up at Tim as if he were his son. "I tink I know you from a time and racial links. Was your fadder a policeman?"

"Yes!" Tim shouted. "He retired as a precinct captain."

"Yeah, and he retired from da U.S. Army as a Captain too. Pretty brave guy. But you and he no getta along good. Dhatsa too bad. And dhat may be throwing tings off for you now."

"Huh?"

"You gotta spiritual master, right, Tim?"

"Yeah, Prabhupāda."

"Do you love him? Are you close to him? Do you follow your rules? Is he pleased with you?" Giovanni was speaking warmly from the heart, not accusing.

"I…don't…know…for sure," said Tim, and tears started coming from his eyes.

Giovanni: "Do you chanta your 16 rounds every day?"

Tim: "No, I've got generalized anxiety disorder."

"Whatsa dhat? It stoppa you from chanting?"

Tim didn't want to talk anymore. He was impressed by Giovanni's powers of insight but thought it would be too hard—and he did not want to tell him the whole history of his illness.

"Here's the five dollars. I can't talk more. Maybe I'll come back another time."

"No, you keepa da money. I understand. Dhis is painful stuff.

I'd like to talk to you another time though, anytime you want to come by. I also knew your granddad, Frank."

"God!"

"His wife was Teresa. You see? I know alotta about you. I can help. Don'na be afraid to cry. You came here and cried, and you can come and cry again. We will cry together. And I will pray to understand what you can do with your dark stars. You're right, you're under the worst stars you have ever been under."

Was you ever in trouble with
this man? Even steal his jacket?
And share jail cell
with him for
political reasons to get
rid of the Brits?
He wants to know if he's
going to bed. I mean heaven
(Goloka) at death. He fought
hard against the gang.

Oh my dears?
Have some tea.
I'd be protected by God
no matter what happens

under dark stars.
People have been tortured and kept
their faith.

Meeney mooey they sing people
uplifted by the misuse of
the music of the soul's suffering.

Through suffering you gain peace.

Chant your *japa* three billion
behind. The astrologer can't

tell you much:
"give a black cow in charity to the
farm." He's
afraid of losing my skin.

You look like Michael Jackson
and Boris Karloff of "Frankenstein."
No straightforward. Only five
minutes to make a
shapely *daṇḍavats* and tell truth. I will
tell the truth.

You can be the friend
of one but not another?
Why not just keep away?

I hear skunks in the attic.
I'm afraid
five minutes.
I'm happy when safe alone.

Be always safe
in Kṛṣṇa's hands.
He will be happy with

my daddy and I'll be
a grown man too
and the *jīva* soul
gone through the fire.
"All that matters
is that you've gone through the fire."

Tim was growing bold, even though he was already in or about to enter a dark phase. He had also been the cowering one in childhood, and even in dreams, but now in his nightmares one gang attacked Gītā-nagarī and Tim flew at them with his fists, kicking like a Hollywood hero. "Phone 911!" he shouted to the other timid devotees. "We aren't getting any police or fire department help. They're going to topple down the tallest tree!" But Tim swung and moved into the gang like Joe Louis[1] gone wild.

Someone said that for the past year Tim had been acting uninhibited. Someone said, "Your writing used to be desperate, near hopeless, but you would always pull through with prayers and cries to God, giving the readers courage. And it was authentic. Now, however, that spirit has waned and you seem defeated. You don't even cry out. You just tell of what you do in a day—feed the cat, go for a walk, get headaches—*where is the spiritual cry!* Can you imagine Trane[2] without his spiritual cry?" Some didn't agree and said Tim was still good except a bit more self-assertive, and that was fine.

Anyway, one day Timmy was eating his supper and his friend Daryl visited and sat beside him. Later Daryl's wife came in and said she needed the car keys, she was going home. She was a beautiful woman. Daryl had told him that she was half Italian-American. So spontaneously, the usually shy Tim said, "Hey Nina, I hear youse half Italian." (Timmy's American-Italian accent was a carefully studied imitation of Chico Marx's. Perhaps Chico Marx was not even Italian himself, but as a Hollywood actor had developed a good pseudo-ginzo accent. Tim's imitation of Chico Marx was good. It made people laugh; it sounded real but exaggerated.)

"Are you really a paisan? You don'na look like one, and you don'na talk like one." Daryl and Nina laughed, but a little uneasily. Bold Tim.

"Can you make a good pasta?"

"Oh yes," said Daryl in earnest.

Tim said, "Did you ever read John Fante's Odyssey of a Wop? He spoke of the prejudicial hardships of growing up as a wop in Colorado. Do you know what the word "wop" stands for?"

"No," said Nina, going with the flow but not so delighted.

"'WOP' means 'Without Papers.' When the Italians came to Ellis Island, they almost never had visas or official papers. But since they looked like strong workers and the women seemed nice and pious, the immigration authorities let them in but stamped on the card 'WOP.' Yes, that's how it came about, but then it became the worst word for them, like 'nigger.' Sometime, if you and Daryl invite me, I'd like to taste your spaghetti. I like it with lots of ground mozzarella cheese, like my dad and granddad served. No wine, though, huh? He winked; end of routine. They laughed and complimented him and Nina quickly exited with the keys.

Yeah, Chico Marx is the man for the Italian-American accent. Tim loved him. Sometimes would you like to watch Marx Brothers videos with me? "A Night at the Opera" is the best. There's a wop accent exchange between Chico, Groucho, and an Italian family of twelve that's the best in all the Marx Brothers movies.

"Is this what critics mean when they say your spiritual writing is waning?" asked Daryl, who knew about the criticism.

"I dunno. I believe that if people think the writing's terrific, regardless of subject, they will say, '*That was done by a Hare Kṛṣṇa person*,' and the Lord will get all the credit."

Hey man, dark clouds could blow away quick
in Ireland. Any place, Italy
is good. Anywhere is Vṛndāvana if you're a pure devotee.

You need some *tapas*. I don't
have much here except my mission.
If I hurt you, just tell me and
I'll communicate or not.

Oh he sounds so *nice*
put stuff in his letter
like I'm going to the dentist
I'm getting two cats
and a room for painting.

I read from your statement on nurturing
and therapy and they jeered.
Thanks for the prayers.
I appreciate you're not

mean, like so-and-so.

You call that a letter or a come-on or put-on?
"I gotta twelve children, six are gone into your
automatic beds!" Groucho:
"How much do you earn a week?"
Fat man: "$25."
Groucho:
"How could you afford twelve kids at $25 a week?"

The dope goes back to his wife (she's twice his size) and says, "The man says I could only afford six children."

She belts him in the mouth
and throws herself down on a bed
wailing out the names
of the "missing" children.
Fiorello! Maria! etc.
They turn on the machine
and the kids come out
from the automatic bed.

Fat ginzo: "Are you makin funna my accent?"
Chico: "No, I'm Italian too, from Naples!"
A Hare Kṛṣṇa did this.

Tim went back to see Gio. It was a dreary, rainy night. But inside the cafī, all was aglow. People were feasting at the cafī tables, drinking their nonalcoholic drinks, and jazz music was playing live on the bandstand and sometimes on the juke box in this vegetarian—What? No meatballs?—Italian cafī of Giovanni Sciortino.

"So, youva come back," Giovanni smiled openly to his "son" Tim. "How cumma you gotta this name, Tim, if your passport says Taddeo?" Gio asked.

Tim said, "I'm Irish on my mother's side, and that's my middle name, so my mother insisted I be called Tim."

"Dhatsa all right," said Gio, patting Tim, "especially in the 1920s the Italianos and the Irish used to marry, you know?

Dhey would come as immigrants to America and had similar ethos and seemed to getta together. There are many such marriages."

"Yes, they're both Catholics," said Tim.

Giovanni said, "Now dhare's Mary—my favorite—she would'av been your favorite aunt, too. Dhare's Josephine, who lost part of her finger in a factory, butta nice lady. And by da way, all dhese ladies married Italian men. Sister Mary married a man named Sal Sessa, who worked in a clothing pressing place. He had a Jewish boss. Dhen dhare's da old brudder Ralph. Ralph wassa wild man. He used to smoke cigars all da time and go out drinkin. He was not a domestic man who would stay at home wid his wife. He always used the expression, I'm gonna flya da coop. He saw himself like a pigeon in a coop unless he could summa da time jus leave home, family responsibilities, and go off widda whores and da bars and wherever his big Italian schnaz would lead him. The other brudder is your fadder, Sansone, the Army man, policeman. I already told you whadda great man he was. Unfortunately, you two split. But I'm'a hopin dhare'sa way dhat even after death you can come back again together and dhis may solva your problems. Listen carefully. Hmm," mused Giovanni, "I tink dhat's all. Oh no. Dare wassa young Uncle Jim. Your father used to say he was a Marxist or a crazy man, anarchist. He wore his hair long and he used to listen to da opera. Quite different dhan da other brudders. He was kind to da younger nephews. I'm gettin summa dhis mixed up, but don'na mind. I do know dhare wassa five brothers. Your fadder is being one. And he, Sansone, used to say, 'Iffa dhese brothers weren't so scatterbrained, iffa dhey could only organiza dhemselves, dhey could make a bigga truckin firm, Dimaggio Truck, and make millionza dollars.' He putta da blame on Ralph, because he was da senior brother and he was always tryin to fly da coop when he could have been organizin a bigga truckin company. I'm sure if Sansone were able to take the responsibility, he woulda done it well. So dhat's it. Five brudders, two sisters."

Giovanni continued, "I know dhem only on the psychic

plain, and da same with your grandparents, Teresa and Frank. Frank, he hadda bigga white moustache. He wassa bigga man. Not fat, but bigga. Bigga belt with brass buckle, bigga white moustache, bigga white hair. I see in my mind one picture of you in his arms. You're a little white-haired boy, and he'sa white-haired also, and you're just maybe a few months old, and he'sa huggin you. A very precious picture. Too badda it's lost, along wid so many udder things. So I guess he really didn't know you, 'cept as anudder one of da offspring. But you mustav inherited a lot of tings from him. Memories of wine barrels in the cellar and big chunks of cheese and the big feasts where he used to say, 'Manje manje,' to all the family gathered at the table. You don'na remember your grandpa?"

Tim: "Yes, I do remember some of the things you said, but there was no grandmother that I remember."

Giovanni: "No, she wassa dead by dhen…Okay, so dhis issa small talk. But now, whad about dhis dark phase you passin through? You gotta any new ideas?"

Tim: "The stars say I'm about to be ruined, but I don't know what to do to stop it. I've always been a good boy and people have taken advantage of me for that, but they like me. But the stars are indicating changes are coming."

Giovanni: "And?"

Tim: "I'm thinking maybe I can take some advantage in this dark sky. I may have to suffer for the first time. People will think poorly of me, but as a result I get some kind of purification. I become a real person."

Giovanni: "Youse reading my own mind. Dhese thoughts you're gettin, dhere actually comin from me, which is comin from the stars. Tell me what else."

"Well, as I told you, nothing bad has happened, but I see some storm clouds, so I was making contingency plans."

"Dhatsa good idea. Jus like da Germans made so many contingency plans to start war. Italy did too, but dhey were on da wrong side. United States make alotsa plans, maybe not as many plans as da Germans, but da Americans are special and dhey made it up. Dhey work hard. 'Praise the Lord and pass da ammunition and we'll all be free.' And so dhey finally beat da shit outta da Germans. Great history! Your dad was in da Army, huh?"

"Yes, he was, and I was too, but I didn't like it. I was an anti-war man."

"Ah, youse kids. But I know whatchu mean. War is not a good ting either."

Giovanni waved to a waiter. He and Tim were seated at one of the tables. The cafī was crowded. He asked for two Italian lassi drinks to be brought over and asked Tim what else he would like. "Nothing else, I'm not very hungry. I just want to hear from you."

Giovanni said, "Bring me a bigga Italian sandwich with cheese, tomato, lettuce, some udda things you tink of, some olives. But no meat. And offer it all to Gaura-Nitai in the kitchen.

"Most important ting," Giovanni said, "is to pray to Kṛṣṇa, 'Jesus' as dhey call Him in Italiano, God da Fadder. It'sa all the same. You gotta pray to Him to be made humble. All dhat matters is dhat you can walk through da fire. So, if you gotta fire ahead, you gotta walk through, my son. Dhat's all. Jus take awhatsa comin. If da clouds fall down on you, dhen you say, 'Okay, Kṛṣṇa had dhat comin for me. It'sa my fate.' If people speak lies against you, jus take it. Whadda Lord Jesus say? You remember? As a little boy? You wassa Christian, right? I tink you still a Christian. Whadda He say?"

Tim: "He said many things, but He said, 'If somebody slaps you on the left cheek, then turn the other cheek to him.'"

"Ah yes. A very hard thing to follow. And whadda else?"

"He said, 'Lord, forgive us our sins, just as we forgive those who make sins against us.' And in a special prayer to Mary he said, 'Holy Mary, mother of God, pray for us sinners now and at the end of death.'"

Giovanni: "So is dhat all dhare is to it? You jus remaina passive and pray to God?"

"No, I have to do things too. I think I did some things wrong."

Giovanni: "You can't dodge da karma. You jus see what happens. But pray to Kṛṣṇa to give you strength. You cry da tears, you accept the lashings, like Lord Jesus did, and you say, 'Lord, dhey don' know what dhey doing. Please forgive dhem.' And you say His last eight words."

"What was that?"

"Somethin like, 'Now I give up My spirit, now dhat's done, I commend myself to Thee.' You give yourself to Kṛṣṇa at the end. He will forgive you, no matter whatchu did. If you go down in worldly history as a cheater, dhatsa one thing; but if Kṛṣṇa knows in your heart dhatchu tried your best, especially to make up for wrongs, and dhatchu were humble, dhen He'll remember you and forgive you.

"And dhatsa why I say most important, you gotta start chanting Hare Kṛṣṇa better. Yestaday you say you chanted no rounds. I dunno how much medicine you gotta take to avoid dhis pain, but you gotta keep chanting too. Now da weather'sa turning nice, you getta up early, chant; dhen in da afternoon go out on da veranda in da sun"—Giovanni sighed—"an' go on chanting Kṛṣṇa's names even if it seems mechanical. Dhatsa not exactly an astrological reading, is it, my son?" He smiled, some big spaces between his teeth and the smell of garlic emanating pleasantly toward Tim.

Tim was going to ask how come a Vaiṣṇava chewed garlic, but he knew there were a number of discrepancies in Giovanni's presentation. After all, it was a cafī and had to succeed financially. He didn't ask Giovanni what sampradāya he was in, or Vedic questions like that. He listened to his own heart and felt there was good advice.

Tim: "Hey Giovanni, tink I ought to try talkin widda 'Talian accent too?"

Giovanni: "What! Dhatsa ridiculous. You jus talk like you wuz raised. New York City. City College. Now you a-bigga scholar, huh? Devotees ask you, 'Hey, where'sa your New Yorkese?' Dhey don'na hear you say, 'I gotta aska my muther if I can go out.' Your muther taught you before you go out, watch your de's, do's, and dhem's. You wuzza good boy and did dhat, and now your language issa clean. So why go back and speak like a wop?" Giovanni laughed warmly and gave Tim another hug.

"So you see, I'm no astrologer or seer. Dhat boy who told you dhat, he'sa justa bluffin. He like me cuz I run a vegetarian cafī and I chanta Hare Kṛṣṇa every Saturday night here. We gotta big group. You come too. And remember da things I say. Dhen you be doin all right. No matter what happens it'll turn out all right."

"The most important thing is, you've got to walk through the fire," thought Tim as he lay in bed that night.

What are the ethics of war in self-defense? Is it better to allow yourself to be eaten by a giant grizzly or escape him? Should you kill him? There are ways. The Cardinal pulled the gun trigger. "No," I argued with Doris, "nothing justifies killing."

But it is inevitable. When the Redcoats entered the town, our worthy Minutemen grabbed their muskets and fought and the U.S.A. was born. Thorny questions. The pacifists would refuse to fight. There would be no war. The Iraqi tank shells bounced off the sides of the thicker U.S.A. tanks. But Harry S. Truman did the best act for avoiding street fighting in Japan. He dropped the big egg.

What did you want, Lord? You insisted that Arjuna kill his own relatives. But that was a good thing. You told Yudhishthira to lie, "Ashvatthama is dead." And you advised Arjuna to kill Karna while his wheel was stuck in the mud.

"These are not the proper military ethics!" shouted Karna.

"Since when did you observe ethics? ... At the time when you tried to disrobe Draupadī and undo her hair during her menstrual period?"

"Get him!"

It may cool over.

The room is silent again. Take shelter of Kṛṣṇa and He will control. You try to be a good boy to whatever happens, react honorably.

We waited honestly on the
street corner but the bus
never arrived. No one lived in the house near
by; the rain poured but we could not enter the house;
it was locked and not ours.

The bus stopped in the garden—
can we get the man to
come and see our Kṛṣṇa visionary garden?
I'm so far away now. How can
I paint? The American flag has
thirteen stars and will never have more.

Can I go back to Ireland and
live in the quiet house?
"Is your ankle any better? Do you like
those new shorts I brought you?"

Ask your friends. Violence—
threat. Say I should not be—
saving the killers round them
up. God how are you controlling this world?
I wouldn't want
to do it. He is a very smart
man. He cried, he cried. I would,
ah, hell with it.
Do your homework and the chips
will fall. You'll be on God's side.

Yeah, it was good.
I tasted mud. God took me in His arms
and now you know a little what it's like.

Stay away from those places.

Put him behind the bars
with Laurel and Hardy.
YOU will kill me.

2

CHAPTER TWO

I knew a girl who contested with me regarding the meaning of "histrionics." I heard that a certain guy was called histrionic for being a dramatic person, the opposite of a civil, soft-spoken, democratic citizen. Is that the right meaning?

She said she'd get me a St. Bridget's cross, but then decided not to. "I believe in all religions," said John. I like the sound of it, but that's like *yata mata tata patha*, "all paths are correct." Śrīla Prabhupāda says if you buy a ticket to Detroit, you're not going to wind up in San Francisco. It's not all the same.

If you worship Durgā for a car, or Uma for a wife charming, or Kṛṣṇa for devotional service to Him—thousands of different paths. St. Teresa of Avila said most people pray for that which if they've got, they'd soon be in tears of misery. Don't know *what* to pray for, said Rev. Gary Davis. Śrīla Prabhupāda replies, "That I may love You."

You is completely different, high brow,
low. Offensive and pleasing.
So Johannes scaled the wall.
And I am a human being.

Mid-January. The Freudians track down the libido, that's their game. Well, I've gone, I admit. I imagine, we've already imagined.

O Lord of Hosts.

O King of Advils. O supporter of both meds and male counselor. O writer to a friend who commutes from Australia to India. And a friend who is happy in peaceful sleep and who often doesn't know if it's day or night and misplaces his pants. In "The Idle Rich," Charles Chaplin played two parts. The aristocrat preens himself to meet his wife, forgot nothing—but to put his pants on!

'Tis not persiflage. 'Tis the story of Us as planned, to going on roller skates on weak ankles as well as the histrionic showoffs, boy and girl together. I find my own merriment.

But are you praying, and for what? Ten faxes an hour to frosty and warm people. Now you'd better stop because everything runs by the clock. No, I still have time. This express ain't moving till the Lord wills it.

"Show me your Lord," said Dr. Kovoor. Bring Him into the hall. Haṁsa smashed him, and Śrīla Prabhupāda made him a guru in return. Ill-fated, but that was something that had to be in the life of Hari-kīrtana Ṭhākura, whose name I sang in a *kīrtana*, just as he sang mine, lowlife, short-timer sailors.

Never Forget
He's one of the most important
people in this book because
he broke the dead end of bebop.

No one came to unlock
the secrets of the Sanskrit language.
Fred is behind doors not
receiving visitors. He doesn't
dress in uniform.

There is no girl with him.
Suddenly he remembers
he's forgetting Kṛṣṇa. Above
all the rules and regulations.

sva-kathāṁ kṛṣṇa. Forget
the spiritual master, don't obey his
rules and you are off the
screen. No one knows
where you are.

I doubt that I care
enough. Now you are blabbing.
"He's in the dark night
of the soul."

And it's such an easy thing
and you have allowed it. They
gave you Ensure to drink.

Oh boy, guacamole and fritters
and corn fries and crackers and
humor CD.

Forgetfulness. He can't sink back
     into the religious beginning. "I'm
not so great on *śāstras*." Well
I was.

Do you think you're so deep into
psychic recall? I don't see you
crying. "Why do you cry?" she asked
and I didn't reply. Leave it open.
Maybe it's because I lost
my editor.

Maybe I just feel some pity for myself
like "nobody knows the trouble
I've seen…but Jesus"—a point from which to seek love of
God for *His* sake.

It's a lie, I don't cry. I did when TKG died and that morning when I blubbered over all my losses. Cry for loss.

Oh boy, guacamole and
corny jokes. No talk on
good dames.
The drum is too harsh.

Manager all day long. You can wake up with another headache, take suds head bath, Radox and *go on with your work* (you silly Vanguard) have a streak taste for "passion" and you'd like to dovetail it into the electronic and telephone age. He'd rather talk on the phone or manage GN Press than write a concentrated paragraph.

You don't want to expose yourself as having nothing to say. You thought you would escape through the Gorki Park of "DIARY" and the dark night. You found a fantasy, even if it was not a funny one. It's not Sergeant Bilko.[3] It's chemicals and worries and waiting for the guy who never called up from New Delhi. Start your own political party, get a thousand votes. Your face looks like JFK but you are right wing. This actually happened. He found football and rock music offensive, but America loves it.

Obscure poetry, rats. Where's the story of rats? Who came up with the story of Groucho's movie? It was "suggested" by a story of Antoine Stravininan. Why are the girls so beautiful? Don't be a fool. They carefully pick them out; it's called audition, or meat market. They fall in love with them. Whoo-whee. That last dream was a whopper, but I recovered in time for the phone call from India; but he never called. That's okay, there's always another chance to talk and inspire. I'm the impresario of encouraging, with my feet and eyes that see double lately.

A dream in which the poor cat needed surgery, but gobs of other cats and dogs were chasing him. My mother was suddenly in the car with us and said we must take him to a veterinarian even if it costs $7,000. But we were in a neighborhood of warehouses and no vets to be found.

If you're going to fantasize, I mean if they just come down upon you without your asking, why don't you have fantasies that Kṛṣṇa comes up beside you and says, "Stop the persiflage and histrionics. From now on I want you to talk with angels of *bhakti*." Why doesn't it happen to me like that?

She threw herself down on the floor of her nun's cell. The superior came in and said, "I order you under the vow of submission to stand up and fight." She did so but wanted that vision badly, the way Nārada wanted back his vision of Kṛṣṇa. He only *heard* Kṛṣṇa saying, "You won't see Me again in this lifetime, but you can hear Me and preach plenty." In between headaches he pesters people. Johannes was determined. He had a part-time job just so he could spend money on his own menu at home and not take any non-vegetarian food from his parents or even use their pots. They thought he'd gone crazy but they'd hang in there with him so he wouldn't leave home. Gertrude followed her brother. They became cool siblings and didn't try to preach to their parents. They just went about their own bare minimum, like soft chanting of japa, sixteen rounds. How many have you done today?

WAITING FOR THE BOOTS

You'd never leave me, would you?
Somebody's got to nurture a person
you mean breastfeed?

No? Drinking beer together at
the Standard or in the woods?
No, I mean a six-pack of cigarettes.
We were cut off and didn't know
anything. Bad opinions on everyone.
You kept your secret. "I hear
you disappear into the Village
over the weekend."

No, I am not. I've just got
this mistress, my English prof.
And I always keep it a secret.

Grub, I want to hear what's
been happening in your gut
since you joined the Hare Kṛṣṇa movement.
It's a machine shame when the
speaker breaks down just
as you try to spread cheer.

In India "the world of Hare
Kṛṣṇa" regularly loses power before a thousand villagers
so turn on the generator

and the show goes on.

Try to sell books and make recruits.
Tell them the world isn't exactly
round, Meru-peaked, hellish, many
planets, I'm not so good at it. Go
talk to Sadāpūta.

She asked him a question:
How come you're so sure
you're right if the scientists
are always wrong? What's so special
about these ancient books
where people
have a thousand heads?
He's got a snappy answer because
he's been doing the circuit,
is faithful and his own man—
his answer is so technical it's
over their heads.

We've got everything we need.
The altar's full of *mūrtis.*
Baladeva changes the clothes.
I pick out the clothes.
In my privacy I pray in
a special Urdu language only I
understand. It's called Patnoi and Urbu.

Yes yes they will send for you
we will send slippers and sneakers
tie-up boot style and then this
adjustment will make you happy.

It's all right. She said, "Read some of it to me, it must be different." Yes, Fred just uncapped, but this isn't a masquerade party—but neither did it happen. Wonderful title of Stafford's poem collection: Stories That Might Have Happened—the ink spurts out all over the page like a Rorschach test. What does he see? The map of Ireland. A target for nukes being planned in the general's room. Just patches of wet ink.

He keeps telling more people the nature of his illness. Dear folks, come to the ball game; the mothers' club den party for cubs and their bosomy den mothers who bend over to offer the kids a cookie from the tray.

The boxer dog who rushed out of the house and attacked our Mickey. Mickey's curly tail finally uncurled and he ran home humiliated. Gosh, a boxer is a powerful dog!

The birdie robin in our yard.
I will not be happy living alone
with you everything that you are takes
better care of me. Take your medicine
fool! I HAVE YET TO HEAR
YOU PRAY and you have been
up an hour! Schmuck.

Wednesday night horror show.
It will not last long.
He will not have to sing the
bird pecks on your shoulder and
squeaks for seeds and ladhus.

She likes being with Fred
goshes Dondi we were on the
same piece of track as we were in Detroit—there's Grand
Central Station

Do you know what to do now
to keep from being mugged,
going to the subways?
I hope you don't flinch
from some unintelligent move.

That God work kicks at you
in the dining room of the
grim house and you'll never forget
you had a softer plea
for service.

It's for the gun. Some other.
Yeah, but I can't do it in my way with
some prizes in it.

She's like my sister.
She's my
Madeline, who I so much loved.
How bothersome and square the parents are.

And what she learned at Hunter
College. But I was miles ahead in knowing
what to write and leave the *karmī* world—
they would never dare, afraid
they'd wind up in a shack
like Charlie Chaplin so they worshipped
money and regular
subtle life for the goals
one can venture.

We stopped our intimacy just,
you and me
even our best moments when we Catholic siblings watched the horror show on Wednesday and I gave her a little protection in between laughs.

They choose to remain unmarried, dedicated to dis-entanglements from the opposite sex. It saves so much time. Pure and simple. Nurtured by the Lord Himself and His mission. Yes, he's a male human being, but he doesn't need "it" because it's an insignificant thing, and one is better off without it. That's *sannyāsa* talk. I fit in there, in that big doghouse-like structure, the writing shed, with the sign, "Danger—beware of bull" tacked to the outside wall.

"I think I have understood myself right," said Zed, as he peeled potatoes and onions, "and it's just a matter of sticking to my guns." When you hear "sweet lelani, heavenly flower," don't think it's an invitation to embrace a lover in a secluded place (condemned by *Bhāgavatam* as being chained). Lelani is the name of the flower, and it reminds him of the Lord. All women, children, men and dogs respected alike. Leave me mostly alone.

RELAXING

You may invite your friends
to hear "Relaxin' at Camarillo"
where Bird[4] recovered and think of
recovering yourself here or the
year of taking it easy.

Squeaky. Yes spanky. The monks
have a good time realizing
self-humorously they are not saints.

But they take seriously the proposition that it's "hands off"
and love is saved for
the divine Lord. Above the sex tussle
that's an eternal fire of devotion. Thump—thump
his heart is
steady, steady in failing and
success. Keep your nose to the
flag of *bhakti*. And also
don't forget to *honor* French
toast. Don't eat it like
a dog and talk of your food
as if it's all prepared for you.

It will work out in time.
It will happen.

Hare Kṛṣṇa the matrix of all eastern
spirituality in the 1960s and with me now
in '03.

Moon Mullins got his notes ready to talk with the doctor. Nothing much new. How long will I live? Doc can't tell. King Khaṭvāṅga wanted to know that information to get his affairs in order. Say last prayers and try to drop garbage in ballast. It can be anywhere, anytime. Drop drop. Keep hearing the same lecture tape over and over. It was important. People are after new cars, women, but not concerned with the most important thing: *Where do I go when I die?* So Bhāgavatam tells it and Lord Caitanya manifests, Lord Nityananda manifests the easiest method.

Oh but it sounds sectarian. Don't think like that. Sing praises of worship, have high domes like the Cathedral of the Holy Bean-shooter on Comm Avenue, Boston. Look up at gargoyles. Some buildings have nothing but a pyramid. See God (minus speculation) everywhere. The all-powerful, all-loving pursues me everywhere...balderdash. This is one of your problems. You don't believe in your dogmas. But you were born into this world with them at 26 years old, like Dumbo dropped into the lap of his mother. At least hear it out and know that is your biggest problem. Not libido, not lack of self-assertion, migraine, but weak faith. If you can straighten out some material problems, maybe the spiritual ones will go too.

THE LITTLE RED ROBIN

Lady bird robin is our friend
picks ladhus out of seeds, has a sweet beak.

All videos used up, all persons defective sit by the roadside.
I'm okay. This is nothing to worry
about. Oh ya!

You have heard rumors and
seen meteors flash in the night
rehearsed your play with
twenty actors in the hotel recreation hall and then
it went on without a flaw.
The good guys and women
won. Don't quote corny
clichīs. Grope out there for something new.

Oh feel your truth. I
won a jeep in a migraine raffle.
I rattled my grandfather's sword.
I was born too early for the wars
and got into the bean movement
with emphasis on collecting money.

You think Kṛṣṇa is just going
to bring it on a silver platter?
Wait.
Don't con people.
Groucho didn't wait and he
didn't have a minute to spare because
the house dicks were beating down the door.

Had a bogus suicide awaiting them. And then Harpo
fell out of the closet
with a knife stabbed in his chest and a suicide note.
They prayed to God for best destiny
of the souls but the *karmīs*
were restless. They just wanted
their money as soon as possible.

Lady bird sat on my shoulder and squeaked for ladhus
and seeds.
We won't deny you, although your voice
isn't so sweet. You pray
to God Almighty the

sweet Kṛṣṇa Parameśvara—
can You help this little
mighty mouse
recover from his cold and
his laying in his bed? Just send
him out on a mission/as you used to.

Thank you God, amen. You mean some "younger" person is going to give you back your faith in Lord Gaura? What cat is going to get you excited to the reality of Nṛsiṁhadeva? No gods but these. He scared his sheep. He went to bed early, after watching the others. Oh no, hilarious, *Father Ted*[5] banned in Ireland.

Imagine a satire on ISCKON. Could it be that far-fetched? They called him a racist because he had made a comic impersonation of a Chinese person while Chinese persons were looking in the window.

Would you be the same scriptwriter? Could you think of forming scenes and ironies? No. Just this scrub-a-dub.

"Write more about Prabhupāda," said my doctor. Prabhupāda was an army general, chief of staff. Led the war against *māyā*. Could yet chastise his own troops until they cried; "Rascals, buffalo-brain." He was annoyed with them.

Dumped his best disciple. No, she dumped him. Astounding, because she gradually noticed he was writing about his self, art, writing and not so much about Kṛṣṇa Himself. Did he ever believe? Did he go to Mass?

Waning, dwindling, hell no. Just give me a little sleep. I'll break the mystery case and come to understand we have to live in the cold for being honest. It's worth it. Still, bring him tea.

A PRIEST GOES TO BED

Now's the time to go to bed
with eyes open a bigger
cocktail to help you sleep.

And not wake up so quick. You take

it yet? No. I took milk
ice cream and bread and Wheaties
and wrote no facts.

They know, however,
he's a nut.
Believes any rumors by hearsay. Where's
the dogma? He's supposed
to be part of it.

Contained, yet wild. I can't write
it. I look at it, the expanse of sea
(photo taken from helicopter)
then down to the
old sod and fenced pastures
of Ireland and an old
stone rectory where some Catholic priests live and are
waiting in the crowded, small church
for the Mass to begin on time.

Open with the *kīrtana* and open
the curtain singing *saṁsāra-dāvā* sometimes someone
is full of devotion,
most of these things are elsewhere.

But just drop the worry
and take it across the line to the island.
They'll think of something
sincere and pleasant enough to
believe
the main belief in God
when he learned from his swami.

He is in accord and ready for bed now.
Please apply cream
between his crotch.

The audience jeered when the master of ceremonies said,

"The show is over." They wanted to hear more Trane. "But that's our rules," he said. They jeered and called out. Then he said, "Listen, Trane wants to play his very best for you, no clichīs. He's tired now and doesn't want to repeat himself." They applauded.

Bacon said he can only paint two hours a day. Different kinds of audiences and artists. I hesitate and don't want to be pushed. My father in 1966 said he would throw in the anchor of attachment to me, but he didn't. Wish he had?

"I think," said Ferdinand the Bull, chief of the air commission amortis, "that angel girls are played out. Their proximity cannot be experienced."

It's like explaining why two empty cartons of liquor were present in the rectory. "I can explain it," said that rector, but then he said, "No, I don't think I can." The parishioners don't mind the abridgments to rules if the priest can produce more liquor.

It's funny serious, and I can keep merry laughter. Guinness lager everywhere advertised in Guyana. No, we can't drink if they say; "We don't care if you are a racist, dumb, sectarian or whatever, don't believe in the 'beast.'"

Has this vignette made sense to you? It was told to me by Sarah Vaughan,[6] like "April in Paris," it's a few holiday tables under the sun. Who can I turn to? What have you done to my heart? Sung by human being robbers for money; by transforming bhakti into it we can actually dovetail it to Kṛṣṇa.

Peace. I don't break your CDs
or hurt you. We are never separated,
sit down sometime to chant *japa*.
Lord Kṛṣṇa accepts us as most fallen.

A not beautiful friendship and for the sake of money he kicks him out when there's danger, he fears.

CHAPTER THREE 3

Lady bird in me,
and the Blessed Lady Rādhikā and
all Her *sakhīs*. How could you forget
Mother Yaśodā and Rohiṇī
and the cows—
you know...

I want to love and
be nurtured—please Lord, by sky and the hill
how to lure the soul of the Lord?

Beer was vile tasting. Nothing you would want to drink. This was in about 1950, *From Here to Eternity*, starring Burt Lancaster. But never mind. Many many films today show the same thing. My Esterbrook pens are junk. My Max Eastman films do not contain enough footage to do redo takes, and they have no money to pay stuntmen.

PARKS DEPARTMENT SAVE YOUR SOUL

Go man go wave is enough to ride on
those Schaefer pens are bunk ride
the inner and outer waves
move leaking too fat my black
the Pilot 7 stare I told you eighty times.

Please don't be angry with me. The Greek Parks Department supervisor looks like your own dad, almost as dark, smokes cigars, but the other soup, Frank Bobbin, was obscene. A fellow worker lent me a dirty he said he found in the street. "Give me that book," said Bobbin.

Every Thursday I had to go from the Parks Department to the Naval Reserve, the crucifix around my neck. I knew the

Apostles' Creed:
  The creed for how to die if you are captured
  as a POW, the need to pray
  to Mary at the last hour of your death.

  How to cry for Her Mary Mary,
  how to use a .45 pistol and kill a Jap or German with a jab to the neck with a bayonet.

  I just want the Allies to win I just want
  to win the war to get out of
  the Navy without broken ribs hunt out last happiness how to lose your spirit.

  You were *proud* to be
  in the Navy so skinny?
  A tiny bit of free will.

I just want to get home to be at the park job again in the morning and do any job except on Sunday when we parked all the cars.

I can't remember wop fool? Do what you're supposed to.

You know how those lawyers and judges are when they amass evidence on you? "I heard it said that you are the greatest clinical hypnotist in the world." Milton Erickson[7]: "Yes." "On whose authority?" "My own."

"A lion is better than a mouse" (approximately Mussolini). Throughout the house were holy pictures. I'm going to change that *too*. I'm going to become holy and you don't have to worry about my pains and anxiety anymore. Let's both just work on our Kṛṣṇa consciousness.

  She knew I was due to a
  slap and Durgā came to deliver it.

PREPARING FOR AN EVENING'S ENTERTAINMENT

You are lucky when you
are down and out thinking did I say the wrong thing?
Fork in my mouth? Will they let
me go easy? "Two hundred pounds or a night in jail."
"I don't have
two hundred pounds!"
"Father!!"
"What?"—Father Ted thought he was accused of holding back two hundred pounds in his pocket from a cheating scheme by the innocent junior priest, but all *he* intended to say was, "Father,
your fly is open."

Scripts for the ISKCONites don't
make them vulgar but straight
from Vaikuṇṭha with a twist
he suggested a jazz band.
"No, the audience isn't wide
enough." A film? What kind?
A standup comedian. Standup
comic and now the temple
is such a dirty place and the rodents
chase the cats.

Or try some "our religion is better than
theirs." A skit with Marilyn Monroe.
No he wants something by
sincere devotees wearing uniforms
speaking from *śāstra* but not
with embarrassing gaps in the Sanskrit,
he should be decent. I'll be surprised
he doesn't slur or cancel. Say "I've got nothin'
more to say."

Groundhog tomorrow. I'll be peeking up. "Is your head round, oblong, ears at angles and sticking out, specifically misaligned?"

"It will take a long time to forget this," he said.

No more pilgrimaging to Kathmandu because ISKCONites go to collect their *śilās* there and get slaughtered. Why did you go there? I went to see if I could find my true love in the Gandaki, but they chased us away with submachine guns. Charlie saved the bank, arrested all the thieves, was congratulated, given money, given the girl he had fallen in love with, but then he woke up from the dream, cuddled by the janitor's mop.

Me too, always dreams I'll get better, if I do if I do. I get better more times because I am a bloke with a talent to fight and I pain too in this sun-pouring rain. Give me quality of life to get the action of my life back. Let me revive to the upswing of the roller coaster again. Does that mean another roller coaster downswing is right ahead?

They've got a new Easter Day arrangement in the church. It's a symbol for resurrection. But
Under the weather. You don't know for sure.

Egg me no eat. On the lookout for
forbidden food. Wheaties, Cheerios,
Raisin Bran, this. That's outer, not
substance. Things perfectly
sublime. I keep waiting to hug Wayne Shorter[28] but
he's not on
this cut, right?

I can keep the rain out of cover
but the bus doesn't come.
Still I hope surely he'll come it
couldn't be such a long cut without a tenor.

The American flag. I've
got all this stuff. Here's
Shorter! I told you,
I told you, we need it—I was told the bank would be open for sleeping. Please make it here. I've seen the oblong hero, he

hit a double all our heroes got to second base and further, all the way home.

One—two—a third guy got caught—what the hell—

Holy holy cowherd boys not much
interested in robbers they
know just what Kṛṣṇa wants,
make them spray a fine
squirt with milk, create a barrier
against the *gopīs* with their
strong arms.

These are not stories or dreams
or scholarly teachings by
historical balance of dating.
But if you choose to believe
Matthew, Luke and John,
that's all right too but I prefer Kṛṣṇa Goswami,
the Gosvāmīs, the Ganges, the
nonstop dancing. The man
who never stops, never stops,
running him won't get him chilly.
They caught him but he doesn't stop
it's not true, he wakes with the plumbers' mop
like a turban around his head.

He walked into the woods and found a long rock to sit upon. It was surrounded by phlox. He picked up his lute and began to open the wonderful flute beside him. He played the flute and a wonderful feeling passed him on the rock. He played the flute and a bad feeling crossed through his body. It was always the same. He can't outlive fun. He's cast into the rough sea. Let's see you do it. He tried the story but it didn't work. You better get your eyes fixed. Everything is getting worse. I cry for you and I see you kind of cry for me. There's no curse. Try to push it for him. I can break out of it.

We're a club. We'll help any member of the club. "But I led my life helping others. Now I want to take care of myself." Yeah, we know that guy. He's in the brokenhearts' club, and sometimes we cry together. We don't cry as we should. He's spiritual but covered by heaps of rocks and sand, the modes of nature, deep within the soul cries for God. How spiritual! Wish my cry was more toward the top. Oh Kṛṣṇa, hear my calling to You. Please come and take me. What use to me are my tears? Imagine, he cries like that and blows his nose. The bad jokes of the comedians. They like being on the air. Getting some recognition, get a part in a new movie.

All three will be lovers. The foolish congregation, the intelligent congregation and a magnificent priest. They're all gods and goddesses.

(From "The Masquerade Is Over")
"I'm afraid
the masquerade is over
the words don't mean
what they used to mean
they were once inspired
now they're just routine"

"I'm afraid the masquerade is
over and so is love."

"I guess I'll have to play Pagliacci
and get myself a clown dress and
learn to laugh like Pagliacci."

"You look the same
you look a lot the same
my heart says no, you are not
the same but please—the masquerade is over
and so is love."

Oh boy ago you know I
don't want any part of it—

I burnt out. Do what
you can.

Do what you can. Rest on the couch,
play a poem, I know it will be over by the time
the tune has run.

At death he'll see maybe nothing. He'll just run out of gas
and start to decompose—oh
the dew. Then there is nothing
there so why not burn it into
ashes in the first place?

But the ship passes in the first place.

The saintly ones deserve no bundle of wood.

I know a *sannyāsī* who wanted the body cremated and thrown
from an urn into the Ganges. Not a body or monument,
just look to my books.

Why give tomb and stone to an
ordinary guy? Just do like they do to
ordinary blokes. Burn the outer covering.
The skull may not burn—watch out—
the whole thing will catch in eiry
flames down to the fingernails.
Do you put kerosene on it?

Ask the local *sādhu*:
"You can't burn the *guru*."

He prayed out calling on all the saints and creeds of his religion (the only religion) claiming with sincere-sound that he did NOT kick the bishop in the arse (which he had just done). The bishop was so shocked he could not believe it one way or another. He said maybe he'd been working too hard and needed a vacation—while his arse was stinging from a good kick by

Father Ted. Funny how you can't believe something so obvious when it's pulled off with such boldness and nonchalance *and then denied in the name of God, the* śāstras, *and all the saints by a priest!*

The Irish bishop then left the house in shock and hurried up the bog to catch his plane for a lineup reception with the Pope. When he got to his turn in the queue, he was introduced in a soft voice by an assistant to the white-robed Pope, who raised his ring so that the bishop of Ireland could kiss it. At that moment the bishop broke out of his trance and said loudly, "He *did* kick me in the arse!" He swung into action, didn't kiss the Pope's ring, brushed passed the Pope, ran into a hallway with his cellular phone and called for a plane back to Ireland, where he immediately kicked Father Ted hard in the arse.

Nothing like that would have happened to me. I am not surrounded by such corruption, a 75-year-old alcoholic priest who drinks all day, a mess of housekeeping, cheating, and a complete simpleton of an assistant-priest.

Bala told me this film series was produced by British producers and banned in Ireland, but it is immensely popular in Ireland, where 60 percent of the population is in the youth bracket. They love hearing the bishop say to the simpleton, "Don't call me Len, my name is Bishop, you prick!" Blasphemous by the score of the Holy Roman Catholic Church, but the youth of Ireland love it, and the ban has been lifted.

Ted's rectory reminds me a little of this place, but I love the hill, the lone-ness, the fact that I can walk again maybe and take pills and therapy. "I have spent most of my life taking care of others, now I'm going to take care of myself," the burned out man said to his brother. "I still want to help, if you can call this help. Have you seen those canvasses? What do you think?"

Keep your heartbeat normal
if you can. Doctor says get out
man—*fresh air!* I don't like
that music, she says.

I have nothing to say. Why should
I go trying to beg for those hearts?

I've saved them all, ordered
them, accepted their worship
it was all part of the job.

Yeah, smoothed out a little. "When I see you cry, it
reminds me...." So vulnerable.

Brokenhearts' club, Charlie Chaplin leaning against the walls of the Church of Hope. He's hearing the singing of his sweetheart—she's a looker.

(Women are better fully dressed) when he wanders in, sees a few other bums are there, later winds up becoming a policeman and clears that part of town of the nemesis.

I wish I could become
a tough guy too and fall in love
can male saints?
I want to walk straighter. Oh Bala thought
the committee is keeping such a tighter
hold on his spending
it's ridiculous.

4

CHAPTER FOUR

You are admitting your spiritual defeat. You must die, said the Count, her father. Obediently, she took a bare bodkin and stabbed it between her breasts, and that was the end of the Mozart opera. But this is no opera and the nun eventually forgot her order, forgot the Count, who was her father. "I shall live," she said. "On whose order shall I admit I am a spiritual defeat?" He then began to show new styles of Charles Chaplin roller-skatery, sweet bashful smiles, abilities to become hard as a policeman and knock brutes on the head with his nightstick. Most important, he knew, was substance of rules and regulations and "preaching is the essence." To help people. To be humble. Oh what a wonderful book. He expected a fresh loaf of French bread for his children, which he would carry home on a bicycle, but what you could give us is also helpful.

In Chicago the reporter described Prabhupāda as traveling around the country having "philosophical chats with his followers." Chats indeed. If you don't know what *Bhagavad-gītā* is teaching, your life will be wasted and your next life degraded, and the next and the next, unless you truly receive the knowledge and become a knight of faith.

The treble boy is singing, but I cannot tell her. I am not a drug addict, but I cannot tell her. It will never be the same because that's how life and persons change. Tragedies.

I would have to view it in a different way, and so would you, but you would both say, "You were mean to me."

Ricardo was an Italian tenor and his lady love was mezzo-soprano. She sang "Alone, Alone" to him as the ship departed and he was not allowed to go because the musical director considered him "lacking reputation."

These are the random remnants. Śyāmasundara dasa said, "In South America Prabhupāda was given a guestroom, but asked that the crucifix be taken away. Śyāmasundara shed some tears as he told it. We can't comprehend why they would worship a crucified man. But billions of people do: "He died for our sins that we may attain salvation. He is the prophesized savior come to save the sins of the world." But another scholar said the Old Testament did a hatchet job on many races and ethnic groups and the Israeli-Palestinian-Christian-Protestant-wars go on.

And the man who wanted to be a believer fought and fell and just accepted it when he said his life was nothing but 24 hours of sleeping, bathing, defecating, eating, taking more sleep, head aching, and scribbling some random nonsense. As I told, we do not accept that gunk. Here we are with the troubled boy and the Italian tenor and the chorus and violins and don't care enough about the spreading of Lord Caitanya's movement. May we somehow do so! Get "out there"! It's not so jolly but at least I can walk.

All right the angels, the Gandharvas
are all shit said Archie Bunker[9]
but he's dead and so is Abe Lincoln.

Saints and sinners due to bad
and good association. Fortune,
luck if you catch on to the right
group. Depends on *karma*?

I'm not sure of the details anymore.
High theology doesn't even interest
me or Rādhā's removal of the thorn
from the particular calf's nose. Why not
remove from all calves?

People will soon know by writing to this address they'll get
no satisfactory answer. It
will be slurred and disoriented.

The guy is taken wrongly.

But you can't prove yourself
right to a hardheart.

And you *were*
slurring, isn't that enough proof? My
doctor took me away from pain
and soon will do so without
slur. Trust the guy, don't think
a guru is wrong by outer appearance.

You think you're a spiritual master?
Yes I contain a link in disciplic
succession. So see it that way and
I will come through
in a prayer.

It's not a stigma to have a mind-rooted disease. A knee broken from football (while making a touchdown) is cool, heroic. But a post-traumatic anxiety disorder is something you'd better keep to yourself. Freddy did so. Just told one or two and let it out with them.

Now listen here, this is not about myself. It is about Freddy Redd, a person mentioned twice or once in EJW. Don't you know the characters in that book? Hello to Hollywood!

Now my cast includes a few higher-ups in the church echelon. I have no time to read books! I wanted to read the Book of Luke commentary. They say the Book of Luke is the most beautiful book in the world. I do read *Bhagavad-gītā* and follow Bhūrijana hopefully in what he says are the ever-revealing depths of Śrīmad-Bhāgavatam. I'd read *The Making of A Love Supreme, John Coltrane's Signature Album*. But there's no time. All I do is sleep. And sneak in a little rest. And try to avoid lapsing back into EJW daily diary. Edna Purviance, co-starring with Charlie Chaplin, 1915 to 1917, movies... How lovely she is! Purviance. Chaste-looking, yet flirtatious at the same time.

Freddy received his first Holy Communion. Read some of

the prayers sincerely. Similarly, Howard, Professor at Ohio State, sincerely read *Bhagavad-gītā As It Is*. We fought for it in our lectures. Raya-Rāma was an ace.

The meadows were frozen. "The wild hare was limping through the frozen grass." Wild animals have it very tough. The editor Dat said he could come and join the crew. They said yes!

FW Words: crotch itch; holy angels; Brooklyn Dodgers; wide experience; yearning to return to my *sādhana* but not guilty about it; ideal behavior—when I'm giving a relaxed lecture on prayer and the two *smartest* intellectuals in ISKCON walk in, my attitude is, "I don't give a damn." And that is my attitude in general toward all of them. "I am serving Kṛṣṇa but *my way*."

Tumbled down the stairs. Superstar "male" sissy singer doesn't even have a penis. It doesn't matter, all God's chillun got wings. "Suffering is selfish," Donald Hall. That's his opinion. Starvation, homelessness of millions in the world, is that selfish? Boo hoo. This heart yearns the entrance into the original Kṛṣṇa consciousness. "You love me and I'll love you." He hesitated in loving him. You "love" pretty girls so easily. It's a trick, a masquerade. I'm learning my lessons, school of hard knocks. Come to my house. Peep, dab, pray, pray. I'm a loyal follower of the Kṛṣṇa consciousness movement. Be sure Kṛṣṇa is God and His expansions. The people who know this are fortunate.

The scratchy sounds. "I don't care"
Charlie on the streets often without
a coin but he's got his schemes.

You're thinking this is too abrasive?
Not spiritual? But I have to
stay awake. I want to go out
in the flaky snow. Ireland
is a great place. We said
come at once!

The butterfly bush is growing.

When I am growing but he's dead now. They would turn
purple again in the spring.
The newcomers figure
through the books.

Books so deep you
grown tired to get
smart. Just go
with the flow "father, do you mind
if I play the radio?" "No."
But it was a sad song and the priest
had to talk him out of suicide.

Nothing hard so they invited him
to the toughest parish in America. He backed out
and returned to his cozy improvised mad place.

I want to tell you, you'd better
ask an intellectual question of the guru-stumpers.

Just pray simple, I've forgotten
my *dhotī*, I'm sick, I have
no *ślokas* to remember but
my heart is good.

I take you guys and
girls and children even if
you are mushy.
Suspect the guru if you like, you can. It's only a short ride.

And then I walk
breathing
GOD's fresh air. This Wicklow
is a cool place. I'd rather stay
here than go back to New York. I'm
63 years old and feeling at home.

You either live with me or

not with these poems which have odd
shapes and take several
cups of herbal tea. Go back to bed and pray for reviving.

God is visible in the
air and everywhere to those who have double vision.

I know so little. Why fake it? Let all the fake and true characters, subpersons whom I know, come through. Why completely avoid SDG? It's silly. Why avoid all day? He's got a stigma at the point of his nose, and all these years he didn't know, he didn't know he was accumulating all the posttraumatic anxieties.

But the joy bubbles are true also. Yesterday I saw one fly by and burst nicely, a rainbow-colored one. He stood at the edge of the beauty and he threatened to burst. And the marijuana-smoking, LSD-taking, heterosexual flirt with camp. Endurement of the Navy. That was pretty good. Johannes tried to survive and he can appear again, especially as his legs grow longer and he can reach the pedals of the church organ, "I may never see you again." I'm starting to see double. The least the best. They can take your money by diagnosing "double vision," go on a retreat, count your rounds. Can you advance in literature without lust? Unusual. Bullies and muggers in the street. Shall we call on him and ask how he's doing? Ah me oh my?

He gives us ideas how to get out of trouble. Pray to God, God is Kṛṣṇa. It's getting simpler and attractive. It's a Kṛṣṇa conscious–produced play. A wolfish reporter next to me asked the name of the beautiful devotee woman who was producing the children's play, asking me her name, she who was feeding them lines, their costumes, movements, etc. I said I didn't know.

Wash up your eyes. Listen alone.

There's no way to appreciate but alone and you know what to like.

I think for sure you can go to Gaura-
pūrṇimā on the festival.
Go that actual day to say Haribol this
Thursday Gaura-pūrṇimā the moon is full.
Oh the sky is filled with full full moon
kill the vampires while we
can. There's nothing to be
afraid of. Chase the bats.

Kṛṣṇa is missing you and you are
missing Him. He wants you
but you have to let Him
go deeper and deeper by His method.

I believe he can do it, nothing stops the soul—the tiny
flame is powerful.

The Lord has caught us,
He caught the last layer. Kṛṣṇa, I saw You
in pursuit of all demons
so poignant and doubtful.

And then I say forgive my sin
how can I find You? Please take
away the stigma
or how can I give a shit
for it? He took my hand, he was against us.

But live with the Lord and it will all be gone for phonies.

We are all sitting around singing these Bengali *bhajanas* of Lord Caitanya Mahāprabhu. God, the sunshine was insufferably hot. I sang, "Cut it out!" I wanted to sing, but I thought I wanted to serve with some coolness in the water, so I went back into the Ganges. I wanted to see my sister, but she was in the mud. Too bad, such a beautiful girl. Three years older than I. They walked up to me so I said, "Hi, hi. Don't forget we were siblings and we can go back to Godhead together. Do you believe in God?"

"I'm not half your life. I gave up God. It follows. Brings in so much among books to print." Then we were squashed together in the sand when it comes to God's heartiness. The person was becoming hotter and I was half covered in mud, rocks and sand. But the hospital tried to help. It's worth three hundred Euros and a lot of footnotes. There's much to learn and so I prayed "Help! Help!"

"If a woman isn't as good as a man in spiritual life," she said, "it should have been figured out by now."

He didn't want to be bereaved by a bad
band. I don't want bad players. I want
good players.

I want God. He says it so often you
don't believe him, right? You imagine
priests just sitting around
playing poker
for high stakes, bullshitting and talking
cynically. It would shame you.

They're all pipe-smoking,
"If I Fall in Love" on the radio.
While I never imagine it could be played
that fast, no clichīs. Go over
to that beggar and ask him for a donation.
He sometimes remembers a poem
that was written by a maniac.

Just hear a heart beating and you go on
and be happy. You don't beg to him
do you? You and I pray
to the Lord (where were you again in the power?)

He says, He used to play it the way we expected it. He gave a splendid performance which he did at first when unheard by his siblings, then they heard him right.

Keep willing, trying as well
no jokes
and slapping asses with wet towels in
the common bathroom.
My my that has to be monitored
and our proposed worship of Gaurāṅga hurts
when it's false in the shape of fat priests.

Open wide, "Ah," that's O or AUM to you. "You chant *Oṁ*?" she asked me. I was surprised she knew *that* much. I'm talking about a co-case worker in Dorchester, Massachusetts. It was very embarrassing when the boss phoned me and I had returned to the temple. I was so dedicated, however, I didn't mind it much, as long as I could bring the money home to the temple.

Today, Fred got his $90 Nike shoes. The insert cost 350 Euros, the two visits to the doctors cost 200 Euros each, plus extras, and there's no guarantee that it will work. Where is God? Wait for God, wanting for God. Tired of studying the scriptures, aware it's the most important thing in the world. What next? When you dig up the clams of the past they won't be as bad as the recent ones, boo hoo. And the ones of the present. Are you trying to be happy? Is that your goal? Forget it! As for the search for Kṛṣṇa, just be content with your identity, "I am a crumb of a crumb of a crumb of a Vaiṣṇava." Why do you need more than that? Besides, it's not enough living in limbo.

In the morning when you look into the mirror, will you detect a pimple, a bubble of joy? Getting closer to death. Give me more time. Let me tell you my truths and feel rich from it. Give me strength in transcendentalism over humanism. Oh! But where is the proof? He hit the glass with the little hammer and the door opened and he pulled down the lever of the alarm. Very soon the trucks came. When they arrived, he said, "I didn't do it but it's right over there and you'd better hurry up."

Take your time. Wheat flakes will assemble

a team. Ty Cobb at third base. Got him caught by
luck. No more Aunt
Mary with Uncle
Sal and his frilly breast
shirts and cigars. Drinking.

Pretty soon I've lost, got bored. Big thing for us kids was that we liked the meals but I also liked Aunt Mary and her daughter Mary and Jackie (a girl).

You could have fallen in love.

All Catholics. I was in with them until the generation gap
appeared first in me.

The best I could do was a junior college.
I pretended to like Shelley and Keats. Did I
like anything really
except the teacher and her sandals?

Where was the Church? Your own
father didn't go to the Mass, tended
his vegetable garden and says to Mom,
"on this particular item, get
off my back. I'm a Catholic but
I won't go to
Mass."

That didn't help Mom in her corralling us
to go. We *had* to—until I
cheated on that. Screw it.
Go sit at the train station and read Dickens or an assigned
book like Stendhal.

This was the life for Fred Jones.

An extra poem because I
can't get to sleep. It's the ballad
"Loverman" and we apply it to Kṛṣṇa
and how He is so tender and loves me.

And so selfishly when you saw love—
suddenly confirmed.

Lovely Loverman, barefooted
Rūpa and Sanātana with no possessions
except a scroll and love for Kṛṣṇa and
kindness to share whatever they knew
with others.

To hell with tenderness? If they hit you on the head
with bottles we just
talk about Kṛṣṇa in a home shelter,
my brothers never giving up.

We speak in Sanskrit, they speak in Latin or high-class Persian for the Koran or Hebrew for the Torah. Which is the best? It is that spoken by the sincere lover of God. Then he will be free, he will be able to see again.

With my robes on I speak standing behind a lectern but more often sit on the *vyāsāsana* and represent Vyāsa, the incarnation of Kṛṣṇa. You don't say anything he didn't originally speak when he composed *Bhagavad-gītā*, *Śrīmad-Bhāgavatam*, and other Vedic literature. The *bhakti-śāstras* are superior to mere philosophical distinctions, but we have to learn logical philosophy also.

Cheerios come from the box. Don't allow your Godbrothers to look into your pantry (as some of them love to do). Oh why did He get shot in the foot? You are confident you can explain it? Why does He have a teenage crush on thousands of women and they go off dancing in the night? Listen to Viśvanātha Cakravartī Ṭhākura and Rūpa Gosvāmī and everything will become clear. You have to have a transcendental brain, and not a mere scholar's or *muci*'s.

I'm good at this? I prefer to avoid it? How do you like to speak to devotees about organizing communities, about seeing money as *lakṣmī*? Do you like comic stories about your own activities?

We can teach you at the theological seminary and then bring it into the streets and homes and hearts. As long as you can do it without tripping off the podium and breaking your walking cane, as long as you can stop seeing double and hesitating to correct yourself and stopping halfway. Just do what you can.

I thought it would be a way in
to the house—through the back door,
as we do in anthropology.

To get a cup of tea served by an Irish biddy
or a pipe of opium shared with Crazy Horse[10] and
talk visions of the
other world.

But he says it's better to *hear* these
phenomena spoken by learned seers who
read with faith from the books
their *guru* taught them to read. You see,
the books aren't ordinary paper
and ink, they are flaming tongues,
brahma-śabda.

God's language, which can be understood
only by the seer of the truth,
my Uncle Sal and your childhood friends
in moments when the mind was
open to the soul and you just didn't give
a damn for judgments of
others who are smarter in their logic historical slice.

CHAPTER FIVE

Our world. The dead leaves. The flute. He said he liked the poem about the call of Kṛṣṇa's flute and my claim that I'd come running eagerly. Pretension—wipe it out, but at all costs what flame you have must be raised so you remain a *bhakta*. Come by calling out—the call. Send me a little wind and fuel, Lord, to keep me going. And could I do it as soon as possible? Oh you who want to reach the rarest goal without paying the check! Can't be done.

Johannes would wear Alpine shorts because in his previous life he was an Alpine man in Italy and took long walks in the mountainous woods where tall waterfalls fell narrow but magically. How wondrous. One could stay out all day in wonder.

But there's a place near Delhi called Brindaban...

Now concentrate. It's a great vision. If you fail you miss a million things that could help you. Johannes, I have nothing in my pockets or legacy but a love supreme buried—the call. And it was answered under the most unusual circumstances. I still have the red beads.

A man can't lay bricks unless his back is strong. A conductor cannot cast up his hand unless he has a flair with the full chorus enlivening child Kṛṣṇa, who is touched, but when every show is over and He is tucked in bed...

Sister, my brother, and artists and workers. Joe visited his material parents and said it was like swallowing vomit. They thought he wanted money.

No shape. Songs sublime. A chorus of Kṛṣṇa's favorites. The dilemma of many religions solved—according to time, place and persons. The Vaiṣṇavas are top, and *me* among them? At least you have been given the keys. I ask of *you*, oh self, hold the *kīrtana* of the selves. Make a nice big book and Johannes' dad will be pleased with you.

Kṛṣṇa Kṛṣṇa Kṛṣṇa, come home to Dvārakā finally, blow the

rose-colored conch by applying it to Your lips.

They don't know the meaning of
Detroit but so what? They know
they have gathered there to
worship Kṛṣṇa.

What about your child? But I told him again. Learn
from me. You're my student.
Do it my way. He had
good chops.

Later, later but I'm on
schedule to chant the *japa*
train, last steam engine locomotive
I'll wash but first call
my friend in to buzz my head with *śikṣā* remaining in
the right place. They say it's absurd in
America and we'll always be freaks.

But some people come up and
say friendly, you are some religion? And you can tell
them it's Kṛṣṇa and most
memories are gone
of rough days.

Haribol haribol. The
dead cancerous, dead
drugged soul is covered
I can feel it, Johannes,
but I'm fanning my best
to uncover it.

Did you see a funny Lou and Abbot film
last night? Was it
funny when Costello was
so afraid of the Frankenstein monster
he couldn't even cry

out "Abbot!" in a loud voice?

And then get ready for bed?
Were all your rounds
completed? I'll whip your ass and
send you right now
to your morning duties—

Last as long as you can
you are triumphant good boy and can't let the
middle-aged or younger mermaids lure you.
Or the authoritative guys.
Just do *your* duty and
be forgiven with yourself—

Well a sad lad is not in a prison cell so why should he lament? Not intimate with his Lord and devotees. He leans forward on a cot. Where is God? Does He really exist? He says he's going through the dark night of the soul. That could cause the girls to giggle, the dark night is for advanced souls who have almost reached it when the bottom falls out. The stuff you are going through is baby steps.

Probably true.

The pen ends up like the guns, empty. Running and running around. I've often seen this before. The long-moustached impostor Count is grabbed by the beard while Charlie runs away. At least he had that flight.

Wealth and power, look forward to it, sing it, earn it, February. It's good enough for you.

Kṛṣṇa Kṛṣṇa, I haven't seen Him around here in a long time except in paintings, in carpets, rugs, hugs over the sofa. The Last Supper, *gopīs* and *gopas*, cows, the Lord Himself looking from the dance. Ah look—there is Kṛṣṇa making a toll bridge. These were drawn on the inside of a cave but the artists have left out the picture of the dark night of the soul. The boy had asked for it. But there were too many *gopīs* with faucets streaming down their eyes and forlorn faces so he didn't want to add it in a dangerous moving car.

This is it people, the fourth floor, women's lingerie, mine ooh ahh smarty prove and say you are convenient thoughts although you can fall down on you frightened toots. This is it, furs, fourth floor, for medication, sorry if it works. This is not fun. Don't fear, women's lingerie, men's underwear—look! Something moved in women's lingerie, Chico Marx, who slept there overnight. Ooh, we're getting smarter, saying deeper, confinement of thoughts in a fighting front.

Around you go copperhead
Warned your head by bowstring
Keep away all black beans too heavy
armed guard awake.

Beaus enter. I can't, chained to electric power.

Social balls, sporting events, event scholastics, all a bore and waste of time. So is religious formality. Of course physical and psychological patching up are helpful but the real thing is *amour de dieu*.

Expressed directly to the Supreme by works of charity, art, peace-politics-sparing animals etc.—yet He can do all that Himself when He sees that you want to see Him and please Him. That's the sure way.

Pleasant melodies. I do detect in the ether. It's snow whitey and coldy and it's God's creation. It's been snowing all night. I slept an hour so far. I am happy. I don't want to neck with Ingrid Bergman as she offered the married man, Cary Grant. Ha ha ha ha ha ha ha ha ha. She threw back her head, laughed, and said, "Then you'll never know." All this junk was offered forty years ago and now it's forty times worse.

In my heaviest coat and sweatpants I trod the pebbled road. Will you really always be allowed to wear shoes even when you go into a temple?

And I must drink whisky, the doctor's orders. Slur slur.

During sleeping hours (he has few of them), he has many nightmares. But he dreamt he became inspired to paint slick and grotesque.

The problem is I can only paint *saṅkīrtana* people because other far-out stuff is only recognized as Kṛṣṇa conscious by the young generation and H. I. Gates and other gentle mavericks. I still can't paint for myself.

Someone's always got a quote or hearsay by Prabhupāda that what you want is not what he likes. I say he'd like it if he knew the circumstances—oh I think! Johannes, are you practicing? It doesn't matter. You don't have to become the greatest organist in the world. Just enough to entertain at a church service and that "mystical" drive to find your way breaks barriers even set by Prabhupāda and then you say, "Look Śrīla Prabhupāda, I did it for you. People will say the Kṛṣṇa consciousness movement produces not just yes-men dolts."

You smile and say, "I always knew you were so lonely and forlorn you must be a genius."

There you are again, back to autobiog and diary. God bless you. Thank God you never met your grandmother and grandfather or you'd be talking about them. Counselor will have me working on Dad and Mom soon. Run, Charlie, run. You are a runaway star. You run away from the law and trouble that troubles our hearts. God bless the holy face and wit of loony ISKCON.

NO MEAT ALLOWED

Winter here in our warmed kitchen.
Three of us so far with kitty in the kitchen.
Wheaties, corn flakes, flakes,
that's what I mostly wanted,
not greens. And cooked by *karmīs*.

Give me a little pepper and salt.
"Take what she says with a grain of salt."
That expression fits Alice perfectly
and we want her that way. The chorus line,

the embrace with men. Why not the blood
suckers "the whole truth and nothing but the truth."

Better to *save* your classics.
I don't care what you think
I've got my memories.
Was a lot of time wasted?
Yes he pushed him in the water and
saved him and pushed him in again
and saved him...

Reparation is not the
worst of it but what it gets is pretty bad. Just argue me
and meal me like a Eucharistic wafer. You guys got to get
it straight. Johannes and Steve both
wear ankle-corrective shoes even in the temple,
    so stupid they look in their pants, so sloppy. Einstein
didn't care.

Avant-garde. Don't primp in a pair
of tommy pants and sweats.
I'm sorry you haven't
reached bared minimums. But I
do see love growing in your
hearts. I see your love growing.

I want to be a person that
responds when they say "here
he comes!" then listen to their troubles. Oh shit
not that. The realistic is too much to bear.
Once a year, Vṛndāvana,
Jersey, don't try to paint
just to make jokes.

And go deep like the sea. Cut to cry to Joseph and Mary,
to Rūpa Raghunātha,
to Santa and to the lowest saint or *jīva*...

I don't have
to pray
really. Just that mechanical *japa* of
the one minute into another and the many
when I'm in a terrible problem—
"God help" and *sakāma*.

Let them recognize me
and my writing and art and
could you wake me from the sleep
and bring me to the eternal show to
eternal sky? You clever Lord, you can't trick God,
He allows you to go hurtling down
past the lower planets and they
laugh at you gleefully to show you
how to pray "Save my skin.
Teach me to love You."

He's not going to be the best *sannyāsa guru* or the most influential leader. He prefers to be the toad in the road. Sturdy Bob was the pride of his dad and mom when he was 6 months old, even though he sucked his thumb. Now he's a bum and they have gone on to another run. We come together like straws at sea and depart at the lee or deep in mid-ocean where no one sees us but the eye of God. The countless *Jīvas* with their wrong conceptions, how sad and misled. It's the Vaiṣṇavas who are meant to save them and if they don't, then who is to blame?

Yes, it is their fault, not the fault of the people. I heard my master say that one day when we were walking on the road in Vṛndāvana-dhama. We sponged up his words and retained them with faith.

Now a friend writes and says he's realized he must practice the Holy Names. Not think of practice as ideal but actually do it. *Hmm*. I wondered, it sounds right: shelter of the Holy Names. But what are our chances? Sitting around the table with scones and butter, the ladies and men confessed their performance was very low. Increase numbers, numerical strength? The *vratā* to stay awake? Well-promised, great fellow, but let's see you do it.

Yeah things ain't what they used
to be. It used to be merry?
We were afraid of rocks through
the window, but visits and letters
from Prabhupāda. And simpler
friendships. Was it not that way?

Things ain't what they used to be.
I could work hard and chant
my rounds with loud strength
and lectures every day from dearest
Śrīmad-Bhāgavatam.

I have a dearest letter, I traveled in a *sannyāsa* van
and was greeted everywhere.

But sure, lots of trouble even
then, she blew so loud and clear
I liked it, Swamiji said, you are a boy sincere,
one of the best; do whatever he says.

But I wasn't always right. Better to
have a day school. Better to have a
fired-up leader who goes into the streets
running after people for a quarter.

Or better to turn the whole thing over to one
who knows how to
manage things. All I had was a
little warmth and *śāstra.* No heavy politics
filtered through the *Bhāgavatam.*
Now good morning breakfast,
nothing cooked by *karmīs.*

You mean you're concentrating practicing the *mahāmantra* as your main means of worship? That makes sense because it's the only method in Kali-yuga by which you can gain freedom from the clutches of *Māyā*? Yes. It's recommended as the easiest. The age is packed with vice, but there's one good thing in this sea of pain—the chanting of the Lord's Holy Names. But to talk about it at a "*Hari-nāma* supper" or "Hare Kṛṣṇa festival" doesn't seem the natural thing to do. Beneath your mask there are other things. "When I chanted at least I began to grieve for how much I had neglected my early chantings."

Go on, tell us more, did you have symptoms of shiverings and rolling on the ground? Are you going to tell all the secrets you learned?

"I have done it, I have been liberated by the toenails of the Holy Name." We quivered in the corner of the room as newcomers marched in in search of us. Then they left. The new men stopped praying. But the heebie-jeebies remained.

You start thinking of these things, how you were, how serious did you receive them? Is your health all right? Seems all right to me except your trust. Yes.

"Ladies and gentlemen, if I am elected president of this temple, I will make major changes. I will punish the ruffians who came into this room. I have a tall bordered wire fence which I will place around us and all night we will have armed guards. I can come here in about a month. Go easy on everyone who cannot do a pinch for improving the mission as long as they are able to do something or other.

"Pray in a church. I know how to pray and I'll teach you when I get back. It is required because of the ferocity of the babies. All morning and most of the evening we will be disturbed by shotguns. Don't talk of health baskets. Know that Dr. Swift is watching your activities. Give over all your life samples and this branch of the church will keep your body—and mind—clean and first class."

Counselor said drink full glass of water with each pain pill. I mistakenly also took a full glass with my supper last night (*who* is writing this? It's "the champion," Mike Mitchell, who wanted to practice *japa* until he became the world's champ and could knock anybody out). What happened? He went to bed at 10:00, then suddenly woke at 11:00 P.M. *peeing*, an involuntary piss on the mattress, the floor….There are three lights in this room, but like a comedy classic man, he groped and could not find any, meanwhile peeing with gusto. He has a urine bottle in his room for emergencies like this, but couldn't find the light. Finally he found a desk lamp in his soaked room, wiped the floods with pajamas, old clothes, would-be fresh clothes, but the mattress won't dry.

I too would like to practice and practice to improve my *japa* but it can't be done easily when you've got an illness, and this was admitted by another senior man. Oh what can I do? It hurts too much. I'll join the Scottish French Legion of ISKCON army. No, no strict orders for me. I'll retire, just on my own. Oh damn the pee-filled room, damn the night without sleep.

Aho, you know, my dearest friend, *my* Jesus (Prabhupāda and Kṛṣṇa) I love you and want to gain you, starting with *sādhana*.

He's got a way to begin a happy day—
by peeing on his bed—it could be
considered a miracle and I am *looking*
for them.
Looking for research on the top hill
two-cycle exercise for a confused yet strong
but weak book boy.

What will you do with
the soaked mattress? Do it
smell? Should you call
Bala? No be a man just
sleep through it.

Admit you can climb on hands,
knees, the other guys did it they
said we tried and our spiritual life dwindled.
Tell that to

your tall pal. It can help.
So throttle the top. I'll find
a ghetto somewhere with waterfall
and say my Hail Marys there, like you did.

My famous night, ankle still bent,
no headache, but on the human
heel with wooden hammer
the little fellow—he's religious too.

Let it be. Don't need an old Count like he. Go deeper in your hurt and petty disable. Think of the great ones and the little ones. Those who are free from addiction. Those who believe in God and don't ask payment back.

Why are you not able to smile when you pass urine in your pants and suddenly your bulky shoes and weak ankles cause you to freefall and crash against the shelves? Are you still alive? And a friend doting on you all day and you're too tired to rise. Hey I think it's getting better. I don't feel butterflies itching in my drawers, I think my pancreas isn't poisoned yet and the liver is alive, heart in upper drive (or once it used to be), and we've got some banjo memories to make them cry.

So chant while you can. It's a humbling thing and perhaps not true to say I need my concentration, headache-free and no flu or constipation—they took away my drive to be in love of the Holy Name. Yet it don't seem true to me except for a sissy. And that's what we are. Lucky we've been picked up as high as we are. Now hold on tight and do something every day. Don't think, "Maybe this isn't for me." It's a shame you've fallen so low and I only wish you were attached to the Lord more. But you don't cry enough for me. I don't hear a peep. Does He think you're asleep? Stevie, what happened to your God-seeking sorrows? Where is your *kīrtana* joy?

He's my man as B sang to
Porgy and Porgy sang "You is my
woman" and that's a shadow
reflection from a man.

Can we have a straight Rādhā,
You are my Queen, my Empress of Vṛndāvana, straight
from the lips of the forest King?
And Kana, you are My one and only, whenever I even
think of you leaving Me, My body
is stunned and My *sakhīs* have to lift
Me from the ground.

The poetry of old with
clichī-sounding imagery
to us non-Sanskritists could be made
by a pure devotee.

Who is actually *there*, and Kṛṣṇa—
as He did to Vyāsa—
gives the words appropriate
for this time.

Just because I had a physically weak day and said I was going to write, he said, "Going to write the blues?" I resented it. The beauty of the gray atmosphere seeping in the half-open window. The room otherwise darkened. Lying all day in bed. Took two kinds of pills. Those people who say not to take them. It's better not to talk to them.

But feel,
wherever you are, let the feelings come,
don't hold them back. ("Oh that's a woman's thing.") Man meets woman. They fall in love, mate. Maintenance daily life lovers dwindle to pals, then arguments.

Go to Kṛṣṇa church together. Children start to come. Why don't you hold a lecture before Gaura-pūrṇimā? I'm resting. He's on vacation.

The famous robin who squeaks in your ears. Our Dear Cat who daily now returns with scratches in his ears. But he's quiet about it. Baladeva is definitely his caretaker now, I wanted a pussy pet.

Yes this is the diary pit. You'd rather some history? When

the American Civil War generals reported to President Lincoln that U.S. Grant was drinking whisky, Lincoln replied, "Find out what brand it is and drink some of it yourself" (you wimps).

You want some religion? Kṛṣṇa's footprints all over Vraja. Some are big, some people claim they know where they are and they show them to you. I was shown and tried to take it seriously. There was a tiny puddle in it and I put my hand in it and touched it to my face.

Enormous lore.

Enormous info in Prabhupāda's books. Outline them. Study them. Are they getting ready to go again? Sit and listen to the lecture. Ah, I detect his old age. God he's become a frazzle, but is that wisdom or just an ordinary old guy (as the *New York Times* wrote of India's P.M.)?

Wholly personal. Sorry he's not God conscious. He's cavalier about his lack of God consciousness. Someone—a college official—once wrote to a Kṛṣṇa temple that we devotees were acting cavalier, I forget why. Maybe because we are the cavalry of Kṛṣṇa. The cavaliers (meaning soldiers, not the other meaning). The musketeers who sell the books by hook or crook, the Marx brothers, Chico, Harpo, and Groucho.

I got it. We got it right
I was in Newcastle temple
underrated, he's actually a
good guy, doesn't go out
on the streets without a cane.
Just a regular one.

Just a regular one.
A cane with no fancy black Irish wood.

I need it before I fall
into the gutter and mush
my face looking up at
the spire of the Cross—
God—no, it's the

half-moon of Islam.

When shall "we" buy one of those cathedrals
for a St. Patrick's Cathedral–style temple with *cakra*?
Don't need it.

Practice at home. Listen to him
play, blow, sit around the house and be who you are.

I can't get to sleep
it's already too late.

I can't believe it. He was so aware
of what to do, yet didn't
follow it himself.

Oh yes, oh yes, oh yes
"Get that smirk off
your puss."

Double lines I caught
you, you bastard! You are growing old.

Twelve dollars in your
pocket and the meter
reads eight bucks.

What will you spend
your last moments on? "Take me to the inner self—
let me face the Creator—
the *mūrti*
the *guru*, the Name
in essence
regret
forgive, wherever
you want to drag me I
deserve."

I think if you can get one sentence in, you can get two, then three. He told his brother, "I'm going through a dark night of the soul." Everyone uses that phrase as a clichī for having a bad time spiritually, but no one knows what exactly St. John of the Cross meant by it in his scholastic and mystical journey. But brother was intrigued, especially because his father mentioned it, and he said, "I am questioning everything in my life." So he bought a copy of *Dark Night of the Soul* to read himself. How much could he understand? At least enough to scare him and give him nightmares.

CHAPTER SIX

Your libido is acting up. He was a tracker of libidos. Castrate the monks. Impose abstinence on them. Hide them from girls who wear tight jeans or flouncy skirts and especially who are young or handsome and intelligent and *especially* who are spiritually minded. Body measurements and facial beauty are important, but we won't discuss that here. I just want to think for you...whatever it is. Short-term memory shot.

Two Veterans talking in the dark. Two brokenheart vets commiserating and speaking of it from the withdrawal stage. It's not just medicine, it's not just "holistic" tricks (as I drink these two cups of water with my aspirin, the *water*, not the pill, will remove the headache. Report this each time you medicate.)

I'm shooting for the heights. I'm grabbing on the shooting star of *hari-nāma* in an exclusive way. It's all I need. Too bad you can't join me with your med-addicted, sleepy-timed, brokenhearted "dark night of the soul."

It is a good place, I will never deny it. In one sense there's no reason to leave here. Haribol. Haribol. Watch the latest funnies. Don't be a bad guy. Don't gorge but eat a little more.

Fred Jones was denied entry at Trinidad Immigration. So what? It's a rotten country. Just jump over the wall and they'll never catch you, Adi-keshava coaxed me. Come on, try it. Your Trinidad friends will support you. Really? So bold? I didn't dare.

He's switching around but knows he has to pray. Dear Lord, I believe in You and not atheists, even if they can out-argue me intellectually. Stay with simple arguments. Big words. SK[11] I don't know him well enough. Tell me dear, who's the best, Him or you? Milton's Satan was best, better than God, because he was so human. But God Himself, Kṛṣṇa actually, is the best, and I thank Him. Please protect me. Please protect me. Give me shelter in Your arms. "Speaking of webs...guess who came here two hours ago?"

Speak of angels, do they exist? Sadāpūta, please explain how Bhaumāsura could shoot a thousand arrows. Explain the other realms. Admit defeat and ask it from the big brains of ISKCON. It will happen, but not in this generation. I am a harbinger from Great Kills. I gave the whores money instead of sex. But...keep it to yourself. It's all right. I'm standing.

Like flying high in fearless plane
it's like hidden mirages. They went out and looked for the moon. Please—I want the
spirit as servant individual.
There's another one referring to
individual. I can't find it just
now (in *Īśopaniṣad*) where it seems to
emphasize more that you
can *use* yourself *your* way

for Kṛṣṇa (I did it my way)
but this verse he gave me
emphasizes free will is
done *His* way. Then how
is it your own will?

I want to pick up the brush
and smear it on the face
of the monkey canvas and say
this is a parchment called
"outsider." I did it for
Kṛṣṇa but I am an insider for Him.

Do you see the subtle
difference? Does it matter?
We are all His puppets:

Street person alcoholic
paperbag lady

prez of U.S.A. prez of Lester Young[12]
all were pulled by the
strings of *māyā*.

Those—Prabhupāda—who
cried—please let me dance!
truly wanted to use whatever
He gave them in His service.
I am more independent
and less devotee
but there's still a little time
if you'll guide me—come here you
dolt! Give it to Me
straight without taking credit.

Would you read this at a meeting, little John? Oh why? Better to shed some soft tears when you see Charlie Chaplin losing Edna Purviance once again. He sits alone outdoors by a fire heating some water, but then gets up and starts to walk away, receding from the movie viewers. Halfway out of sight, his dejected steps suddenly take on a jauntiness, the cane starts swinging and the man and the little fellow is "up" again. Because life is life and worth living.

"Hallelujah I'm a bum, hallelujah bum again
hallelujah give us a handout to revive us again."

"I'm going very inward," Meera said. Is that good or bad? If you have unusual powers or you're very simple, as a child, and you are childlike, wholly approaching the Lord, maybe it could work. Pray and pray the recommended Holy Name. But how dry it is and occupied by tiredness and your obligation and pains and duties. Oh shooty! It'll pass.

Yeah, life will pass and I'll be left behind. That was Franklin's fear. Let's make a sophisticated MGM movie about it, who will write the script? They do it themselves. Never heard from them again.

Henny Penny the sky is falling,
the emperor has no clothes

Rumpelstiltskin is his name
and only the Shadow knows.

If I could find the precious
jewels and slay the wicked troll
I'd cross over the bridge to
freedom—but if you're looking
for rainbows look up to the sky
never look to the ground, little girl.

A special Oscar for his inventiveness. A special pooh pooh if his systems improves. But if you're looking for rainbows look up to the skies, never look to the ground my dear.

He sent me a *Bhāgavatam* quote saying the pure devotee has a little freedom but he surrenders it to the Supreme Lord. Śrīla Prabhupāda printed so many writings, conversations, speeches and words that they create a field day for proof checkers. So I have long treasured a statement in the *Īśopaniṣad* which has a slightly different nuance of meaning from the Śrīmad-Bhāgavatam quote my friend sent me. It says we are not dead stones; the Lord gives us a little freedom to use in His service. I favor a spontaneous discovery of what one really wants to do for Kṛṣṇa and he does it. Does what *he* loves for whom he loves. Maybe not a realistic painting of Kṛṣṇa, maybe an abstract. Tell them send your case, even to the intelligent wife of the intellectual man, whether they accept it or not. I will not give up the Brooklyn Dodgers, but they are Kṛṣṇa fans.

Is this enough for now? It's 3:15 A.M. and I'm in a rare clear head—that is, Ted is. I'm not writing diary. Tough young priests are willing to minister in Watts and Harlem. I can't even walk out the door, said Father Seamus.

Don't just listen once,
hear the bass line again, then
listen again to the piano,
then hear the drum.

You must little girl, if
you want to follow

me and kick. We must overcome these doldrums.

And the occasional tears
are excellent.

Excellent. Lord Kṛṣṇa ain't no clichī.
He's going to pick me up
even from here. Even
without a monkey's
tail in my mouth.

No no you better go for a *tapasya*, he teased
me. I didn't know it
was already over.

I "disciple"—that's what we call
them—do we know what we're doing?—
says "you paint mush, Prabhupāda didn't want,"
says, "autobiography is for the egomaniacs
write a śāstric book." I sat
alone with my toy dog.
Let's hear what Lord Kṛṣṇa was doing.
What kind of toys did He have?

Where did He play, what clothes
and toys did they wear? "Did you
get my letter of apology when
I said I didn't believe American
born *sādhus* when they speak of Vraja?
Did you understand me?
I don't believe nobody" (this is Tim).

He says "I believe in my
personal religion, all religions."

The "stories" disturb
me—I want to live in the pure
present moment of peace—
call that God.

TIRED POOPER

You get happy talking to supporters. He was not a confrontation man. Old shoes get comfortable. Buy it for me, buy it for me, a man is thinking, a baby consumer. And his mom supplies. She was a good smiler. Slide into third base—"Safe!"

Toe touches the base, head touches the shelter of your God. Read the sacred literature about the Boar and Kūrma and the half-man, half-lion, and Matsya and Rama, but *kṛṣṇas tu bhagavān svayam*. Haribol. There's no one home. I had a message to deliver: "Can you type for me?"

So foggy you can't see on the road. Just go to Geaglum and then come back. It sounds like enough overendeavor. They taught us to write in school. Stay after class and write a hundred times, "I love God, I love God, I love God and the Holy Roman Church. And in Jesus Christ, His only Son our Lord." Was that only a dream when Jon saw John Young dressed in *brahmacārī* saffron but wearing a Christian cross on his bead bag? What's this?

Reaching, reaching by your mercy, he said. My mercy? Just give out a few chips for a few people and mostly take it all for yourself. A little prayer in your group and die. But I didn't die, *no one dies*, we change bodies, understand it, stupid. You're so pooped out.

In Arabia, sand and oil
and Kansas
the corn grows for
cows to eat and be killed.

In a good man's heart he
desires good acts and carries them out.
You gather all this together.

He's worrying over the pet dog, can he stay a few days alone? It's getting late at night. So he's expected to see double. Bless me Kṛṣṇa, I am drying out my pajamas with a nice big nap and when I wake I'll kiss Your statue and say the mantra twice.

I can't tell you it's approaching spring. If you can actually *go* to America next December to be nurtured at your birthday party, you could at least wish for it. Wishing is good. Prayer is simple in one sense. I believe the man who wrote the two-volume book *Conversations With God* is a phony. But how do we believe his "God" who answers as God? There's no guru he speaks to, there is no *paramparā*, there is just his legal pad and some good God consciousness (I don't remember right now if it was good) but I think you cannot simply make up conversations with God. I once created something called "As If." I asked questions and gave answers "as if" God replied.

His actual status is given in *Bhagavad-gītā* and *Śrīmad-Bhāgavatam*, if you've got some more questions. Approach the *śāstras* and *sampradāya* of His many *ācāryas* (I understand by faith and logic—they are all in allegiance to His football club), so pray to accept the Lord by asking questions and looking at the various verses in lectures and the *śāstras* that he savored. That's a good place to start.

You see, you have not died. Any advancement helps. Help. We'll show them Dumbo can fly. And you can throw arrows or even snore.

A Drunken Sailor's Poems Are Hard to Dictate
Early to be enough
early the Central Park dancing there
alone without fear that muggers might get me
I was prepared dancing
all night naive to the well-being of the dangers.

People taking you now I don't understand
please let's be friends
"two bourbons please!"
You're shouting ruins the music.
I jumped to where Charlie
said I contribute only because he did want the
kids to laugh at the boring
lectures all over the world.

Noble Noah? Unable to fit
all the animals in the boat
taking care but
laughing makes it easier.

How could it be I said
it's not my spot
of talent to fill the boat of Noah.

Swans keep walking up the blank plank
we're making progress but
the rains are unabated.

Kṛṣṇa, Prabhupāda taught me the Holy Name
carefree unbelievable to believe
once you're on their side

and they have that remarkable
way of attaching you
with the guy or the whole
śāstra's now backing me with
a drummer and I think that's dumb if
he wants me to give it up. She's a beautiful girl
with an egg he gave to her
he's the star of the show again
(Charlie Chaplin and Edna Purviance play bluff
Holy Couple. It's an allegory for Rādhā and Kṛṣṇa.)

The people who survived wrote some books or just lived happily somewhere in the U.S.A. I certainly shouldn't worry about critics. "Sticks and stones may break my bones."

The Supreme Lord should stop and listen to your laughing, chanting, remembering, serving the nine ways of *bhakti*, each absolute. Bye bye, just don't get caught exchanging with *māyā*, with companions of His. One way you can do this is by giving food to a 5-year-old tow-head boy who knocks on your door with tearful eyes: "Please give me something to eat." Just then, the rains began to fall. Oh Ester wants you to rescue him.

LOST THE POEM, INCOHERENT.

We have to go after the variety in God's creation, right? And it looks random. But it actually has much more architecture than the Parthenon columns. I'm trying to sell you this new car. Trying to convince myself too.

But where is God? Is He in the desert, in the *arcā-vigraha*? We do know He is in His name, but who perceives it? I'd become very jealous if you told me you'd achieved *śuddha-nāma*, perfect chanting; then all my complaints against your cruelty would be null and void.

Why should I feel that way? If you are doing well, I should appreciate it. I'll try. I'll send you the quotations from Bhaktisiddhānta Sarasvatī "to paste on your refrigerator door" even if you then surpass me. It will make you go faster than I. You are better. Accept it, I was always one of the *shortest* kids from class grades one to eleven, but jumped up to five foot ten and a half in my last year of high school. I'd tell the people I'm six foot tall.

This is the resume of Freddy McDermott because he's being considered for becoming an in-residence student at the Rādhādesh Institute in Belgium, and they are well-organized there. He really doesn't know what his I.Q. is. He thought he overheard a teacher whisper from a card that it was 114 and he was very disappointed, but he may be wrong. *Does* know that he's dumb and crippled in a plethora of fields, especially the whole science building and anything with his hands. Can't play music or cook, do carpentry, drive a vehicle. So way down on the scale of worthiness. That's Freddy, not me. I'm the tops—yet that is irrelevant because I'm the author and no one cares about the guy who wrote the book.

Hesitate then get going. I wanted
to tell you to buy *Man's Search for Meaning*,
by Victor Frankl
but didn't know if I was allowed to.

My friend told me this. He's always beating around the bush. He can't breathe life into the story he's telling because he's afraid of passion and silliness
and blasphemy.

Afraid of confused thinking and
being criticized. Oh it's nice when they
are going. I love to watch
from the red bridge like in the best years.
Please let me do it again in a new way,
oh Lord.

I'm in the boy's
club now, take ease. But that's
where the monks belong.
Unless they are sophisticated like Meister Eckhart
who preached mainly to women,
as did St. John of the Cross.
In fact, many priests specialized
in preaching to nuns and pious ladies.
So what do I know? Did they fall
in love with pretty girls in the
front rows?

So I told him if you want to be a
writer (artist) for Kṛṣṇa, don't
beat around the bush you
think Kṛṣṇa wants only sissy
writers who can't bleed onto the
page? Take me, I'll take you.
We'll then overwatch the holy health club participation—
all of me, liking all of Thee.

You can do that without dirtying
thyself or getting punished.

Spend your money before you die. Don't let a trust get some or an obituary company. Use it. Be happy and produce some process.

Hold my hand. I'm sorry for all the partying and reuniting and all the investigating and monkey faces. But you've got to do it my way. When Kṛṣṇa (*śāstra*) sees we have a little free will but it should be *all* turned over to Kṛṣṇa, what does that mean to you? What does that mean to me? I'd better go back to bed before I get another lion ache. Roar! Please phone and ask what pill to take. We know. And don't get up too late for a lot of *japa*, new *japa*, before you collapse short of sixteen. Wait until you see me go on Gaura-pūrṇimā. It will be the simplest lecture you ever heard. With faith, depending on Swamiji, which I first heard. I know a raw egg before you throw one at me and I'll duck. "My self worth is not diminished by your opinion of me."

You'll come out before anyone even knows it. Driving your station wagon past the temple long before *maṅgala-ārati*,
quiet and down the road. No one
discovers until after breakfast
that little Mary has gone off to the
new outer and inner life.

Does anyone know?
Inner:
Wants to remain an *inner* more
person with prayers.

Keep out sounds out
everyone: you know what? I like that.

Rolling along miles ahead.
But it hasn't been put together yet
the brilliant thing. Do it as you like,
this way.

I was born two hundred and three. He'll catch
me. There aren't enough counselors
to go around. It can be done overdubbed.
Don't punch me. Just
go right in don't be

a friend of written scores.

Look for the cat under
the top hill call but don't
wait too long without them.

Pray to your Lords, They
hear you. They are the
protectors of the pious
and we say to hell with
the reductionists. Sorry
no party but that's your *śraddhā*
and I thank you Mother
when I was a baby.

Frost is froze frost February people don't like little kids because they are mean to each other. That's often true. They pinch each other, take turns calling each other names and not letting their parents see their harm to each other. Sometimes a 9-year-old boy will even sexually abuse his sister 2 years younger, put his fingers in her private parts. They torture animals. It's all *karma* coming out as soon as possible. It takes a lot of loving to correct such material meanness.

Big Jim found the goldmine. He was kind and cut a share in it so that they both became multimillionaires. Watch us become millionaires. I don't care. I mean to say wake me up because it's getting late now and I'm getting up early to call my *japa* partner.

This is the heavy-handed road past the chords of the base of the tree where we want to win an outsider art prize, but a picture would be nice.

Dibbly dee doo. They don't know the value of things. He offered an ice cream cone in one hand and the Romanoff jewels in the other. The kid chose the ice cream cone. "In me you see a man alone… A man not lonely/ Except when the dark comes on… A man who knows love isn't what it seems/ Just other peoples' dreams." (From the song "A Man Alone," sung by Frank Sinatra)

Pedal pedal you learn to ride against a smash to your face and cry for the daddy Kṛṣṇa. You now use new faith and you have careful supporters.

Now I'm going to teach you things
never learned at Harvard Business School
or in the tough streets. You need
smart and kind friends who
don't want to keep it all for themselves.

They want to give it too.
We were up so early and went to bed late
and yet we continue where
we left out, not so brilliantly.

This is called teacher teaching
school and among tons of the art.
Please tell me how you learned it
so well. Please.

I've stripped all ambitions and can't
let bazaar centuries like they do draw
a picture to see them in museums.

Dr. Sax. Ouch zig zag,
all the schooldays' fun we
went through but how come
you didn't have a girlfriend and sex?

I guess I was raised Catholic shy
(dammit you are writing about
yourself again!). No, but what if I
was? I am breathing life into
a story about another person,
Romanoff, who lived with me and who was
shier than even I and not gay.
And I admired that we...

We what? We could get along
on the waves and did not get smashed
as yet I hadn't even heard
Mahler or learnt to paint or love of a girl
only my old teacher and that was over.

Mary our Mother of God pray
for us. Jesus on our wall purify me.
And I want St. Therese of Lisieux—
if they could only be a
little more nonsectarian
and accept me with
delightful Kṛṣṇa.

Can't get it all at once
Prabhupāda will fight it out. I'm in the
doghouse and he just wants to see
me straighten out and then he
will straighten it out for me.

CHAPTER SEVEN

I'm sorry to tell you this but your overall grades do not qualify you to enter Brooklyn College. I regret to say that once having signed a military entry form, there is no way out. You were sane when you did it, of adult age (17), and you can't claim, "My father forced me."

Woke up suddenly on Harvard Square seven years later with a new identity, a mold broken: "I'm distributing magazines as a Hare Kṛṣṇa devotee!"

Raw Vision they decided to call their child. They were high on marijuana when they decided that. The next morn they changed their minds. The mother decided on Yudhiṣṭhira, and that was that, although dad had a lingering liking for Dharmasya or Lakshmideva. Baby names, they later grow up and jack them to Yud, Green, Bags, Yurks, Screw-em, Juddy, Buddy-pops and so on. No obscure Sanskrit or "Hare Kṛṣṇa dāsa" (gosh!).

As he grew he lost his blondness, and then a tooth loosened. He became attached like mad to young women. Consummated it. Looked for more. His parents didn't know it. He was part of a promiscuous Hare Kṛṣṇa underground. Dopey parents had only the faintest notion, but then they smelled the pot and smoke. Serious lectures about the law, career, and dangers of addiction. Didn't stop the offspring; it was only a question of money and accessibility. Boy, getting high was sweet, even if it was not "forever"!

Stayed friends with mom and dad, who began to accept him. Send the kids to college. Their "quotas" of chanting diminished. "Never get me initiated by one of those guys."

Prabhupāda maybe, but not one of his sons. He'll probably fall down and I'll be stuck with it. Just a private faith. Prabhupāda, not Sai Baba or Swami Schaeffer or Johnny Carson, such a *baba* or ISKCON showoff. Just leave me. Maybe these decisions—

marriage, initiation—will work out. For now I'll sell Nathan's hotdogs in the street.

This idea of changing religions was brought in by Johannes (and Gaura—these three or four shared all intimate thoughts along with Johannes' sister Gertrude, who was a very nice trooper, and later in the book I hope to tell you more of her). You can't change around all these histories and cultures and theologies. (But he liked the pictures of Jesus and his followers, even modern-day ones, chic, like Therese, the Buddhists wandering in cloudy hills, Li Po, tossing down saki handouts, Wing Wang, ancestors, seclusions, miracle-making poems, mantras, great humorous and powerful analysis, Caitanyites—humans! All hall-of-famers! I like them all, hall-of-famers and little ones.

Wives talking about Weiner, a new buddy of Sal known because he played in Johannes' straight-edge band where lots of the Hare Kṛṣṇa music floated around. Weiner was impressive on harmonium, playing all the *bhajanas*. The girls liked him, all blond, but he was somewhat indifferent, so caught up in the cult vibes. Not to say he didn't have a swelling libido and enjoy the applause!

It was the best development yet, even though they weren't so scholarly, like the very first batch who read intensely in Prabhupāda's books...all of this is not true. But I'm just giving a thumbnail sketch—Weiner was about five foot eight, 130 pounds and not very big in the chest and biceps, and not very active. After all, by this time they were reaching 60 years old.

I've waited a long time before going back to
visit our homestead. One of two
giant front lawn oak trees was felled.

Aside from that it looked the same. We went on a tour just before going on a summer writing retreat. Planned free writing—the idea—which suggests writing alone within ten days
some open to bigger
just like it used to be. Within ten days Charlie's son

punched a bigger
neighborhood son until
he knocked him down.

I don't know what Kṛṣṇa
thought about this. Did He want more or less fight? Guys spending time with no girl. I'd punch or be more of a gentleman, depending on the situation.

"That's him! The missing man from
the fireman's family, the one
who joined the cult and now he
goes his way a lonely song."

Pray all the prayers you know but not to false golden calves and to Gaṇeśa. I use Gaṇeśa for another purpose, recommended in *Ayurveda*. The Hail Mary is sweet to me and all forgiving, surrendering to the Lord and all risks on her behalf—"Behold the maidservant of the Lord" and "Holy Mary mother of God, pray for us sinners now and at the hour of our death" means to go inward. They ask to supplicate. Believe. Do good works. Be open to people and think the love that you hanker for you want for them and for the saints who you have faith in. You wish they will have it in you. This sounds like holy talk, and so what? I don't want barroom whore talk. Just a few pills and talk.

Penelope got married and buried in the same church in Eltingville within a few years. I was a few years' younger teenager than she. She was Episcopalian and a close friend of Madeline, my sister. All this was mostly over our heads. How could a woman, with a husband who had quick tendency to grow a beard…how could a woman with a sweet flirtatious vivacious smile marry a man and then die because of cancer or something? Could it be explained by our God? Over my head as I heard the lovely organ twice within two or three years, once for marriage, once for the funeral. It was a footnote to my life because I had other things to do and it was a mystery. When did Penny die? What can you say? She was the nicest person anyone ever met. Then you go home awkward. I never even thought about it deeply. Did your sister feel it deeply? Who feels for whom? The quick, moving mysteries of God. The pastor is hard put to make some sense out of it.

Now this pen is the worst they say, and spring is coming, but the answer is coming soon. Don't expect me to be prolific or to evolve. This is maybe all I can do. As Dhanañjaya dāsa said, "He's a hype," but I don't believe it—I have fun and do my Śyāmasundara and Rādhā-Kṛṣṇa.

Distract your thought. At the first stop after
the funeral, stop to study the full-color
commercial of the girl with an attractive
rear. They banned it.

Think if I ask you oh what voice I don't like
it. "Voyeur's step"—what does that mean?
So many rehabilitations. Be optimistic
I boldly request. Hate songs by
ministers with scriptures to support it: Muslims
hate non-Muslims, "Catholics are
pedophiles."

Find a little pal some people who believe
who see love and peace despite the
many complaints how we're all corrupt.

He attempted a stopgap and made a prayer, didn't jump off. Just sat chanting his very last beads. Could you chant a new set?

Or do it on your *japa-mālā* instrument—what does it matter, rosary or *japa*? We ask for love. Love will find it even in a dung hole. God will appear in our dream and when we wake up early. That's what she has been saying to me for sixteen years
and I still can't understand it. Will you ever?
A man sent a new book with
iron chains for you to

sing throughout always
good Samaritans.

It was just a matter of days before Prabhupāda was to pass away from the earth. But by the insistence of Tamāl Kṛṣṇa Maharaja and Prabhupāda's own desire to preach, he decided to make a last visit to London from Vṛndāvana. He went in a jeep with a mattress to the Delhi airport. Just as he was leaving, some devotees from Māyāpura arrived and told Prabhupāda about a disastrous thieving occurrence that had just happened there.

Some Muslim *guṇḍās* had a suspicion that the Rādhā-Govinda Deities were made of gold and that the decorations were of precious gems. This was hardly a fact, but so the rumor spread. One night a band of them attacked with spears and knives and other weapons. Seeing them coming, the *pūjārī* scattered all the keys on the floor so that you could not tell one from another. He then hid behind the curtain. Ironically, his feet were sticking out from under the curtain, but the *guṇḍās* did not notice. However, they took the opportunity to lift up Rādhā and Govinda and run off with them across the fields. When word of the emergency spread, Bhāvananda ran into the field with his government-authorized shotgun and fired several rounds at the dispersing thieves. He shot and killed one of them, who dropped the Deity, and the other Deity was also dropped along the way. But in a bizarre twist of fate the government officials arrested the *devotees* because they had fired the gun. So the temple president was taken off in chains and put in the local prison. The devotees then rushed to Delhi to tell Prabhupāda this just as his plane was leaving. He felt great compassion for "our Māyāpura men" and assured the ones who had come to him that Kṛṣṇa would protect them. It seemed that at every moment there were catastrophes for Prabhupāda, either in his own health or in the protection of his temples. Prabhupāda already had his plane tickets booked and so he went to get on the plane. He noticed in the newspaper that it had reported the *guru* Bhaktivedanta had not been present at the time. He said, "This means that they would have arrested me too." The devotees then dispersed, some back to their Western centers, some back to Vṛndāvana, and a small traveling party with Prabhupāda to London.

Śrīla Prabhupāda one time had to stay in quarantine for ten days at the Bombay airport hospital because his secretary had failed to bring Prabhupāda's inoculation card. There were other occasions also when he was confronted by officials—they denied him entry into Africa—but he was never rough-handled because everyone could see that he was a saintly and gentlemanly person, and so even if they had to check his entry because of some rules and regulations, they did so with utmost care befitting a religious personage. Even the bums who blocked his way on the Bowery because it was their sitting perch used to move aside when he came, and they would give him a little greeting. This was instinctual. Devotees saw a few close calls when Prabhupāda was walking on the walking machine and some *mūḍhā* was gaining ground on him, but it never amounted to a collision thanks to Kṛṣṇa's and the devotees' protection. And during private or on-the-air conversations, when Prabhupāda was talking with people known for their insulting wit, Prabhupāda's own sharp wit averted any insult or embarrassment.

At the Bhaktivedanta Manor, while talking to a mini-skirted reporter:

She: "Why do you people have bald heads?"

"Why do you have bare legs? Better to have warm legs and a cool head. You must have a cool head to understand this Kṛṣṇa consciousness."

Gone just as well,
and here's a liberated guy who knows
all the signs on Rādhā's feet
and can talk in
Sanskrit and Bengali, is a
citizen of India, and other places.

Tell me your shit, were
you the GBC who shot himself?

Are you the guy who wears a scarf
and shoes in the temple and
who loves his mother and
wants to kill his Boy Scout master?

Where exactly did your Kṛṣṇa
answer specifically? If you never did know this then
how the hell are you a *guru*?

You I like, your sister I like better because she is
soft and younger with
a pretty face.

She's Edna Purviance and you're Charlie Chaplin
it's a tough call, but I'd take her over
you even if she has no
shotgun
and you are the official tramp.

You see what this has done to me—I
grope for drink at a moment's
notice and search for a cigar butt under a table.

Yet Edna's moods are swanlike,
a girl with a craggy face she'll be and sing "why
did I sign up for
the jungle?"

I'm a rich man but didn't know
if God is black or white.

I hope these messages make sense to them, said the director, I hope they won't start walking out in droves. They had planned quite a number of short intermissions, like seventh inning stretches. And nothing broke his heart more than to see small groups conferring and deciding to leave. Have you seen that take place in a church or temple right during the sermon or lecture? Or just as a feast comes out? A bold *brāhmaṇa* approaches them and says, "The best is yet to come," or something as outrageous as, "it is not the proper etiquette to leave the services at this time."

"Shit it ain't," a small group might respond.

Or "I am terribly sorry but we've left our children with a babysitter and have to go now."

But it's *your* fault for not holding them to their seats like a magnet so that they forget their children at home or their overbearing rude natures that don't want to be told what to do. If you find fault, Father Ted, for making your logic rock them to sleep or bother them with tediousness, who's to blame? The head pastor's thinking, "His dogma is okay, he has some charisma, but he's not good at asking them for collections."

The best preachers hold thousands of people without air conditioning in the desert or until he multiplies loaves and fishes. Or backed up with a full orchestra at the coliseum for Verdi's Mass.

A humble kid says he is speaking what he's heard from older kids, ducking away.

So while the lecture goes on, Betty is wondering when her FedEx will arrive in the mail with her sneakers. It's been over two weeks! Lost in the mail! Get on the computer. Look around the inner theater TV for pickpockets and interaction. There's an old woman crying. Outer face of the soul—can you depict it?

He wanted to be a minister, a religious,
a private person with God. Know Him
in some private place. Can you? That started
after awhile. It took St. Theresa
of Avila thirty years of living in
the convent to get off the socialite track
and talk to angelics.
Most never do. Therese of Lisieux
walked right in on clouds of flower petals
and it seems heaps of tolerance and

blessed teenage rapture for Jesus
of the perpetual good looks.

For the rest who plug away. In ISKCON we get fired up
at *kīrtanas* but all that fault
finding. And for form
mind drifting out the window and
taking in the fears and
landscapes—but I really, says Bill, am in love with
Jane. Should I ask
her for her freckled hand
in marriage? Jane knows it and
doesn't want to sit like a decorated
Christmas tree at the marriage ceremony.

You get a lot of money on that day. Yeah, and then drag ass to work for IBM for thirty years in Kali-yuga, trying here and there to squeeze your *japa* in.

Stay a *brahmacārī* and take the orders from the Vietnam
temple commanders. Just leave the scene
like a low-profile man for "our religion."

Everyone is like that, with kids picking noses,
then wanting to pee, begging ISKCON managers
fingering the peas but Śrīnking to save
from the traps of the latest law case.

Lord save us, fix our right single mind on You and save us
now and at the hour of our death each one of us.

One *gāyatrī* upon waking, one *gāyatrī* before lunch, one *gāyatrī* after dinner. Regular short breathing time outside during waking hours. No fixed schedule according to the clock, be final. He wrote many signs like that around the house. Then they started seeing a lovely deer in the pasture, eating grass. But the farmer hired a hunter to kill him in fear of foot and mouth disease.

Frankie and Johnnie were sweethearts. He was her man, but he was doing her wrong. He set up a Jagannātha altar then was praying for her. Jay's counselor made an analogy of construction for him. Build a house. Build a boundary. Don't let in who you don't want, open gate for friends. Read mail but once a week. However, eliminate bad mail. Lead the life you want and don't worry, you'll get by, but you will have to work for it. He could understand, he didn't know what he was doing, but the mob was after him. Those persons and their fuss.

When it was time to go home his parents were annoyed, for they wanted him to stay longer. Clean your eyes like a rabbit. You are too ashamed. At the graduation party they all wore their mortarboard hats and spritely colors. But Joe hid in a closet to chant silently.

You mean call for
Philip Morris? No I mean he was
like a high priest on the tallest seat in the temple room with all plush and velvet
silver and gold.

Oh, Nellie was happy to see a Kṛṣṇa picture
in a pawn shop, and she bought it.
Even if she could not stay in ISKCON they couldn't keep her from the London Ratha-yatra, a pot of flowers every day before Them, hold a little *kīrtana*, do her rounds. The institution can't grant
condemnation
for cooking, any kind of *prasādam*. You can't be stopped
from uniform, rings, beads, books. Yes maybe you are not allowed to have them.

But you can walk through the daffodils
sing "al leu cha" and in an earnest voice cry for the mercy of the Lord.

CHAPTER EIGHT

I can't even remember her name. It's Rādhā, you fool. It goes like this: Rādhā is the most attractive, worshipable goal of the Gaudiya Vaiṣṇavas. By their chanting the Hare Kṛṣṇa mantra they please *Her* because we chant the name of Her beloved. So She's pleased with us and we receive Her powerful mercy. Boy, do I need it. And we chant Her name directly, "Hare ... Hare," which is pleasing to both the Queen of Vṛndāvana and the Forest King, Vraja-bihārī.

This little fellow, the tramp, decided to wear his saffron uniform for the trip to New York. Wear sweatpants underneath. Nothing to be afraid of. Don't be a burden, apologize in advance, ask them to tell when I do something wrong. Some people will come and see me, but I can't see more than one or two a day for an hour each. Yes, they know that, hmm, hmm, hmm, hmm. The eyelids droop down. Not another airplane, please.

Vasanta Pañcamī in a few days. Okay, buy tickets. Take that "icon" picture of a boy holding his hands in prayer. He prays to God for "allowing me to love You and serve You."

Thumbnail sketches—he was the brother-in-law of Advaita; she was one of the maids of Mother Yaśodā. He was a favorite tree. Do they have lilac trees?

Can a man change his life past 60? The little fellow announced to a friend, "I don't get headaches." Yes you do. You mean you abort them. "Yes, that's true. I get several headaches a day." I can't keep this up. *Vasanta* is coming with its joy and the American lilacs.

Try it again. Maybe you didn't
like it the first time because
you had just hit a rock.

No, I don't think that's it. You just weren't
into it. Kṛṣṇa is for you favorably.

You advise thousands of people
how to reform.

Now you hypocrite, you have to reform yourself.
Tell them "*just hear.*"
Be attentive
as you fall asleep.

I see their estimation (of me) begins
to lower.
But the Lord
will up the promise. That's the
top and priority for a sleepy-always fellow.

Don't quit, Jackie said, you'll be back on top,
struggling to the peak, at least your quota. You don't
even need special ideas.

So my friend, see you in Chicago
when you are doing sixteen rounds
and looking better from your
exercise. Maybe you can't
do anything immediately except not
quit and do what you can
straight, huh?

Well that's all for this one.
No clowns, rubber noses
or high tightrope walking and somersaults
just straight to the fulfillment.

I don't know the time. Phone Francis and ask him. He says, "You woke me up." I say, "Then begin your *japa*." The foggy *japa*. It is the most important and easiest thing. We try to teach our pupils. They are interested in everything *but* Kṛṣṇa. So life is wasted. Maharaja Parīkṣit asked that question: What should a person do, especially one who is about to die? But that "person who is about to die" is everyone.

Simple: chant God's names with devotion. Practice for a long time and you can be accustomed to it. She fainted at the shack. Her grandson who had learned so much from her picked her up and placed her into bed. She was sorry that she was dying. He couldn't help her now.

Varoom! The steam engine entered the station of Des Moines. It was a small stop so they wouldn't stay long. Harold[1] kissed his fiancī and his grandmother. He was going to the big city, New York, to earn a living so that he could marry his wife and have a house. How could he have changed in so few days, so that he could go out bravely? He had always been a coward, but now so much more would be expected of him.

His grandmother gave him a carved "charm" and said that whenever he was afraid, he should take out this charm and make a little prayer to it, and he would gain great courage. He happily took the charm and placed it in his pocket and then ran off just in time to catch the train.

You can't play the same thing
over and over. People have
things to do. For example, *japa*, even
if you have a fulltime job.

They chant car-*japa*
and other poor performances.
I want to be the best carrier of newspapers
door to door. But what, what
good will that do—can you click your
God's names in a pocket clicker
while no one watches? I
don't pay attention. "*Just
hear*," our Guru Maharaja taught.

And a deeper plea. I don't know—
out of the false ego? I'm not asking
to tell that I'm a saint. But wish I could
concentrate and laugh
a little about the absolute nature.

His Lord is in His heavenly
home. We are like pigs but
He will not abandon us.

The Union admiral explained all the reasons he could not enter and take the Confederate harbor of Charleston. Wind too heavy, coast too fortified, etc. Abraham Lincoln said, "And there was another reason, Admiral." "What is that, sir?" "You did not think you could take it," the President replied. So I'm praying for strength not to back down with a logical reason not to move to God Bless America, said Freddy-of-the-month. I'm sick here and I'll be sick there. But a sea change may occur. I'm going to try for it. Let them even see my Zen tricks. Boo! to the tigers and vampires hiding behind the bedposts. Feelings flow. Crying to God. I will tell people more what I think when it's time to, but when it's time to deliver a *bhakti-vaibhava* lecture, I'll listen (if I can stay awake). Watts was conveying all this to his close friends, who were in similar situations, sitting together in the forest. Some were staying at Wicklow and some were making a physical change to see if that might help.

There's nothing to be afraid of
if you are a hoop-skipper who
believes in God. Think of Haridāsa
Ṭhākura defying the emperor and going on calling to God.

Sleep is a closer enemy because it is *in*
yourself. I think it can still be
overcome and you'll be like that
excited young girl in a 1920
movie—her disease was that she had never been
excited. Now her heart was going
bumpety-bump. Life was real!

Oh if that could come
when I speak His names.

Swami Mullins was ill in bed for a year, and when he started taking tranquilizers, he felt less pain but forgot all the *ślokas* he had memorized. He stopped giving lectures. Meanwhile the senior devotees organized seminars, and some of the seminars were very learned, technical, like M.A. courses in *bhakti*. Swami Mullins realized if he ever did get back into the game, he'd be an old-timer (like when Sonny Rollins[13] took a two-year sabbatical and returned only to find Ornette Coleman,[14] Cecil Taylor,[15] and Anthony Braxton[16] miles ahead of him).

So you do reminisce, if you can even do that. I recall the time Swami asked if I could go on a walk with him because it was Saturday and I had a day off from the steel mills. "Oh yes!" I jumped into the air.

1920. An organ is the only background music of the movie. Years and money speeding by. Bodies rotting. You're going to just pick up and leave the house a wreck? Plug in three days just for himself and for two days, save himself for money-making. I don't remember the girl being the cause of a fistfight, but she turned her nose up and favored the rival. The characters in the movie were billed simply: a man; a woman; the rival. There was a dog in it too. Our hero lost the girl and became addicted to Coney Island rides alone.

They sound the same
a man buys his girl a heart-shaped
box of chocolate candies and she serves him a mothball.
(Looks like a *sandeśa*.)
The rival also bites into a mothball. They
barf. Fighting for the hand
of a dolled-up "princess."
Love isn't what it seems
mostly other peoples' dreams.

"You're on the far side of Uranus," I told her and she was as far away as that. Or was she as close as a branch scratching at the window?

Peace. Is Daddy going to drive the
car? Who has the tickets? Aer

Lingus—I'm just a
citizen in their family.

You lied to him.
You left his country?
(Why did Maharaja Parīkṣit
leave his country and people?)
To seek out yourself
in a new place. They say it's better
if you try that.

Dogs and sirens, we'll have hundreds of noises. There's only one God. All he wants is to follow him. His friends are the devotees picked up by Prabhupāda. I don't want the interview to myself.

I see.
The hands on the clock are moving slow.
And they speed up. Prabhupāda's God, baby
Kṛṣṇa, that's all. He grew up
so you do this too.

Seclusions, people seeking a little privacy in different spots of the globe. "He's been incognito for five years!" Another won't receive visitors and wears civilian leisure clothes at all times. Amy has gone back to her mother, who loves her, "a real Mom." "No Bull Browns has made a singular, surprising-for-him move: I shall go to the state of my birth, New York, and live among sweet young people I don't know well."

My mantras. How many old videos does he need? Learn to play the movie organ along with the videos and spend your last years in the perils and smiles of Harold Lloyd. No, that is only to cheer me up. And dammit, I like it.

Most important of all is chanting God's names. But Ginsberg said, "Why not an American chant that truck drivers could use?" Śrīla Prabhupāda replied that his disciples were Americans and they were chanting it, we don't need an American mantra—"give peace a chance"—"go man, go." No, *I* have to build faith in that one great mantra and practice. Don't sleep so much.

Who's this "I" who has to transform? It's the congregational I. But what about the sermonizer, what's he doing with his beads? We'll talk about that later; we'll talk about it now. Rising from the flames, the baby phoenix. The gift of baby human shoes given to him by a seer in trance. The seer said, "Lord Nitāi showed them to me. It represents your progress." Will you leave your teddy bear behind? You know he's coming. I need my amulets. And a picture of a 5-year-old curly-haired lad—looks like Jesus—praying with his hands "in prayer." Take him! That's you.

Will there be room for all these articles? Yes, and they will come alive in a new setting.

Swims' mystical goodwill charms. Kṛṣṇa gave it to him. Remember, however, even if you may lose them, the goodwill remains. When a boy lost his *japa* beads Prabhupāda had chanted on during the *dīkṣā-yajña*, the boy wrote to Prabhupāda to ask for new ones. Prabhupāda said all right, but it is not so important; once the blessings are given, they are immortal, not the beads. Swims has an extra security need, so like Dumbo with his crow's feather, he's told, "Hold onto this and you cannot fail." But it's God within him that causes his success—to soar.

What is there to say?
It is a big venture, and you're
asking why am I leaving such
a lovely county of hills,
quiet streams for
the place of sirens and
mockers? Lots of reasons
but mainly *the change*,

the American base is bogged
down at the top of the hill with no one
to visit and love him. Ha! You
can't expect him to cook for
himself or drive a car,
he never did.

How can you not panic
when you're in a room
with other peoples' energies?

One counselor said he'd
teach you. A different life, but not without Kṛṣṇa.

Not so fast, take deep breaths.
Kṛṣṇa will do it for you but
use your life skills with confidence.

Booba-dee-boop, sing and amuse yourself
how sad it all is, you'll not
survive more than twenty years,
so what are you worrying about?

It's your mouth. Put in new
dentures or not, go to Vṛndāvana
or not soon. Wink in the
mirror. Don't worry, you
ask, everything is predetermined
to work Kṛṣṇa's way and
He just wants to see how
you act.

Sleepiness from the steeplechase horse raced in first because he hopped over all the bushes. He was meant and trained to be a steeplechase horse. The young man spent all his money on the horse and his fiancie considered him loony when they discovered the horse couldn't run so fast. They didn't know he was a steeplechase horse.

Anyway, I'm boring you with this. "There's a hell of a lot more you're denying." Pleasant words, huh? The counselor was more supportive to Fred the Nerd. He said you are seeing a counselor openly, and you write openly. You don't seem so "denying" to me. What's "denial" anyway, it's just a word.

Dear Doctor, I'm taking the pills. Dear Elephant, Dumbo did a great service to your race. Dear little children who pray to

God with faith, and dear old people and middle-aged people with *śraddhā*. Straining to keep their eyes open. Oh Lord, we'll get all you need so they don't laugh at you as you speak with Harold Lloyd.[17] Write home to your mom and tell the truth: I'm failing in my grades; I tried to get a job but got fired, I've got no girlfriend, I've turned to drink.

Then they go to the city and track him down as a *harināma* member dancing on the street. They accept it, at least it's better than the aforementioned failures. He is favored by God.

The last times he played he was
physically shot on heroin and other
bad health but he played excellently.

Look up, a sad horse.
Never look down.
Do you know how to pray?
I forgot the names of everything.
Come and take all you can and
sell it. I'm going back to
America, land of the brave.

I sold my hat and wore a *dhotī* boldly
on the plane in a self-asserting prayer
to God.

Hey, you be courteous to me. Remember we said that if either of us uttered something that was a little acidic (contentious, the new trendy word) or I didn't agree, that we would tenderly mention it and try to patch up? Yeah, I remember dhat, but youse is going to New York now so you can't expect those courtesies. If I say you are now *in denial about a hell of a lot of things*, and you don't like it, then tough nuggies. You can run to your friends for support if you like, and if you have any friends. Oh these clichīs and jargon words! I try to be original but now I seek support and deny I'm in denial and forget to hum "so what?"

I still can talk to myself (I can hear what he says and talk back). "You're full of shit, you're completely wrong." Counter reply: "I'm on the right track, but in baby shoes." I detect a streak of the heroic and let loose—I won't go so far as to call it devil-may-care in Jeremy Jones, who eats Shredded Wheat for breakfast two days in a row, but at least he's on the upbeat.

"You think God says it's okay you dropped chanting your quota of the holy names?" No, he'll accept your sincere I.O.U. and *struggle* (my most used vocabulary word; "life is a bitch") and will bless me one day with return to the norm and even beyond that.

There are thirty-one flavors among the lecturers. I'm not the best, said Swami Dodger (Sandy Koufax to himself—or let's say Ralph Branca,[18] even humbler). But I have unique tongue. Just open your mouth and speak what you can. Throw the ball. Remember you're an improviser, like Braxton. You can stop in the middle of one direction and suddenly change and say, "That's not what I want to say," and get closer to heart and humor. You can choose, you can, it doesn't depend on holding the "magic black feather" in your Dumbo elephant trunk, sweetheart. We love you. Do it for Kṛṣṇa and the Swami.

I trust myself and my dependence in Him; I trust my affirmations about the old days' ring of truth, "he recalled."

Now if you don't mind, I'll call for my chauffeur. Dammit, the walkie-talkie doesn't work. All right, I'll just limp by myself downstairs into the bath and good luck, a cup of Radox and delicious country water.

Music and abstract,
seeing double early in the morning,
haven't picked up the beads,
but I'll get there soon.

We've been through the primary
of this not convoluted intellectual
talk. Show off beyond
your realizations, sister. We are on the ground and
need to have compassion. Help others.

I'm very grateful for the help my
family gives. Me am dependent.

Even God doesn't like to be alone.
We may have special friends so
don't be jealous. Dear Lord,
include me in the number.

After the six weeks' training
course at Naval Officer
School in Rhode Island,
they posted the scores.

Everyone milled around, I was toward the back but eyes peered through. I had passed. I did not fail. I could come back next year.

But I had resolved I
wouldn't. Rather be a
two-year gob washing
floors in humility.

I was on my way to Kṛṣṇa
not to Lieutenant Commander.

A formidable yet pained (why?) interrogator put Watts Swami into a box (bulletproof like Adolf Eichmann stood in).

"What is your goal? You don't seem to know."

"It's to hang in there at Prabhupāda's lotus feet even though I say things like, 'He feels distant to me.'"

"Seems to me you're more a Christian than a Krishnite."

"I never go to Christian church, I don't like their "once-only" theology. And I can't connect with the whole Judaic-Christian saga. I have a soft spot for the story in Luke, and the Master's teachings are wise and Kṛṣṇa conscious."

"Your own writing seems to have lost its aspiration, desperate-yearning in prayer."

"Maybe. I've been physically and mentally sick a long time,

teacher. It takes a lot out of a man. At times like this he seeks support, not put-down. It's also part of a not-uncommon story, shared by saints and certainly all ordinary devotees—we flail, we go through dark periods, we ask ourselves, What is my goal?"

"What is your illness?"

"Post-traumatic anticipatory anxiety migraine. That's a mouthful, huh?"

"Why do you take medicine for it?"

"Common sense. The doctors say so. It gives me relief. What are you inferring?"

"You're psychologically addicted, junkie."

"Anything else?"

"I'd like to hear higher things than the morbid descent into the self, the daily dreary. I want to hear not just about the all-too-human *guru* but the eternal teachings in *paramparā*, the learned, luscious sports of Vraja and the intellectual derivations thereof. I love you and dare you to rise from your many malaises."

They let WW Swami out of the Adolf box, but nobody cared to shoot him anyway. He was planning to go to "God bless America," but what good would that do?

Wave the flag of *hari-nāma*, Swami Watts, I do stick with you and so do others. Pull out all those spears and throw them as weapons.

Night and day the melody
haunts him. The hills of
Wicklow will fade,
and so will memories of
hermit's romance.

He prays to increase in
prayer night and day
night and day he's
attached to the All-Loving
who won't abandon him—so many graceful
mighty saints. "He did

a few services and we won't
forget."

He's got no reason to cry except he's got only two days to live. Then he goes to the kennel. Leaves his royal situation. Uddhava says he'll try to find a home for him. The cat's owner is Catowner. The cat gave him less affection over the years, but the human inmates gave him more attention. His eyes. His demands. He didn't give much. Wouldn't sit on your lap. But they stayed steady in feeding him the best vegan chips. He seems to be aware he has only two days left. "Cats are intuitive." Food, warmth, he's dry, he passed stool and urine, still he's whining a little, although he doesn't know I phoned Abhaya to come with the cat box on Thursday.

Excuse me for the direct cry. It's not *me*, it's just a cat. "You don't want to worry about him so much or you'll come back next life as a cat," U. laughed. Whose cry is it then?

Catowner worried if he was doing the right thing. Some people said he was ruining the remainder of his life. He mentioned examples of people who seemed to be doing well. "They're having trouble too," was the reply. Who's through-and-through happy?

Jittering withered skin. Moving back to the modern country, to a new community. His skin hangs under his chin, big magnified eyes...even U. said, "Everything is going smooth," *but* he crossed his fingers in the air. Yeah, you've got to live that way. Never sure.

Hari-nāma is as far away from me as my Uncle Sal. It's like a dream I woke up to. Don't worry, don't worry, God will forgive you. Say His name longingly just one time, "Nārāyaṇa"—KṚṢṆA.

I will be tender, noncontentious.
Why rile them?
Stand your ground. "I've been
getting a little cheeky lately."

The big preacher invited him on
a tour. He said, "I've got my
duties taking care of my wife and children."
Preacher sayeth, "Are you saying I should
be doing that too?"
You said it

And how they made an underground to
undermine the peaceful *guru*
but it collapsed, all these histories
we bemoan and laugh at now.

I heard the present GBC men like to go for
a round of golf now and
then. "What if the nasties
hear you watch Laurel and Hardy?"
I defy them to sit beside me and *not* laugh.

Yes but that's frivolous and we should
be studying. Give us a break.
I'm no big *sādhu* as you are.
I will not be complacent.
Kṛṣṇa, I will struggle
out of this one. Follow the path
of medicine and therapy of *śravaṇam* and
kīrtanam and if

some upstart three- or four-star
general doesn't like it.
"What will you *do* then?"
"I'll think it over. Maybe
go for a walk in my jeans
and learn again the thing I
most want. I don't need
your authorization to reach Him.

CHAPTER NINE

9

It's an old-fashioned locomotive with the most erratic, very long long line of cars following behind precariously. They called it the zig-zag line of truth. Passing through these mountains, it's the best you can do to approximate a straight line. You are going into total darkness (that has been carved out by dynamite and periodically checked to see it's holding up all right). There's a cow-catcher on the front of the loco, but men and trucks are not always so fortunate when they get in the path of this steaming electric beast. (Steam engines are all in the museums now.)

The zig-zag line of truth. The geography predominates over the locomotive; if there is a tall hill, he must go up and he must go down. He must go across the Verrazano Bridge and the bridge across the Platte River and the countless other bridges. But always progress, faster or slower, or it couldn't have been engineered for that part of the country. It is not always pleasure or even truthful; with sometimes breaking track from the direction or goal we want to reach, making a back loop, but all in the service of the truth and the goal.

That's all I can do today, maybe less than sixteen rounds, maybe it's not the best, too much or too little sleep. A locomotive should not be in anticipatory anxiety. He slammed away, crying "I know I can! I know I can!" But sometimes he tears his pistons and hammers and moans, "I think I can—I think I can," and then even an occasional gasp, "I cannot make it, I cannot make it. It's too hard. Oh mercy, hold me." And the Lord replies, "Do something *more*, every ounce to deserve the mercy which is coming. It's coming now. It's coming now." Prayer work, I oil and work the worn men who are fried at the least.

"Heard someone walking about the stairs," said Janie, who sleeps in the house alone, and she became afraid. She thought it was the servant coming to forage for his favorite big candle and matches because the electricity went off. Then she heard him leave the house. She searched the rooms for flashlights and candles and matches. She mis-peed into the urine bottle. She used the walkie-talkie. Wild Bill came over. It was only twelve midnight, day after the full moon too. Bill answered and the electric bulbs all worked. Jane said, "Jane must be going crazy."

(Eventually I'm going to want a complete roster of the residents of Happy Hill House. I thought to start it out with two people. I don't want more than five! Tell the truth. Maybe some vagrants have started to live in the nearby hills.)

I feel I'm getting a bit fired up about my religiosity, spirituality. I still don't bow down and say my prayers fifty percent of the time when I pass Them first thing in the morning. But I still feel a spark. I'm not getting buffaloed into the blues. Get more Ornette, even if it seems you've lost them. Now the house is quiet. If some bum or the cat was prowling or the electricity was off, it's corrected. I'm sorry to have disturbed Willy, my ego and subpersons.

I don't mind saying something about
me, but I do like to stay
back on this hill.
They like to say he's doing nothing
for ISKCON because "he's always sick."

She was probing him, "You write
wonderful books." And your servant
does your typewriter and you
sharpen your own pencil.

I'm not sure Fred has
any more heart. I heard they put
foo-foo and gelatin on his thin burgers.

So there. I'll work the streets begging

water, Laurel and Hardy arrested for vagrancy
"but the jails are too
full so I'll let you go."
Does that mean we can sleep on the park bench?

You get the hell out of here and
I'll give you both one hour to leave town
and I don't want to see your faces again.
But he *did*—with his wife in bed!

The holy prankster Nityānanda did
joke like that but He made them light,
clear and even singing
holy names chanting climbing
trees jumping to other trees.

I too will recover. You'll
see. I'll get the cat off my
back and kick her out
the door. We'd really go hunting
and trap the
bad men, so what? I have nothing much
to say but chat (imperative, good
advice) Hare Kṛṣṇa.
(I'm doing it right Prabhupāda
will you forgive?)

Wow, what a letter to lynch a mob.

It's essential for *sannyāsīs* to have male friends. Not gobs and gobs of them. And they have to be "just right." For example, suppose one *sannyāsī* struggled with his loneness. He'd have to have a friend to talk to, and not one who would slam it to him from one point of view. Shall we put on snowshoes and search the Arabian Desert looking for the man? He'll appear, Kṛṣṇa will reveal him. But the first friend he reveals might not be the one, so don't give him the full confidentiality.

They will have to drag off Wicklow

the blind *sādhus*, see
how they run, see how
they run. Not long for them.

Death can catch them at one second.

Carlow was searching his novel in his Carlow dorm at Carlow College. He thought, What if I die? Will I go to heaven for cows? He thought with anxiety that he still didn't have the new shoe for his ankle insert. You have to buy shoes in the shoe store, not that they match. But he's trying another blind mouse. He ran an inventory of things missing in his room—beads. Would he be compelled to use them if he found them? His poems, some on a typed tape, one missing. But so what, "I've got so many, there's plenty more where this came from." He thought of the double-bind he was in—I *do* love my disciples, but it's a bitch to travel and reach them. In one picture he's around at the temple with the *daṇḍa* excited and looking as angry as hell.

Keep talking to me. Explain how your—oh I can't see again! Eyes going double! Trouble. Scoundrels, trouble. Going to America from the airport. St. Patrick's celebrated smalltime in Dublin. Loud, loud speakers with loud music. A corny St. Patrick mingling around the crowd with a rubber snake. Chamber of Commerce persons with candies in boxes—but one wonders whether they're giving them away or out for a sale. You hesitate at the "hospitality." AND a sixteen-year-old colleen flexing her calves in between her dancing set with the other girls. You were rushed through the airport by your chauffeur and didn't get a good look at the plaid-skirted dancers.

Oh Mother of Mary please pray for us now and at the hour of our death. Do you mean it? How much?

You said pastiche. Did you mean when materials are taken from different places and patched together?

"No! This is all original. I should have looked up the word I was looking for...I mean, like, abstract. No, not abstract. You have to see it to understand it. Go from one subject to another category. Don't show it to me before it's published if you don't want it criticized. If you aren't contentious to me and I am not contentious to you, then I am willing to have a friendship. But if you come attacking me, I don't see the point."

Well neither do I. I didn't see much help in what he said. They don't know what he's going through.

The man even cut his own competition but he prayed down flat *daṇḍavats* and hid his tears; he's flat-out, he says. He says he's so anxious he may be able to get out of it if he can delegate it to someone else. God delegates to the devotees if they love to serve. Sure! We'll do it, just give us a chance.

Chuga by you forgot a poem.
It's in my pocket. The father leaves the
house and the boy
and girl are left alone but what
will they do? It's a kind
of teenage Vaiṣṇava dating. So they
don't have to mix in the
city in the bars with the fast-movers.

I didn't hear what you said:

You've been hearing the *karatalas* too closely
never look down, he's got to get out of
the memories of all evil. She looked in
from the snowing outdoors
with a signal. They have stolen the
Romanov jewel again.

Do you worship Jesus, you hip?
Say Kṛṣṇa Kṛṣṇa, don't mix up
your worship John, just because you've got anxiety
jitters. I'm sorry it happens

that way all the time.
Charge 'em $1.95 and I'll pick up the
check next time I come around.

Tell them I'm a good friend
of Swami Jones. I'll pick up the tab.
Tell them it's all a fraud.

He counted so many *aparādhas*
he is not working to remove them
but just sits in his nap room singing some blues.

Hey writer, I'm glad we're not dating because we don't want people to know you've been hiding and unable, under the covers for a week. The world would know artillery has been flashing over your head (barely missing you) and you, like Harry Langdon,[19] have been scared stiff and hanging on for dear life. So much so that you have not written any of it! And you won't either, right now, until you gather your wits later. I saw craziness in a man and it frightened me, and I'm frightened to see him again, even though he was such a buddy. (Oh! Stop the "I"! Langdon said, "He was my closest friend in school, but I would not live with him now.")

Other explosions. In World War I they had these see-through sparkling hand grenades—you held awhile, as in World War II versions, and then threw—kaboom!

You are pampered but not arrogant (laughed the nurse) yet when ordered, he climbed the "suicide pole" and was exposed to enemy fire. They didn't hit him but dropped the pole down lower and lower with each shot until there was nothing left but Jack the survivor. Stay under the covers but don't suggest.

So the man has been taken away for closer care, and his friend may be going later this week. Jack Langdon graduated from the Citadel and received highest, perfect marks on the code-breaking exam. They wanted him, the U.S. Army, and he wanted them. They gave $10,000 just to keep him interested, and he signed the papers. But when they found he had a heart murmur—that is, an attraction for chanting the holy names of God—they searched for a way to drop him and found it by the presence of another malady in his body.

Dusky night of the *jīva*. Similar situation to Harry in the army. The doctors said to him, "We don't think we can discuss a serious assessment of your offers of 'yes' or your rude 'rejections' because we don't think you're in a healthy enough state to make a real assessment of yourself.

Our friend (similar cases) set the speedometer at sixty miles per hour, but he was exhausted and fell asleep. The car spun around one hundred and eighty degrees and hit a ramp. This was in India. He was completely unscathed but the car was a total wreck. A woman came out of a nearby building and said, "Do you believe in Jesus Christ?" He said, "Yes" (although he was a Hare Kṛṣṇa devotee, he didn't disbelieve Christ). She said, "Do you know what would have happened to you if you had not believed in Jesus Christ but died in that car crash?" "Yes," he said humbly. She smiled and hugged him, and they helped him to get the car towed, and he received complete repayment from the insurance company. Then he took a bus to Vṛndāvana.

Death at any moment. Do you know what will happen if you don't believe? I don't exactly know but have an idea. Something unknown.

So much change I thought I could write more to face the fear over the loss of a crazy friend and my relapsing. I thought I could not write because you can lose the continuity of the book after a week of lying in bed wondering "what next?," afraid to write because writing requires art and honesty and clarity—but really you just have to try and Kṛṣṇa will help.

He wants to see some Kṛṣṇa hosannas in return. And mental strength and self-assertion. Haribol.

Well I believe we have a vague direction
you write the letters M, W, E, A, S on
a piece of paper and then you
walk around it and
figure out, maybe some sun shadow.

But he was so ignorant
people

kicked him down the stairs.
He didn't have the guts to call a man back
and cancel the appointment.

Failure *low* on a life status—
all that's all right, all you need is
tenderness for God's chilluns
and love
for the Supreme.

Broke there too? Just looking for cigar butts
and ways to cheat people?
Then you need reform and pray
to Nitai to help you open
your lips and stop quitting.

The holy scene in temples and
rituals, but especially in your
feelings and exchanges with them.

You're working for Him under the
guru's orders...that will get you there.

Don't pick my pocket again
don't smash my hands. Don't cross the red line
I warned them, I am God's eunuch.

Mainly the fellow—Chaplin called him "the little fellow," as in "the little fellow was ill-suited for romance"—was looking for a peaceful spot to do regular writing. The idea was to sometimes see supportive friends, but not persons who tried to shame you. When you are confronted by them, then *fight*. You will know how to do that. Do things as you want, not pressured by others. If you have a planned trip, little fellow, to Schenectady, but you don't want to go, then cancel. If they schedule a lecture for you but you're not up to it, then cancel. But do things nicely. Maybe give a short talk in excusing yourself.

You've decided.

Don't pull girls' pigtails.

At first he wasn't sure what the reader understood but now it's clear. The eyes are too heavy.

Shoes too hot, friend says
he has an achy knee,
they're drinking in the bars.

But came back flying, I'm
glad to say.

You can call anytime or leave a
concise note or talk longer
as when Caitanya's friends got
together and stayed up all night

as He told them details of His
South Indian pilgrimage. No one was
nodding in that audience.
If *you* were there, you probably would
have nodded.

"*Kīrtanas* bore me" said the society
girl. She preferred pizza parties
with *prajalpa*. Hari drove her
there and left in disgust when
he saw it was nonsense.
He had his only car crash
on the way home. Don't
run around looking for many
counselors. Your spiritual
master is your first helper,
even if you've got a gripe.

And a trusted Godbrother. Can
hardly keep the eyes open
but believe heart is strong
and God still has
place for me and all of us.

The priest in cassock said the thing he missed most was wearing trousers. We sympathize. But we don't make the stupid conclusion to visit bars and pick up women. The economic needs. "No time" or attitude for holy prayer. Don't miss the newspaper. He said the highest U.S. alert is colored red, and when he arrived it was on orange. Oh gosh, it will be hard enough staying away. A rough spot for McDermish—while passing through Kentucky he was stumbling like a drunk. When he took his shoes off and placed them on a security belt, there was a jingling sound. Nothing like it! The security men became serious. "But these shoes cost me $1,000. You're not going to cut them open." The nun sat and muttered on her rosary, felt protected now and at the hour of her death. Mary would protect her from being cast into hell by the agents of Beelzebub.

Hello hello operator, I've been cut off the line (Kafka's title, *The Castle*).

Now for him this is risky. "All right mister Surveyor we have rechecked your files and it is all right for you to stay in the land. The people in the hotel treated him with more respect. Now here, the sun is in a mild sky, it's 6:00 A.M. and the fathers are up against the wall. You forget me?

They simply wanted to test whether he was valid.

We think he'll pull out
of it as long as he
keeps climbing. He didn't want
to give up. You know how it
can happen.
But those first signs after
breakfast that maybe he
should fight instead of sleep
but he keeps sleeping in a
wonderful spiritual drug,
sleep.

I melt down. He was a good friend
of yours, wasn't he?

Yes, he had much more work
to do, he just finished his Ph.D., a translator saw
Prabhupāda tugging him in the
sky above Mayapur Mandir, saying,
"Come out. We've got
more significant work for you
in the movement."

Jealous! Most of that clairvoyant
being able to see it.

Waking suddenly
Kṛṣṇa is playing with His friends at
breakfast. Our time is dwindling.

The boys were in the backroom, nonalcoholic, but smoking and talking *prajalpa*, friendly old coots. One said, "What a character he is!" They were all vets trying to recover in different ways. One had an iron leg stump, Pop had rheumatism; they had a password from the previous war: "It looks like it's going to rain" when an attack proved imminent. So we're passing that word around and sure enough the mob boss sent his *guṇḍās* and they attacked the old trolley, which at night was the good old boys' hangout. After the long fight, the casualties were eight broken noses, several broken ribs and legs, a broken iron leg stump, scratches, etc. The mob was driven off but they had a quick plan to return and steal the old trolley. Don't mind if you don't understand all these details as to why they were stealing the trolley, etc. It's confusing enough for all those who took part in it.

Freddy was a leader and veteran of that fight but had since been licking his wounds for ten years up in the hills. Maybe he'll continue to do this. But he was planning to take a three-week visit to a quiet community in upstate New York. The purpose would be more therapy, more rest and getting "unstuck" from his present surroundings, which were perhaps adding to his depression. Get out and see some new faces. A new nose?

Perhaps come back to live in the country entirely alone and do his own washing and drying of clothes and cooking. You always get a few phone calls. Sound attractive? Live with yourself where God begins to be and ask Him, "Who am I?" Freddy with a greater plea, "Help me, Nitai, to improve my life, get rid of these headaches and cry out your holy name."

Yes we can get some juice
always from the Lord. He
won't desert us. But
what's this priority of
poems before *japa*?
Shouldn't every ounce go into
the holy names first?

Names, Jane, Jiminy,
Raghunātha, Billy, Alice—
yeah but Kṛṣṇa, Hare
Kṛṣṇa, that's the matrix
the motherlode, all you need

and you keep yourself in the desert
eating M&Ms from a parachuted
CARE package?

"How many rounds are you chanting daily?"
He's cool.
"Yeah, but I won't tell" said Frank Sr. "I just have
a slower pace since that
concussion from the iron pipe
in the trolley fight."

He has all intentions and *wishes*
(they are very important, as are *prayers*)
for recovering to average spiritual status

and that's pride too? One might stay
at the long-ride end of the row

wearing a potato sack as
Francis did before they tailored
and canonized him?

The little fellow walked to the edge. A new persona. He didn't have to live all the time in his reclusive chateau in Switzerland. He's from America and all his connections and operations are still from there. So go live there, his Irish neighbor suggested, and come back and visit here for breaks. Oh it sounds exciting. No improvement in health but just climb a hundred-foot flag pole and step off. These are our new plans and we may execute them in a week. It is better to tell you this way, indirectly. So many—just a handful really—but it's all I need, *well-wishers, advisers, real helpers when it counts.* But the little fellow has to do his part and not get alarmed when there are bumps in the road, delays, etc. Pampered. Patient. Stay in touch. By indirect I don't mean it's not from the heart but saying more by stabs.

Tenderly if you can to whoever
you meet but tough too, the
inner resources you knew
you had when you must
call on them.

He practiced eight hours a day.
I'm down now to almost nothing
but I can recover.
Thirty-two a day, sixty-four a day. Does
it matter? A friend said,
"Prabhupāda won't count

the numbers at the end but
will hug you and take you to him
grateful for what you've done."

"Hmm," I said. "I hope I'll be
with him." People come with baggage.
But some have too much for me,

these days of recovery. Therefore I
discharge them and seek comfort—
to chant the holy names.

10

CHAPTER TEN

Can't even stand up. Wakes up at 7:00 A.M. and thinks it's time for supper. (You might too if you lived in rain-dreary Ireland. Oh, ya putting down the old sod now, yank?)

"Don't put me and my doctor down," said Shorty. He was hiding all his FDNY and "God Bless America" T-shirts and Tommy pants because he'd live in more formal circumstances. It would be better. Yet the crocuses would grow around the beech tree in the back yard in Wicklow. Okay, you can't have everything. One or the other. I am going to a young community. The professor put his shorts on backwards. As a *sannyāsī* he wasn't supposed to wear shorts. It's true. The quality of life is crappy, all you do is nap. The patient can say to the doctor, "This is too much! I want my life back. I can't sleep all day."

We'll teach you some tricks—how to squeeze sixteen *japa* rounds in, in segments, through a 24-hour period. It'll be yours again. Winter is ending. I'm hoping and I'm following the doctor's orders. So cut out the crap that I'm a dunky junky.

This was the rhetoric of Swims Swami. He was shouting into the phone to his friend, who was saying, "He was enchanted by the beautiful sight of the Napa Valley, where he saw a sign, 'Wine Is Poetry,' or 'Grapes Are Poetry,' and thought of the frail poet. Sleep better, young man. If you heard a strain in my voice, it's because I'm using my cell phone. The cat sees I'm packing suitcases and knows what it means. He'll be left behind. Please find a home for this beautiful cat. I can't live here just for him. But I love his beautiful eyes and hope he can find a place to live out his routine of eating and sleeping and pissing and pooing without getting attacked by too many other cats and rodents.

We are happy despite the shit.
We remember God and get joyous

again, even though in chains.
We are not meant for this world.
Lying on your back ain't bad either.

At least you get in one poem
a day. "Tag on Kṛṣṇa?," he asked,
a fledgling. "How do you
do it?" I told him it's the
hardest thing to do without the poem
looking artificial.

Because our love is artificial.
Poems of St. Theresa seem
all authentic in outpouring to
Jesus. But I have to talk out of
the side of mouth.

Street man truck driver
who did once become
so excited standing and dancing
in *kīrtana* and seeks it
again. Trading fours
with the drummer at
high speed, "Oleo."[20]

Now he cannot dance, but
heart dances—I will
love my Lord and He'll let me
chant precious names.

As if the world were made to spend all your time reading, causing eye strain and finally blindness. And for lack of physical exercise and economic development work on liberation and you miss the greatest opportunity. But me and my comrade can't help but think of creating a Niagara Falls of Tim's Kṛṣṇa conscious books. At least it would be beautiful to look at. People could go there on their honeymoon and walk in the tunnel under the falls. (They say the Falls is getting smaller, like Govardhana, but it's still got plenty of kick.)

And maybe while these young lovers and business persons were rushing through Niagara, they might stop a mo' and read some of it. You can read in *Ripley's Believe It or Not* a small list of those who have read all of EJW. I'm not complaining. It's just me and my comrade were thinking, Why not unload the whole bomb—it won't be a dud—and whoever reads some is lucky. Why leave out thousands of words?

And then SDG's new book.

Plan-making. No hard hats allowed.

Before I die. WCW[21] told Alice B. Toklas,[22] "Print one big stock of Gertrude's[23] writings and throw out the rest." They were aghast because they thought all of her words were immortal. Miles Davis'[24] motto was "leave it out." He asked Coltrane, "Hey man, why do you play so long?" Trane said, "I've got a lot to say." We are thankful he did, and we'll never know what Miles didn't say.

Okay, you Zen guys would rather say nothing. Each one has to go by his conviction. I've got a lot to say. I don't say much to people with my mouth, but if they'd like to sit around my "*book āśrama*" I want to have enough if a Y2K comes and if there's no more TV and e-mails, just some thin soup and someone to read, to glorify Kṛṣṇa—because that's what we're here for. So spake Tim.

Pick any one is good. Kṛṣṇa
and Rādhā loves music on lute
and flute. Don't cut us
off yet. We've got a lot to say.
Time is no object. I never
picked the menu. Anything, not too heavy.
Give me a car key for my
"Beamer" and I'll
drive in ecstasy through the Napa Valley
singing "I'm the most
happy fella!"
How ecstatic it looks, but

nothing compared to Goloka,
where "money" grows
on trees and no demons
really come.
So pick any one.
Just give me a little
chance to catch the cat so that
vet can take him away—
today is the scheduled day.
Forgive me Haribol, I brought
you in to kill rats. You maybe killed
one mouse in two years
but we loved you.

The flow of an organ brings to his senses the forgetful morn, but he still doesn't know whether it's Friday or Saturday and he can sleep "forever." This is called the tsetse fly disease, caused by an insect usually living in Africa. You never wake up unless someone plays you a Mickey Mouse cartoon.

Much more dangerous than falling asleep during a Shakespeare play or an august church sermon is actually forgetfulness of existential self. Sanātana Gosvāmī (known as Dabira Khasa when he first met Lord Caitanya) had this deep malady: he knew many outer things, scholasticism, so he was considered a pandit by the society of human fellows, but he *confessed* to Lord Caitanya, I don't know who I am. Please tell me. *Ke āmi?* What is the goal of my life? They tell me not to worry about this, but I am alarmed.

Old and foolish
heard he can't remember
one day from the next. Fritz Perls[25]
died as a pretzel, and they continued
on but they missed him.

You can't mourn forever. You have
to do your master's work. Can't

find many articles in this house, I
searched everywhere but found only
three *sannyāsa* uniforms and no Ornettes.
Do you need a shoe horn? Decided
Donald Hall,[26] "I must bring my
Rādhā-Govinda, even if I must
leave behind my shirt and pants."

Remember: deep scratching
Riley gave as I stuffed him into the
cat cage, something to remember
him by.

Not a stigmata. That I've
completely lost. Oh no your
supporters say,
cry, let your
feelings come, God wants
that. He shows you who
you are. It's a lonely
sannyāsī with plenty of
time to write and read and
learn authentic prayer.

Lord. You came sentimentally to Ireland because your mother came from here. The little people. The biddies. The orange men. More Catholic than Rome. I don't know. Wanted more power in a quaint place.

God. Two voices at once. Tell me the story of the two men in monologues telling the same story. Get me that book by Sanātana Gosvāmī. Everyone's writing today for their reasons. Babe Ruth[27] held the record for many years. Everyone trying to outdo the other. Hear this zap, can you outdo it? I doubt it. They can go play golf, karate, lacrosse, tennis, no need to hear my lecture. I'd rather sleep anyway. Bob thought like this and four hundred thoughts a minute with no particular direction. He tried to stop the negative ones and not be angry at people. Be sweet. Don't avenge. Write intelligently, Jack. A hard command. Everyone's got their favorite sayings and mournings. Riley lives now in a cage. I'm sorry I can't take you to Maine. Sounds good though.

May the Lord protect us. What are you afraid of? Don't you know things will go smooth? Don't be such a scaredy. He put on his brass knuckles and ran to the champion with such strength that the champ began to *run away* in the boxing ring. Our hero was mostly dreaming. How did he wind up so far beyond? Will he find peace, like a discovery from *tapasya*?

Hey, this was supposed to be a poem
but it broke into pieces
Alice in Wonderland looked up at the egg-headed
man who spoke his sardonic speech.

They both had sharp wits but
he was older and sadder and his wit
much sharper.

Come see me. I will try my best
to rest yet love you with the
expected wound. And
speaker of God, somehow for
something you authentically did
for the cause of *param*
padam

Puss is gone, that pest and darling. Brownie. Frantic and gloomy in a kennel. But I would not carry him to America this time, to a house with strangers. There's a superstition that cats abort pregnant women, J. Swami told me. But it's another absence in the head, oh friendly fire that kills your own, there's nothing that can be done about it in this war of life.

But the pure devotee is absolved from slaughter and sentimentalism because he's calling to help for every *jīva* and spreading the word, "Wake up, all *Jīvas*, to the mercy of Gaura-Nitai." His vegan chips, the house scattered with them, let's see how they pack today, the fifty-year-old frat boys. Will Rādhā and Kṛṣṇa fit in? Of course. And will you limp through without too much sleep? No problem. But will you like it when you get there? From the misty, quiet, criminalless (no cow-slaughter, sheep slaughter?) the hills of Erin to the ganglands of the next parish West.

The judge said, "Guilty."

The defendant said, "We ain't going!" and he and his sons pulled their guns and killed the judge and lawyers. Check your body for bombs. Woman's breasts might contain rockets. Check that guy's belt, book bag, suitcase. What are all these pills? The girls told you not to carry them or even take them. How come you stumble, man, and have a glassy look? Because I'm going home. Fred's little saga to live with the disciples of another guru, but he paid his way from his own account, unless they want to help with a few Hail Mary's, Bengali *bhajanas* and Laurel and Hardy's.

"We have seen that one before so I don't want to sit with you tonight again." I had intended it as a friendly last-time get-together, but he said, "I saw Charlie Chaplin and 'The Immigrant' before." I could see Edna Purviance's face again and again and again.

So he stayed in his room, but then a next-door neighbor from the Ukraine came by and we laughed together, last chance.

Packing day. Popeye. They praised my dad's muscular forearms and I was mighty proud. Dear Mother (in her nineties now), I'm sure you'll go to heaven. Go ahead, so pack up your Rādhā-Govinda and go Alabama bound. Does that attorney carry a pistol? Better he not. Even the gendarmes carry only nightsticks.

Your last worry, be calmed. Take headache pills. Suggestion: when headache comes, why not just ride it out with no meds? Let him hold me down as he says.

This anecdote, close to the life of a familiar persona, was brought to you care of Grape Nuts Flakes, Sleepy Time Gal products and no *japa* yet. Let's pull out of it.

Tenderly the day will proceed with
a million things that could
go wrong. Wing and prayer and
computer. Captain Ted Rice
played tenor sax at the
high school dances so
he didn't have to step
on the girls' toes. Combed his hair in
"duck's ass." Sam
stood like a wallflower,
talking occasionally to others,
went to the bathroom to stick it out—
no not one dance—
not until the ordeal was over
by 10:00 or 11:00 P.M.

Why go at all? Why not just
stay home and read a book,
not care what others think,
cry real tears
if they come? Make
an atom bomb, discover poetry, go for
a walk with your collie.
You don't have to be unhappy without a bimbo.

Give me your number, what's your fax? Do you have a residence? No, I've just been living five years in Italy. But you want a long-distance phone. What's your name? I consider that an intrusion. I cannot even find my bills left on the alarm. I just took a 2-hour nap and thought I slept 23 hours, and now you call me up and tell me I need long distance. Three days coming today. These separate notes. I can't remember who they are.

He's broke, he can't add anymore, lucky if he can write. They still have ice and snow here. Do you have long distance? Leave me alone! How did you know my name? I'm just an American and I'm glad you didn't ask my name. I thought I'd have to punch you right out.

Shy. You going to get better keeping and talking to them and asking thanks, buying things. Please get me a video of Laurel and Hardy. Please get me greens and proteins, whatever that is. You don't have to wear *dhotīs* here. Just lounge and recover, take another nap but not too many. Keep track of the data. You could dress Rādhā and Kṛṣṇa? You could take Nṛsiṁha out of bed?

I told him I don't pass the
'60s and '70s. He says he likes the 70's.
I don't know what he's talking about.

I'm just about to start a *japa* round.
He says, "Some people in
the community study *sādhana*.
Some are into taking care of their children.
I have spoken to you,
a swami said to stand and
speak is hard because the children
make a lot of noise.

The motel and racing show they ran.
I haven't skills in them.
The cat is in the kennel. Did I do
the right thing in coming
here? Ah yes, you can have so many
paraphernalia, Barth.

They called me on the phone and
asked me if I had long distance. I said
I'm just a visitor. But you are a human being,
he said, so when you find a home you'll want
a phone.

I have no money. I can only beg for these things. I don't
want so much to be in touch.

Too many people to contend
with, right? You die
screwed up. I don't
think you'll make it.

Take it to the zoo.
Give me a bugle.
Show me the shop.

Do a good job and we'll give you
a raise. Do your work and we won't
beg you to chant your rounds
or listen to lectures. His disciples
love him. Mine don't
even know me.

Just a regular guy—chant,
even wear right uniform.
It will come in the mail next year
and someone will tell us Christ is dead but
the spirit of the holy
eternal Godhead lives on. That boy and his
friends all want religion. But don't preach.

You bum, you gonna stay in N.Y. or go back to Ireland? Stay here awhile. You have no self-assertion. U. told you to go to America, so you went (I'm talking to Henry). Who was really the best? So depressed. You get to just see pretty little 3-year-old girls here. This country kills 11,000 of its own citizens a year, and in Canada they only kill about 50. Go with Saci to the shoe store, get fitted. Doze off thinking of cowboy music, a country nothing. Eyes blue. The whole body is going to fall apart. Can't you see? The anxiety, fearing limitation, can't be made who you are.

Can't read a damn thing, chant beads. I could go to Albany with you. Walk and try the shoes on.

Don't care if he's taking care of me, I'd rather eat alone, but stays like a puppy dog so I'll tell him some confidential things, but he's hearing different versions, so I keep it mild.

I leave out the pain.

My sister doesn't even know I'm alive at 63 and I don't know if she's a Sacred Heart member or a boozer depressed with the children growing up and two new husbands. What about the Hare Kṛṣṇa group—

is he still in it?

The man stepped in the taxi and the driver immediately pointed a pistol at him and said, "Give me all you have got." Both had worked all day for what they had. "Might rules." The sages drooped low. I'll tell who Lord Caitanya is in a simple way, what His teachings are in a simple manner. Esoteric teachings I'll leave to others.

Kṛṣṇa is Rādhā asking you to call for Kṛṣṇa, sort of. *Rādhā-kṛṣṇa nahe anya*. Are you going to take a nap? I can't understand some Godbrothers.

I need peed impedes
I was all right
the parts were not adequate.
Will you go to another place
and leave the present?
He said, Though realizing
each hour of pure earth wrong!

Kṛṣṇa Kṛṣṇa guys have trouble in
Kṛṣṇa because they don't have
girlfriends and move as neophytes
and not enough hope.

The boys gathered in one room drinking Coke and the girls drank sherry in another room. Blink every blink. He says, bring me a brandy, *durlabham* (what's it really called?) that can for constipation, video worth hundreds of dollars of energy for the *japa* and the reading of what I want and enough ability to write it and yet you fall asleep, you wake up when a tender big shot comes. Bounce the basketball, stay alive, send out your talent scouts to hear the groovy straightedge music, which you can't stand to hear anymore but may hire for your company.

There was a signature on the product that said, "*Vaiṣṇava dāsa anudāsa.*" I know those things you find now.

Oh well if you won't do it I will.
I say buy me *all* the W.C. Fields and
Harry Langdon, Harold Lloyd, Del had the bill and said this is too much, can
you condense this? Don't be a greedy swami just sitting in his room.

She didn't know her brother was famous.
He didn't even know where she was.
Kissing the Pope's ring.
We like the praise of the Holy Names
don't tell me too much about it or I'll
be bored on the re-hearing: "The Holy Name
is the greatest thing."

Don't come up here, I'm in a private
position. Don't enter, I'm composing a poem.
I don't want to hear your
kids making so much money and noise.

They give the kids an allowance, one-third for financial investment, one-third for charity, and one-third for *preyas*, chocolate ice cream, your own kind of cellular telephone

but don't go to Coney Island by yourself.
Come with us. There are bad men
who kill at the rate of 11,000 a year
in this country. I can't deny it.

11

CHAPTER ELEVEN

I can pray to Mary across
the Holy Name Hare Kṛṣṇa "The Wreck
of the Hesperus"[28] because I am only a kid
and it doesn't matter yet.

But she empowered Prabhupāda's laws
you grew up hearing
in the city. The saint
is a version of God so it must be true.
I only know that I *want* to go there so
I love to hear her make
the prophecy again and again
that it doesn't matter,
I'll be saved.

It's just a talent of intuition
and she's good to find it so.
I listen to it with great joy.

Yeah, begin.
Tell me who will go and
it's not important if I'm
tired or sick and can't even read.

She was given a full Vaiṣṇava name at birth but it turned into a nickname, Bidge. She was weeping at 2:50 P.M. just before the counselor phoned. No, actually, Budge is a boy, grown up in his forties. Forgive me. There is a baby girl with a nickname similar to Budge, but she wasn't weeping; her mother and father are her counselors. But this male Budge was weeping because at breakfast his friend was talking about a *sannyāsī* he very much likes, and he said, "His vision built this place." Then he said the *sannyāsī* had another even bigger vision, and he described that one. Budge was later taking one of his many naps, and he awoke with the word "Vision!"—the word hit him. He had no vision. He was too disabled to have one. He could have a *wish* to have a vision, but couldn't work on it now. He wished to be a special kind of writer, maybe a painter, to chant 16 rounds—that had become not an everyday routine but a "vision" of health for the future. So he was weeping that he was devoid of the ability to carry out visions. But then he "snapped the rubber band" on his wrist of weeping and told himself, "Your complete lack puts you in a good place to call for Kṛṣṇa. He's all you've got and He loves you. He doesn't want projects or even special writing from you. He wants you to serve Him and please Him."

Stiff upper lip. Be a devotee as much as you can for now. They may catch you weeping. Budge, you're lucky, it could be much worse. So he was on his own with this nourishing vision and wet face.

Yeah he's a funny guy,
said "Hello boys and girls this is
Uncle Don." Keep it going,
dry your tears,
use your musical ability.

Get into it. Today it was
just a brief spell of tears.
It would have been a good
time to catch you. You're
the only one I can explain
this too and get the mental picture.

I know the "spiritual" feeling
on it but it's still not heart
and tears for me—that seminars,
theology, forums, awards and diplomas
for the highest scoring on exams.

I'm just a little crumb.
Have you got that stuff
where you can move...

He was fond of "Night
in Tunisia."[29] Would
that release him? I doubt
it. You've got to go to
Confession
and tell your sins to the Priest and
he'll tell you his. Weep and you're
successful. Take a pill.

Just leave me alone. I don't
feel lonely, I just need to know
I have my own time and no
one will bother me. They'll bring me food.

A lecture every two weeks.
That moldy house.
Defeat. The sloping
hills. I want to go back
to Ireland. From there
to the spiritual world.

Electronics makes it
all closer and I can write you letters.

Of course you are self-centered. Not more than average. The priest put these thoughts out of his mind and placed his lovely light-green vestments over his shoulders. The medicine had done the trick once again. But when his host comes (when will that be?), he'd tell him, "You please bathe and dress the Deities, I feel too weak and need extra rest." He had to be up for a breakfast performance with a Vaiṣṇava *sannyāsī*. I wear no beard, no *bhajana*. But he was kind to me.

Who're you talkin about, fella? The priest who sells hot dogs at Coney Island. Who is self-centered. Doesn't want his secrets revealed. "You can make some exceptions."

"I'm afraid of you living alone in that house. You might fall down the stairs and no one would know." But who will live with him? Not a woman. A menial pal. Hard to find. All those cruel jokes.

Beep-boop. Ten little toddlers running around the room while the *sādhu* remained oblivious to them and sang his wonderful *bhajanas*, "Very popular in Vṛndāvana," from a private book. For therapy you can watch W. C. Fields, not for sense gratification.

I got the wrong number
again. You're safe here.
You don't have the strength
to bend over and pour the
water and dress Rādhā and Govinda.

And miss that fun and purify yourself.
A healthier man works, a sick man rests.

Why don't you work harder? I can't.
I'm just going with the flow.
He smiled disbelievingly.
Your father was never lazy like
you. He drove the fire truck.

I sat up straight and bluffed
the *bhajanas*. A baby was pulling up
his tee-shirt, exposing his belly
and chest. He wore baggy denims and
appeared very happy in an "idiotic" fun way
for hours while the bearded
sage sang
the *rasikā* harmonium tunes.

Fred Swami sat up straight in his
long-time convalescence pose.

It's safe here but you could die at any moment.
Would you like to draw how it
feels? There are massive books
that tell you, like *The Death of*
Ivan Illych, who finally saw the Light

and we mixed Vaiṣṇavas hoping we could
reach a higher stage than Buddha Nirvana
on precarious stillness from which
you have to fall down.

Meanwhile this world
is on a little spin and it doesn't
matter if you are in the Hall of Fame.
You have to become
humble and no faking.

Frederick von Braun, did you catch the flow and tight construction of this book? Did you realize the complicated characters? Did you appreciate the scenery description and the beauty of the high-cheekboned girls? Do you like the pet dog? You'll see, he becomes a hero.

But you have to study the book carefully. Listen to the man on the harmonium, you're aching back against the wall while the children play wildly. What would I have done instead? I can't juggle balls. Picture of children so beloved. Will they love them when they grow? I should talk, they don't know what a cad I am.

"What's a cad?"

"A rascal."

In Vaikuṇṭha on earth, they love the Lord but can't see Him face to face, so it's not as good. He assumed I read *Bṛhad-Bhāgavatāmṛta*, he assumed I follow the rules and regs. They assume I'm a good boy. This is what John Maharaja wrote home to his sister.

I got better when I got home. They eased up on the torture.

But you're a tortured man. Five minutes it's one thing and five minutes later, another thing.

I'm not even allowed on the grounds. They search my shoes and ask me questions, and some of them say, "No, you can't see the President." I reply, "What makes you think I wanted to see him? I wanted to see Śrī Bhagavān and adore Him and His *brahmajyoti*."

But right now you are so shaky you can't even tell the time.

You don't sound that bad to me. Gladis drank down her absinthe and gave him a wonderful, encouraging smile.

We are in New York, our old
state. John lives in a
house built in the 1850s.
Poor section. They make
additions, but the doorknobs
fall off and it's a bit cold.

Underrated, you keep hearing, but
maybe he just wasn't that good.
Christ was not underrated.
You phone a few people
for the full picture but they want
you to tell them everything
about their life.
Why should you?

I have got two people I'll tell
anything to. He runs along with
rhythm and his private spells
searching for, praising the almighty Lord.

He's treating me His own way and that's
"healing" taking place on
the meds and therapy—all night.

This team is Stuyvesant—the new place
where I live, lots of families,

rambunctious children
and the soft giant
concentrating on his
own job. The discerning
will like it.

Oh Fernando, the pancakes won't be here for one and a half hours. The stars are all gone. Bernardo saw that I was sleeping and invited me to take a nap. I said, "What if I tried a writing session? They're always so hard." So he took a walk around the block, holding his head low against the conundrum. It's time we admit we have always been love-deprived. We called it "lust-deprived." But *laulyam* for the Lord is a different thing. But I love you and sit beside you singing. You never sang with Bob Dylan. You never sang with anyone. You should try.

The PTA met and asked the author to be clearer. But he was adamant that he had reached a new breakthrough that *was* clearer, healing, happy, like 50,000 people seeing Babe Ruth[30] hit a home run at Yankee Stadium. Was there an official rule demanding him to change? No. God bless America, the first amendment guarantees freedom of speech, so you can say what you like. That you lose readers brings you other problems but they can't stop you from presenting Kṛṣṇa in the words that come. Of course, to be effective, words of God should come from *guru*, *śāstra* and *sādhu*, but that still leaves you a lot of freedom of soul for Jagannātha to speak differently from Malcolm X.

Did he accept the new son-in-law
because of the official paper from the county
or because, after all, they were now family
and the son-in-law *was* a cow-killer too,
even though he did it more "peacefully."
And he promised to take care
of the daughter so he extended his
hand for a handshake to cow-killers.

Besides that, I feel tired, Sam said, but the cellmates scoffed and swung their sledgehammers, crushing rocks. They knew there was no mercy for the black-and-white striped. Swing the hammers until you collapse and then get revived so you can hammer again. It's torture. Just give me some W. C. Fields like you've been promising, and Buster Keaton—come through with those promises. I don't need women, whisky, meat, but I need my pills, so don't be disrespectful. They think they know better than the best doctor in the world.

I'll do some exercise too. I noticed my chest and biceps began to bulge. I'll become a muscle monster. What do you do. I'll become a *japa* chanter, sixteen a day. Pity pity the quota does ever exist, Mark Twain! Count it down, five feet below sea level. It is surprising that many of the veterans are becoming so slow. He holds his average for a while, praise God, pauses. Gil,[31] come out of that slump! "The slump begins at the end of the bat, then goes to the mind, and then turns into the stomach"—Roy.[32] Where are my beads? Surely they will send me to sleep.

Do you know hippo
was coming to town?
You mean the big big animal?
No I mean the dangerous
snake who gives dispensations
to *guṇḍās* and sinners
provided they change their ways.

Like a man climbing the electric fence
screams out in pain and can you
give him a break?

It's not just a small thing but all people
not just a pang
we want order power fear of shame and scandal,
get the real thing thrown out.

I won't listen to you guys and girls who say I won't recover or who say I'm driving in an invisible car with a small South Korean–American chick. She falls underwater, James Bond resuscitates her and they start kissing. They canceled the case. I don't believe him. So I'm up. I'm making my pampered demands so I'll be comfortable. What's the use of staying here if you don't ask for what you want, if you can't take warm naps, if the food isn't A+ — if you can't get A+ food and you exercise on a bunch of machines daily. Fern was telling us this long-distance on the phone. He still didn't know whether he wanted to return to Wicklow. I wanted to know. Even if it was only for two weeks, let him leave Haribol in the spring garden with his vegan chips, the kitchen, and the sleeping and hiding outdoors. Because once he's back in the kennel it will be for a long time.

How about this for a title (already used): "The Ocean and the Desert," or more religious, "The Ocean of Devotion and the Desert of Desperation"? Sounds like New Age mystical or Catholic religion. Instead—"Popeye the Sailor Man," by Satsvarūpa dāsa Goswami. Or "The Pure Bliss of Working on ISKCON Press: A Memoir of 1970," by Satsvarūpa dāsa Used-To-Be Adhikārī, a memoir of Prabhupāda, who drove us and pushed us into the night. "Produce the books," "Don't make mistakes," "Hurry up," "You're still making mistakes—let me know what's going on."

The awakening at early morning—
no headache! All that pain
he went through,
give him a break.
He'll now commence magic—
pigs rabbits and geese
out of the black box
and appear to saw a woman in half.

It's all sham—"love isn't what
it seems, mostly

other peoples' dreams."
Oh good, if we could get that
faultless sniff of doing something brave for
brave Prabhupāda.

Please dear child, please dear Father, get it right
let me see
You—he refreshes me
(flatters?) "You saw him many times
and he knew you and liked you and
spoke to you and even though
you weren't the best."

No idea of the time. You said the ocean and the desert. Why not a moderate life? The survivors? The half-dead who go to work every day although they rather hate it.

Smooth. Do you like the dinner? Not really. None of them much. How could anyone like dinner? No sugar in the milk. And you can't speak up for it. Did you think the Waldorf School was bad? He said nothing. He knew nothing about it except it was not the school he went to. Why do you think it's normal? Smashed potatoes, peas and gravy from Italy. I want to go back to Wicklow, where they served that, but I have orders to take it easy. Why are you upset? Too much pain to even ask the question. Don? Why do you get good grades on the exams, lie on your back and breathe deeply? Besides, it's almost lunch.

I was thinking you have only got to deal with that task first.

12

CHAPTER TWELVE

I'm not saying just homesick and screwed
up by people continuing
my treatment by the doctor.
They know what they're doing.
Yes, I know them. Take
holy water from the basin and
splash it in your face, genuflect before
Hanuman. I grabbed him in my hand,
greatest servant. You hand bathe
the Deity or say your *gopī gāyatrīs*, *japa*,
bow, look out at the properly dressed
ISKCONites and think
of your own poor standard.

You are going through?
I have six more degrees on
ten campuses. I don't know
if I'll be able to withhold
out have pressing gut
into the saloon. "Happy New Year!"
she shoots a long-barreled
pistol off toward the center
of the hall three times and
they all start dancing wildly,
men with white beards, fellows
on bar stools, up from the cabin he comes.

I bless them. Fellows like him
who get the girls in the fur coats
and gowns and obviously mocking faces
toward the good son of God
who prays to Buddha and

all those who can purify their hearts.

Garuḍa is present. He asked you before.
Care for him while he was away.
Don't you think nature didn't
pull the cabin and the cliff
but he found his gold.

How far back does it go? Chicken or egg, crazy or diseased? John Young, Wyn, and Stephen were drinking beer in the woods, Steve spilling half of his unseen in the nearby leaves, horrid beer. God goes way back, you can't trace His origin. They speculated, "Maybe there is no God." But there must be something that has started off all these shenanigans. (We interrupt this program to tell you that the hawk is decapitating Baghdad.) Go way back way down the early spring home. They were mocking him when he told them he had short-term memory and he was not worried. It's not weird. Don't get worried about it. The missiles are sizzling and killing the top officers and seeking out stockpiles of atomic material—didn't find any yet.

Lonely lonely he just goes into
intro and I can stay here
or go there, it doesn't
matter, just get better
in your health. That's what I
want to see.

He said but in Eire there is
shmere. A myth. You're just as well-protected here.

They say this religion is the only one.

Pāṇḍavas are as "good" as
Hanuman and not as good
—how good is Nārada?

How good are you? Press
your hand on the weight squeezer
and see what it comes out. You might be pretty good.

His real life stuff—suffering
for God's sake and he says I
forgot your name I was
a bad person but you forgave me.

Now in return I will perform
"marvelous" acts according to
my capacity, not just
sit back on my duff in Wicklow.
Maybe I should stay here and
do something big. You've got a big band.

Three men. One soul. Worse
crisis he has been in I suppose.
Lies, hypocrisy, trying to escape
the pains in the ass and the psyche
because I didn't fulfill the One I loved.

Śuka assumed the audience (Uttarā) knew the *Rāmāyaṇa* so he left many parts out. But he told how Hanuman held his white tail as an umbrella over Rāma's head while flying over the ocean on his broad back as a comfortable seat. What a wrecker he was, and the best of all, devoted to the Lord even when the Lord went back to Ayodhyā...

The men read in the beer garden and became purified. They kept on calling Freddy a kvetch because he was always complaining, now of indigestion. His idea of a friend was one who constantly hears all the other's woes but gives consoling replies. A real friend has to hear the other's woes and reciprocate in Kṛṣṇa consciousness. Yeah yeah, but I just want to be consoled. He lays his heart of anguish under the blankets and hears how the words are doing.

Floating along miles ahead, forgetful of my troubles, that's what it's like to sleep. *Instruct* your disciples, the seminar teacher said. Don't tell them made-up stories. Don't be a Jonathan Winters[33] or serious social commentator. Be 'umble. Dress yourself cleanly, use deodorant if necessary. If you are a woman and renunciant, don't dress in rags, appear like a lady. If you are a married woman, dress attractively (eyeliner and mascara are allowed in light quantity, but not a lot of jewelry, and especially not a lot of exposure of the upper bosom). If you are a man, dress smart and clean. If you can press your man's uniform, that would be best. Don't brag about your own achievements. Naturally you'll want to tell stories of Prabhupāda when you were present, but make him the limelight and you the novice, or even fool.

If you attend the seminar, concentrate, don't do doodles, study, try to get the best grades. You can do it if you spend time studying after class. But it's a sacrifice. Maybe one year you'll take none or one seminar and spend your time in the *dhama* in other activities.

First birds of spring in Albany and Kiltakena. I'm lying back on the decision of allowing Kṛṣṇa to show me more clearly. When they put those paintings up, it will certainly look more like home. Har har. One shows a beat-down *sādhu* (1998 style), "me no chant *japa*," and another similar character, but the caption reads," *japa* champion of the year."

Hey, you get some organ music and girls, sing some *bhajanas*. Upper New York State is called the "*bhajana* belt" in mundane guide literature for its underground New Age yogistic stuff.

I wish I could help you more. Here's a desk lamp for your table. Could I have a chair for the desk you gave me, and more time alone? Lapsing into EJW style. Attention! Let's hear those personas. Let's beat the drums. Where's that avant-garde style?

But sir, if I "lapse" back into first-person singular, is that a sin, a flaw?

I just expected more. I thought you found a mountain of gold and were going into it for a long time. I can't dictate your inspiration or lack of it. Just remember: no dates and times, no horseshoes or metal in your boxing gloves, go deep, go religious naturally, cry if it comes, be upbeat. Think of the faucets. Let them come. If you must beat around the bush, find a new bush. Be real. Flow, pray to Kṛṣṇa for the colors of spring and bravery and confidence. Be Harry, Lex, Swami, Sailing, Prabhu, Seminar, invite people to your home, stay alone in a writing shed, pray to God and your saints, please bless me to become your devotee and know you, talk to you, not to ask for favors but to serve you with love.

Don't stop walking the tight
rope walk 50 feet up in
the big top tent. Walk cool
with confidence.

He was among the best performers
but I am just an ordinary peanut vendor
said Charlie, gathered
with fellow intellectuals in the
barn at Des Moines.
It was like old times when
young teenagers but
knew they were children,
citizens decent.

"To hell with them, the governments,
never care for the people,
just trying to stuff their
own pockets and the rich folks."

But John walked away bored
after having been in
so many meetings and to think of
God the sermon in a church
almost never did it.
Cane and root beer.
Peace, rain on the skylight,
a buddy to live with, but

he's got to help you out,
set up your paintings
and give his time to your project.
Not Steve Kowit. Yeah friends have to
be equal.
Just give me a piece of bread
said Fred and he bowed to his favorite
prayer, "Dear Nitai, help
me to become a better person
and get rid of these headaches
—and what? You'll
go on the airplane!

No, I'll paint and write
with the vigor.
It's all up to Him
the Ruler and Director.

This must be understood correctly, the seminar teacher said. It would be suicide: you must do the right thing. When the suicide bomber knocked down the tallest U.S. buildings, they brought about trouble for all the enemies of the U.S. and for millions of people who had nothing to do with it. Students nodded. Some scratched their noses. Paid attention to the birds. Heard memories of old friends now dead. And some fixed their minds on the most crucial present problem. Many just dream of her. A veteran of marriage—and a good manager—said it's warfare, the wife is in charge…

Schedule diary pose, come to breakfast, take your Rolaids. All kids line up. I'm afraid. This is called beating around the bush. You don't want to go right in there where the rattlesnake or coyote lives. So you pretend as if you're looking for them. You hit your stick to frighten away the creatures, use your energy that way and avoid truth-seeking confrontation. Why not just say, "I'm afraid of what's in there"? Hey you, come out! Because they know you are lying.

For confidence, Joey the wannabe athlete wore elastic ankle bracelets. He started telling himself he was better.

He told people he was looking for God, beating around the bush. Held his *japa* beads in his hands to watch the *japa* beads put him asleep. Things got worse. False fiction. You should go to the dentist.

Remember when you went to school and you were not so anxious? Remember being in the Navy, proud of the U.S.S. Saratoga? No. You had the strength to go through all these things, but you didn't like it. Did you like the *kīrtana* dancing with the Swami and the twelve? Yes! It was more to my liking, it was a serious mission, answer to life. Do you see it that way still about the mission? No, now it's like ginger ale left open all night. Or "I'll give you whatever you want, you saved me life," said the old father. "I want her," Buster said, pointing toward the man's daughter, but he actually meant the heifer standing beside her, his face full of love.

I am in the middle.
You can believe it?
And He abandoned me long ago.

Reverse: you neglected Him.
I don't know how it happened,
I slept more and more.

Couldn't you tone down
your hate and anger to me?

"Ornette" he mispronounced
but I didn't say anything because
I mispronounced "Mahler"
and all the Sanskrit. The words
for love—amore, amor,
like that, if said sincerely
I botched it up.

But I botched so many things. There's

no sense going back on it. Stay in
America for now. Don't be afraid
of big bad *sannyāsīs* in armor and horses.

You can take care of yourself
and speak for yourself even
hit a big bag. Build your body.
It's the best thing. Knock the shit
out of the blues.

Bummer boy cry face,
hawk features, tears crying
down, Chief Pale Face
can't do stunt tricks,

oh melancholy—"oh have I
got meds for you! They're 40
years ahead! They will take away
your suicide, your so-aside,
I mean to say your crybaby
stomach." Say, what happened
to the brave, staunch *sannyāsī*?

I just want to read the books
and believe them.
How come this is a poem? Who said it is?

Forty years ago the Indians lived in peace, then they realized it was the white men attacking Baghdad again, with Bush-guided missiles. "We shall be very careful not to kill the civilians." Oh man. I hear the hammer and slingshot. But what about my own woes, so tiny in comparison? Why don't you take care... *you* decide. I did. Mish, mash, I'm sick of such stuff, proud to prove to himself he was fireproof at the burning stake.

What about Ox, Woxy and Tim in the back room? They are playing poker? No, reading *Bṛhad-Bhāgavatāmṛta*. Hanuman is praised as the greatest servant of the Lord. Each servant, when praised, belittles himself. Praise me and I think, "You're right." But I'm barred from attending all meetings of the inner circle, "I can't sing or dance or feel happy." said Ox. This was the Melancholy Anonymous Club. Woxy said, "I love the girl but she was already married, I took to drink." Tim said, "I turned off all hopes for women—I feel hopeless to approach God, although that's what I want—and I'm just living in a little cabin hideaway." They bawled over their beer and happy statues. A mad bulldog chased Wox, and he never gave up.

A guy who doesn't know the date is nuts. Hearsay. Huge amounts of hearsay, better stick to the recorded and printed words. They went to war, the Pāṇḍavas. I'm sorry about forgetting those dates. They're just numbers, and I do have a calendar. I think today may be the sixteenth.

Joe realized, "I'm living in a sanatorium." When he realized this, he purposely broke his schedule and slept late. "No one here is confident with me." Call some in. You are a self-centered bastard. No, I'm great, really great. Those who criticize should be ignored. "The low opinion others have of me has no effect on my self-esteem" (muddily paraphrased from therapy book).

"Now it's almost time for breakfast," he'll say, but he doesn't know me. Read the book while I eat. I will think to myself. Existential anxiety. Who am I? What is my death? Where do I go? Who is God? How come I don't ever worry about death? You don't feel guilty—but you should.

He's my guy, the Lord will guide me to
the top. I have done many wrong things,
but He will guide me through to purity. Books
coming out but
no energy to read them.

Get the course right, tight angles
about the praise Hanuman,
Nārada flying but Hanuman
grabs him by the ankles so
Nārada can only dance in midair

and shout joyous while Hanu
continues reading and reciting the glories
of Rāma, Uttarā sitting quietly by.

A riotous, joyous way. Not the
melancholic
"le penseur" who
can't figure it out. They *know*
Kṛṣṇa in His supreme.
Most delightful—go to Dvārakā and
see Him day to day.

Please excuse me please
pardon me for losing
falling behind 10,000 and
many more.

His bicycle parked nearby
danger at every step, especially in
this neighborhood.
One black boy was
getting rough on a white boy but
at least they were mixing peers.
Door falling off the bathroom,
lightbulb blinking off, a poor house.

Don't you matter, we will get a new
house maybe next year.
Wouldn't you like to see me?

Blow wind and scorch your cheeks
it won't wither my soul.
The books may scatter pages
all over the earth,
but one page of *Dear Sky*
will be left behind and
inspire a lonely boy who
finds it in the New York gutter or

an archeologist in Africa. You have such aspirations.

Why not just say, "I tried
and hope it pleases my
Lord"?

Oh time goes slow sometimes, you call the betrayer, and you go back to Ireland. I think they pamper him too much. Let's do what he wants to and care for him so much. Like—let him go to hell, who needs him? Paul was venting in the Sixth Street bar. No one was very much listening to him but he was talking on. *Then you will never understand him*, he said, and banged his fist on the bar. That caused some concern.

"Shut up down there!" a stool-sitter said. *Never, nevermore*, Paul muttered to himself. The ultimate betrayer. And he could never understand it except to accept he was such a vermin who had done very badly. Well I don't agree with that. No, I shan't accept that version, mumbled Paul. And he sat upright and ordered another beer, but quietly this time. He was a timid man. Nevermore (Poe, "The Raven"), betrayer of worthy souls and you can never understand why. This makes me more confused, but I'll get back to my life as best I can.

Sweet it seems to dance
with the beautiful girl but
she disappears like a fairy
from your arms.
Some big guy takes her away,
you stumble.

You don't remember the hurts
you went through in many lives,
turn to God, they say, prayer
improves health—

proved in 40 universities by
23% averages but others
are skeptic. Well something

happens. And what is prayer?
Parade magazine did not explain it.
All I know is that
prayer eludes me, wish it was
in my heart to share with others.
It's to the One
asking Him, thanking Him for existence,
the chance to get back on the track.

Keep your mouth shut
(says the self-centered old man),
just give me a place to stay
and I'll chant Hare Kṛṣṇa there,
why not Vṛndāvana it's
a good place if you can take
the noise and monkeys.

I can't take this torture.

13

CHAPTER THIRTEEN

Oh Lord, oh Lord—I used to think the word Lord was so corny. Now, despite hip vocabulary usage and time trends, I like it. Not as good as Kṛṣṇa, however. Kṛṣṇa! Some devotees familiar with Navadvīpa like the name Nitai or Gaura. Jaya Rādhe! "The Lord," "the Supreme Personality of Godhead." Prabhupāda used them all, but *especially* Kṛṣṇa. The *Kṛṣṇa* book.

The Supreme Personality of Godhead said...What was his name? In the midst of thousands of God's names, he feels an urge to go to the bathroom. That's all right, just keep saying those names. We want a *nāma* revival. Fight back.

Kṛṣṇa in the park, squirrels (breed with rats) scampering about, up the trees, Kṛṣṇa in the screech of a girl just playing, the car engine, in the quiet neighborhood of Stuyvesant Falls. They treat ya' nice. Sign on a porch: "Go U.S. Army" and black flag with skull and crossbones, bombs over Baghdad, like looking for a needle in a haystack to find that bastard. Kṛṣṇa, the woof and warp of all things. But higher and higher, be loyal to your form of Bhagavān, as Hanuman was; he wouldn't go to Dvārakā and leave his post in Kimpurusha. Even when Garuḍa was sent to get him by the Lord, Hanuman knocked Him away. But when Kṛṣṇa dressed as Rāma in Dvārakā, then he went...loyally. Stay where you are needed by your Lord, who may call you to fetch wood or kill a demon, and you should be nearby in your heart.

You can't go so fast
as a man in a rocket
but who cares, my scars
are showing, grow hair
gray, cut it off.

Well, you are the Lord?

No, not even His servant.
I'm fallen, starting tomorrow will
make it a real temple.

The Lord will be at the house
and the police will break in
and He'll kill them all.

And I told you, *practice*
practice, even if it gets smoky
and burns your lungs,
don't give up, keep it, you'll
reach your 16 again.

Anghts Charleston was
so happy about his new
hopes. More headaches
but less pain and the
mental story was getting better.

He's playing a good villain,
that moustached one. I'll grab him
and give him a good shiner.

Now keep moving this
circus of horse-pulled
carts, this loco,
this jet.

Prayer can change
ill health. Here's the data—
it all can come about
if you just make some trouble
and I can see what I wrote.

Oh what a night!
Couldn't sleep,
meds didn't move me.

I was consoled by
my counselor, so don't ask anything from me.

"I am one who wants
quick progress, 16 rds in
a day. " said Smirk and
we kicked him in the
rear as they do in the
old-time movies.

He responded like a pig to the porridge in his bowl but was finicky with the chocolate drink. The boys got together and lowered the basketball net to six feet so they could dunk it and sink shots. That encouraged me. Why not lower the standards and have more fun? I gave him a good suggestion. What was the best response to demands from the hired help? Find a place where no one will find you. When you give out advice, and you don't take it yourself, what's that called? A religious minister. But they wear beautiful vestments to suit the seasons. Filipinos get to press the officers' uniforms. No worship of the Father. Old ancestors did it going to the pyramids. We used to have a version of it, going to an Italian restaurant. His eyelids failed again, and two Mexicans and twenty-five striped elks escaped across the border into the United States.

No wonder they slip and fall, these children, they are so wild, so happy and fast in this loving community where Lakṣmaṇa and Rāma are common words, and Sītā, and when they go to school they will hear some more of Śrī Rāma.

The road to Baghdad is open, like hell. Open to death, mayhem. "Fierce resistance," P.O.W., U.S. Army, black Muslim traitors, U.S. plane bombs down a British plane, Bush's popularity dropping, dripping in the pants. What shall we do? Oh it will change. The stock market. Use money for self-defense.

At least I can write for a while, but it may not be published. There was never an atomic bomb there in the first place. I phoned him, I can rest. He's warned. What do I have to do today?

Your ballet lessons, your drink, pills, stand on hands, go through the mill and ask how it came out. Oh by the way, I want a printout of that letter I sent to Michael the Archangel. Celibate. The sexy chicks who turn men's heads make Michael just look at the ground. Boom, blast, it doesn't sound good. They've killed a hundred of the "right" guys and the home team is blasting away.

He kept a notebook of flying.
"I'm coming into the sunlight of Baltimore."
Guy almost accosted him.
He was hitchhiking when
they saw him, innocence
personified on the street.

Lucky they didn't slit his neck,
a Jack Kerouac disciple slept
curled around the Lincoln Memorial.

A dangerous little voyage
with no car when you're
underweight, have no knife
or gun and a cop
could tell you "go home
to your mama."

I lived on the Lower East Side. I
slept curled around the curve
of the Lincoln Memorial
but the next morning was
accosted by a gay
bum and ran from him.
Finally decided, "this is far enough"
and took a bus back to NYC.

Know nothing of the rigors of life.

These things can be found
and I'm trying to get him.
Yeah baby grow up.

Fight to a draw. His strong right swing, he's able to duck under the punch and fast comeback at the belt (not below). Round they went. One of them would stop in disgust, but so far it wasn't he, the Irishman. This was all behind the scenes. Don't talk bad about me and I won't talk bad about you. "Mum's the word." Why? If I want to talk bad of you and it's true, I will. Oh yeah! He was helpless there. You can't stop a mad talking fellow.

All this was on the silver screen and the children watched enjoying until their Hare Kṛṣṇa moms came in and said, "Turn off the TV set! I told you it's only for *Mahābhārata* and the Japanese *Rāmāyaṇa* cartoons!"

"Shoot. Let's go out and play basketball." There was no question of them wanting a quiet grotto with a *mūrti* where they could quietly pray on beads. They were only children. And what were the elders doing? Trying to herd the children into a semblance of civilized behavior. No one was in any *vandanaṁ* mood. There were, of course, schools, institutes for higher learning, and a guy or girl here or there interested in *śravaṇaṁ kīrtanaṁ*, even outside the institutional framing.

They would open Prabhupāda's book and stay awake, fixed to it. Sometimes one would read to another. When the phone rings, who shall it be?

All right. It was not to be.
I wanted a horse but they gave
me a cat. Less trouble.

Go to church and come home and
pet your cat. Why can't you
be a truly transcendental child?

So many layers of *karma* and

the kids you associate with. So it's a shame.
You get all right
to get shut down.

Not so radical—just
give them a good dose
of Hare Kṛṣṇa mantra
either locked in a cell hearing
it or taking sumptuous food
and hearing a well-spoken
lecture on the spiritual
nature of all things.

Arjuna and Kṛṣṇa and we'll introduce
you to *Śrīmad-Bhāgavatam* and the
entourage of poor saints in
Nadia and how they were
fearless and mad in
joy nothing like it.

They climbed trees
embraced girls and cows.

The old man was a good fireman. Too bad he and I split. I used to adore him and then I desperately sought a way to get out of his clutches but didn't have the self-assertion to do so. Hail Mary, Marie. Those girls in the playground. At least you didn't have to be afraid they'd punch you. But they ignored you and you never entered the top ten billboard charts of any of the popular girls. No one cared about religion. That was for the "Catlick" kids down the block at St. Clare's School, the kids who wore green neckties and white shirts and the girls in heavy green pinafores. We were all rather mild. No big rivalries or gang fights. Well-policed town.

No prayers except the psalm recited once a week in assembly, "The Lord is my shepherd, I shall not want," in the public school. Secular school, Spaulding pink balls, punch ball, only one capable baseball pitcher, Stevie Rogers. The Tottenville Pirates would have had to forfeit a game if he could not pitch that day.

Why all this? Tell us about Michelangelo and the lady who said, "Call on Michelangelo, Lord Caitanya, and Kṛṣṇa or Rūpa Raghunātha to direct you." We identified the right-eye pain as "Jim," and since that chasing of him by the three deities, Hanuman, Lakshmana and another, he has not appeared. Besides that, I've got a big arsenal. First the pills, and then the prayers and patience.

Water from the conch, blowing the conch, you can be head *pūjārī*—I'm willing to wait.

I can do it but how can you be my meaningful friend? Harder to write—KR says, "Drop the longhand and go back to block letters." Dreamt that I was in a Chinese ghetto and the kids stole my tickets and gifts. I lost everything. Anybody help a 63-year-old boy in China?

The holy voices are sometimes people dressed in ordinary clothes. But they've got the communication through to the pure devotee. Believe him, maybe through a rep of his. It's too important to break that link. So I'll stay a man of the saffron, even if I have to fight for it. But don't lie. They may line him up. It means to work. I was talking to this guy with the black jacket, white New York letters on it. By surprise I offered him my beads and he took them on loan.

There's a somewhat spontaneous Kṛṣṇa underground all over the world if you could find them. They're not in the yellow pages. Will you know if you hear about them through a government rally? I doubt it. But you might meet one through the secretary in your office, a man who goes for silent walks and sometimes meets and talks with people. It's not the biggest in the world, but effective.

You must understand this properly. I'm not going to e-mail anymore. I'm going to write you a letter privately by post. It'll blast you to pieces *because I have a more powerful intellect than you and justice is on my side.* All you can do is fart and snort and bark at me and use your new-found scattered humor you're so proud of.

Sad to see devotee family members fighting. They have a *mahā-harināma* party every Friday night at Times Square in front of an old Army-Navy recruiting office. They stay in this one spot and blast away. If you'd like to come and sit in a chair with us, you can drive six and a half hours down there and clap your crippled hands. "He's back, our old friend." Causing you to crack a smile, realizing again this mantra is best and all powerful.

This won't bring together all individual differences, but it will at least create a temporary ambience, "we are for the Holy Name," and possibly we may think we are *always* blissful and always cooperative in love with each other and think, "I wish the whole world was so blissful."

Deep in your heart, some semblance of the Holy Name ambience. The individual differences are not as important as the *jīva's* link to the *mahā-mantra*, desperate, afraid, embarrassed, mockingly, whatever.

I am not the only one
in a helmet
who got busted.
Hanuman
no matter what armor you use
they can get through—a tiny microbe.

So eat grain healthy food and
sleep late, it ain't gonna to make
you physically immortal.

I hankered for that once
words to look strange from the corner
people stopping to watch,
then some good
friends and hip girls,
and doctorate literateurs come

across the street and buy
the books from Nitai's
books on his little card table.

They think, "This is wonderful." This
is not going to decay.
I can see it was written
remotely but it will last.
They say don't hide away but
maybe I could.

Let's get this guy back to Ireland
where he writes and paints.
No guarantees it's any better

but *begging to God*
he will chant 16 rounds, that's
an impediment isn't it?
You are now going to get better
and lead the circus with
a whip and smirks
in the big room. Sit up
and say something simple about
the Holy Name.

Where will the money come from?
The honey of love, are you mended?
Can you expect to *always* feel good?
Down some days.

Cold and bold
that's no painting! It's just a child's smear
go back to Wicklow and *paint*, make
a new schedule, but
scones and butter
and the right medicines.

Oh I don't know

only the inner one knows what
he has got in store
but that's his decision to work out
as I have said before.

The date isn't important but the intent. Could you go internal? The local shopkeepers were sitting in Pop Lloyd's trolley, which was not used after hours for transportation. They played cards, music, and drank. An elderly, jolly group, full of memories and enough hope and *joie de vivre* to keep up for the evening and the next morning.

Alex the tailor had a copy of *Caitanya-caritāmṛta* (as I said, I don't know the date, timeless). He was describing the beginning of the confidential meeting between Lord Caitanya and Rāmānanda Rāya. "What is the perfection of life?" asked Lord Caitanya. Rāmānanda Rāya replied, "It is to follow the rules according to *varṇāśrama*."

You have been busy, I have been busy carrying this Cross.
What's he talking about?
"That is external." He wanted him to go deeper.
'*ke āmi*,' who am I?
What shall we do, just give up, renounce?
No, do not see everything that way. Don't give up.

Too much. I asked you to phone me but
I'm afraid they are plotting against me,
to throw me against the wall with this toxic anxiety.

He loves you, he wouldn't double-cross.
Still, what does shame show me?
How you are unable to use beads.
Eventually in your heart
they formed a twist and it worked.
Say at the end of the short hand
they dropped the hook to him.
Now not so much interruption.
We have to bear up

to our *karma* and Cross
to purify.

God will recognize you.

The seclusions are not always jollies. I mean, taking time out for a writing session. Sometimes you do it because there's no one to talk to. Everyone is busy working or they're not confidential or they're the ones that are somehow causing turmoil.

And there's the Biggie's absence—you can't seclude yourself *with* Kṛṣṇa. Heck! If you could, there would be no need for my lamentation, but then, He brings on the highest grief by showing you a little of His sweetness and disappearing. And there's nothing left to do but sleep. You know, it's too dangerous to take LSD and get disentangled. You can just...your cat perseveres all day long as long as he gets his two meals.

And there are plenty of people you don't want to hear from. So some can choose "seclusion," and would you like to create your own? Sleepy again? The hum way to fade out. It was graduation day but you didn't yet know what grades you got, like when you graduated in '61 and you didn't know what you wanted to do... you were just pushing off the damn alarm clock.

Love of God, the lack of love simple...sayings without love of God you'll go out and see double.

Don't get angry, that's the main thing.
Especially in India in a mob.
They'll tear you limb from limb.

I'm sorry I'm so violent and
gory. I should just go to sleep.
But there's nothing to do here.
We're going to do rowing oars exercise later
and then it'll be fine because it will remove
anxiety and melancholy and all the
intake of pet pills.

I'm talking about Butter Cal baby,
a fellow I knew in Queens,
the first miserable dope I
knew. He'd been in the Marines.
Much older than us but
hung around with younger kids,
told horrible stories, funny ones too.
He didn't want to beat us.

He started to go to church which
seemed strange. We went only because
our mothers told us but
he went on his own.
It reminded me of my father
who would never go to church
though he had an old gun
in his desk. "Keep your hands
off it." And naked women pictures even
pubic hair, and shells from Hawaii.
My mother had to tolerate.
She just went to Mass and he
couldn't stop her.

If I fall in love
it will be forever
or I'll never fall in love
sang from the heart king
whether it had some truth or
not even near but you
kept getting drowned and your
love lost and especially
his Holy Mother.

Girls are a problem as Charlie Brown of "Peanuts" knew well. He would place his head against the tree in agony after they said something sarcastic. And do you remember the football routine? Lucy was supposed to hold the ball in place for

Charlie to kick it, but as he approached it, she always pulled the ball away as he swung his foot into the air, falling on his ass, full on his back, and sometimes breaking a bone. You're not supposed to talk bad against women.

Pure devotees don't see bodily boys or girls. They see spirit souls, and they wish to help them and serve them. They especially respect devotees and all "mātājīs," but when they get so aggressive!

Women like Draupadī and Sati were great heroines in various ways. All glories to the pious women in the world, who outnumber religious men.

The casualties are high. Just stay home. It's safer. You might die stepping on a piece of stone. I can't tell you how bad I feel that Grandma died. In BB we heard an astounding purport that Karṇa and other demons who were killed at Kurukṣetra lost their existence and never have been born again. No one gets away with any immoralities. Kṛṣṇa has His eyes everywhere.

Peanuts and popcorn! Hotdogs! The games go on! Football is over, baseball soon, war forever with casualties high. "Just hear," just hear, pray to come back, at least to kindergarten level.

Thousands of tanks you underestimated.
You are now killing all the boys
in the name of freedom. How
does this give me freedom
from birth and death?

Strong helmet, straps, grenades, camouflages,
big huge gun and plenty
but not enough ammunition.
Casualties are high.

The news is just what the
army wants to report.

14
CHAPTER FOURTEEN

The news is just what the
Army wants to report.
Kṛṣṇa has mixed modes
since the beginning of time and
men have fought for
land and something
called honor, possession,
"land."

Mary, stories, trying to pay the bills, slowing down the bills.
He can't do it, move to a cheaper place fast.
Overheard him saying, "I will help you paint
only in a passive way."
You have to put the canvas up yourself.
"It's a hype that
they treat your doodles as
mahā-prasādam."

It's just childish scribble. He
should know it's more than that.
So easily hurt. Kṛṣṇa played
in the forest. Wherever He stepped it's a *tīrtha.*

A higher *tīrtha.* Now I can't
tell you more. It will be decided
by a private council
of nuns whether SDG
falls on his back—trust Nancy.

No phone call. The man dug in. They could have stayed outdoors longer and absorbed the sunlight but decided to make a phone call. I wanted to reach Kṛṣṇa but what would I say, especially under the influence of pills? You have to be at least clear and holy. There can be no confusion. You have to be honest. You want to remain a cadet *sannyāsī*. Stand at attention and salute Old Glory as she goes by, avoid shame if you can, but if you can't, take it on the chin and use it for courtroom medicine, "the truth and nothing but the truth." I painted a big white stripe down the rear of Mrs. Joddick's dress and got expelled from school. Twenty years' jail sentence, and when you got out, another twenty.

It didn't make it there
were mistakes all over the
place, my cat had to
be given away.

"This is external." Did
the barber give you a good
haircut? No, he messed
me up.

Persiflage and then he suddenly remembers he wants "heaven"
but doesn't know what it is.

Garuḍa isn't as good as the Pāṇḍavas, yet all are great, but the queens are top, but the *gopīs* are much better and yet all come from Kṛṣṇa. I don't quite understand it.

I can *say* I do. I see a picture of
Red Garland licking a double ice
cream cone and understand *that*,
but it's just sense grat and soon gone.

So *you* tell me. Gurudeva *has*
told you but you're dull
sullied brain can rarely go
beyond "mythology" or "I *think*
I understand it."

Now the house stands in
Wicklow waiting for you.
Shall you go back?

Billy the Kid[34] was an
historic monster
but Kṛṣṇa's the real narration
and the *śastras* prove it. I sat
with Saci lifting the weights.

He says in three months my
bodily physique will swell noticeably,
the girls and boys will see
when I wear a T-shirt. But I'm
thinking, what is that, we
should be talking
of how to know the Lord in all
places and chanting our rounds
as Billy did today,
more than 16.
It's going to get better.

I've been dreaming about Mrs. Mulligan off and on for weeks. She was an actual person in this life, red-headed school teacher at P.S. 8 for grades 4 to 8. She taught mathematics, she taught everything. She was tough. She had two tough older sons, a daughter, and I think she lived without a husband.

I don't remember being very close to her, but I don't remember that she ill-treated me. I learned a lot from her. Perhaps she was the woman who loved me when my mother wasn't loving me. And she was a teacher. The kids couldn't push her around she was so strong morally.

Why all these dreams about her? Last night it was revealed. She loved him at one point in the dream like a lover, but then I saw that she loved everybody. I got a deep feeling that this person was capable of loving everyone individually and that this was something I should strive for. Don't go looking for a lover in a particular girl. You are very blessed if you can love everyone and be satisfied with that. That makes you a saint, and you can do it in an ordinary way as a schoolteacher in a dumpy public school.

Land of mercy. Get the strap out. If you're guilty, you'll get belted. The bettors aren't snapped yet. Looking at the teacher's legs up to the garter, a renounced man. And taking too much medicine according to the "amateurs' club." The doctor gets angry with them. What do they know?

Yamuna, you bring the daffodils in here and decorate the court table.

Flying across the country to meet a friend. He better be in good shape to see them smile. I can give spiritual instructions. I wonder if you have confidence in your spiritual master. What rumors have you heard? He has a wooden leg. Wears jeans. For hours I dreamt someone was pounding. Due to attempt he entered his room. How do you feel? Grateful, photo log. Do I trust *you*? Do you understand my trust? We climbed a little far, almost there, "of the absence, of the geese." A little further out of the geese oceans. Names to read. They're asleep. Devotional son where someone rests.

That was most incomprehensible.
That was Kṛṣṇa but you can't
see Him like birds on the roof.

He denounced his earlier work.
We talked. It seemed all right because
we are in the same KC clubhouse
and must come to the same conclusion.

Kṛṣṇa streaked through the dark like
lightning. Ugrasena may see but
Yudhiṣṭhira may not. Bali may but
Prahlāda must see. Uddhava will definitely see
because he is the closest and

Yādavas are closer than Pāṇḍavas,
and so are the Gaudiya gurus, but I wonder if there

is some fellow or girl
who is not rated in the usual
dynastic way but is very, very
dear to Kṛṣṇa, she
can't even talk to Him or
even see Him to worship. Can't

breathe without thinking of
the Lord? Of course that's possible,
I'm not saying it's me.
I can break through the line
but I've only got a few rounds of *japa*
and things blow into them.
My father taught me wrongly and
I never overcame it.

It's time to eat supper. Ring the triangle. Rush into the ranch hall. Buster's first, gobbling down them rolls.

I've been given advice to ask forgiveness to one I've hurt. I'm doing it. But is it just words with the pen? So I asked what action can I do? How much does an air-mail stamp cost cross country? You pay for it. Pay. They're beginning to suspect he's a rat. But I'm not giving up. You can kick me out. Then he'd have nowhere to go, nowhere to live. Might as well give up your life. That's what the *Gītā* says: to one who has lost his honor, it is better to die.

He wanted to see the saints, go out chanting the Holy Names. Don't be catastrophic, there's still hope.

Don't take away my fame.
It would be so unhappy to be fallen.
You have lost everything.
Well at
least you don't have to go

anywhere. You can just
chant on beads with
nothing to live up to.
Live on a mountain top.
He was afraid that leopards might
leap. Always been afraid of animals
and corporations and police and lack of money.

Would someone give a room to stay
in? Yes, I think so. Just a little place
and you could think there and pray
from books. It might even be
better for you.

But don't read newspapers and
TV. Just go think, How could I
reach God? I'm not sure I
could survive such an existence.

I thought I was doing good
but they all tell me now I'm
full of anxieties and always was.
They used to say I was a good guy until
anxiety entered my life.
Why don't you boot them in the
pants and be happy again?

Kṛṣṇa Kṛṣṇa, how I
have been pulled down by rumors said
Charlie Brown.

There seems to be nothing
wrong with me. So I
don't know what to say.
You either are nuts or sane,
lusty or celibate

shame-faced or full of scandalous
petrified wood and your foot

sunk in a stream or a skunk bites it.
Kṛṣṇa! Kṛṣṇa! At least you have the sense to cry.
You have been trained.

Streams of dry tears.
Laurel and Hardy got a
second 200 years in prison
for trying to escape in
painters' uniforms.

Were they praying? That's my question.
That's what counts.
No prestige. But
some kind of service.
All these books.

There's more to this than I thought. I thought I heard one big scream and then it was over and we'd know who the winner was. Very easy. Just go to bed when you want. God will protect you, just a saddened fellow who can't do anything much.

God, please show me the light. The foothold and the daring to take the steps. It is not easy. I am paying for it. You gave me every blow I deserve. But let me reach the goal of loving service at Your feet and kindness to all beings, in utter humility.

Retired. He put a sign on the door. It was unexpected. He was also getting ready for any smear job. Remember when you had to enter the military? You figured it would be awful but you'd have the inner resources to endure it. Feel like that now. Don't be anxious. The opinions of others have no effect on my own self-assessment. Joe. He'll sit on that veranda and chant his *japa*. Chant 16 every day and write these comic books to pay your way through law college. What about studying the religious books precisely so you'll be ADVANCED and LEARNED? Retired. On occasion, if I have to speak, I'll do it; old-time cider. Smile. 'Dis is my contribution. You nuts?

Why don't you look at these books being sold so faithfully by the followers. And your financial position. Stay actually pure. That's it. Tony laughed so hard he had to grab the railing. Very prone to fall.

So he wears funny shoes and doesn't demand. He wouldn't want anyway; seclusion and living off herbs and weeds in the wolf wilderness. Compromise. Wait. Read.

Well I do care if you think
the war is the littlest thing—
the demons are fighting the demigods
and higher planets and the earth is
a significant one. It's big
because God walked here.
I don't care about anything,
Henry thought, but when he
has to engage the Gaṇeśa
method and cuts his fingernail,
then he complains.

The melody is twisted. All your Kṛṣṇa bombs
are going off and
children in uniform are being killed
in numbers. Beginning to think about
the memorial for this war, depending on who wins.

George W. Bush irritated when the
reporters asked him when the boys would come
home. He speaks of freedom and
even God, America more than of God.
But we trust when freedom wins
and the war he started
for fifty cents in Florida.

I am determined to rush 16 rounds
like climbing a mountain peak but
by arthritis asphyxiation by

power and fall by the roadside. Click click click.
How many *japa* rounds
and where was your mind?

They say you're becoming a
hooligan and disloyal mountebank.
You've got anxieties up to your ears:
"What's the big mystery? Is he going
to quit?" Yes he's fallen
exhausted on the candy store floor.
Afraid he'll be headlines of page one,
but actually cool as a
cucumber. Just wants feeling
who he is,
a *jīva*, come out of the hurdle.

My dad's and mom's conjunction
and the hand I may hold onto
very tightly.

Getting more tired earlier. Smooth through the night. How absurd to be called a drug addict. I want life, trying to be obedient, sensible. He says I'm in good condition. So much sleeping—it doesn't sound like he'll be home soon.

Did she fight her captors? American spies. That's all right. The symbol of my dealing with some debts and serving out *prasādam*. But I could clear up my mood and say I'm feeling better.

He doesn't make much money or sense because he's so mean. Walk into the saloon with long-barreled pistol. "Pow!" One dead. From the balcony, his enemy pulls out a shorter-barreled gun and retorts with "Pow! Pow! Pow!" We don't hear more fire. We watched the movie, but the film broke. Someone made a dumb remark.

I just want to be treated tenderly
but the world is a rough

pile of dirt, sign: "Turn back
here or you'll be shot." I think
you love her and she loves you.
Sense of God and the *ācāryas*
is the only sense.
Kṛṣṇa sleeps at night, and
Rukmiṇī hears, "Rādhā!"
as He talks in His sleep.
"Candrāvalī," He breathes, and assumes
His flute and bent-leg position. Don't you
dare say He's forgetting Vraja
because of the splendor of other places.
He never forgets, and Rukmiṇī knows.

He's not as good as Prahlāda and
Hanuman is not as good as Uddhava and
Uddhava is not as good
the *gopīs*, but they're all serving.

The movie is bewildering your mind.
The night gets darker.
Two to four inches of snow.
Swami will be back.
I'll have to wear my
uniform. Hardy and Ollie
dressed as regular painters escaped
jail but not
for long. Don't seem
despondent because
they're jokers.
As for me, I tell the same story of
boy and girl saints
who killed smiles and I have that
narrow fellow in the grass
singing on my mind,

because of all the confusion and

dirty stuff and pay-off, but *Vraja*
vāsīs think of nothing else but Kṛṣṇa
nothing else.
Have all the transcendental jealousy you want!
And if you are a devotee, don't
be afraid.
Kṛṣṇa will reduce you and save you.
You can love Him more. There is not truth
in the bad stories,
only the good ones.
I don't deny it. Please vacuum my mind,
King of the planets,
and His smallest helpers.

Contesting parties. Hook and fish. I'll keep to the side of it. Is there a way to escape? Retire. Don't get worked up. "You're an easy-going guy and you'll have no trouble getting through life." Yeah, my mother said. She meant you're so darned submissive you'll march to war, go to jail, do whatever they tell you because you're a good boy. You know rebellious boys get in big trouble. So you will have no quality of life. Hey, that's not true. I'm getting an aluminum cane.

These words were spoken by me, a member of the low-off-the-ground tree hut. Other guys were much more ambitious, they didn't want to fight but their mothers told them. Harry S. Truman was a momma's boy, but what a mother he had, made of stern stuff. Stevie's mother was a wimp. Irish anyway, I could drink some nights, but every Sunday go to mass. She'd drag us along until I became an atheist by reading and learned how to outwit her. She went to 9:00 Mass, and I said, "Ma, I prefer to go to 10:00 Mass."

The letter of apology goes out today, Priority Mail. Take a snack, chemical and psychological warfare—"it breaks my heart to see you because I used to love you and sacrificed so much for you."

"You liked my books."

"I'm not sure I do anymore. They are too much about the

author and not about the Supreme Author."

"Well *read* about *Him* and repeat."

"I did. I read that He's often away from Vraja and that creates a *viraga-bhava* for them, better even than when He's there." I can't understand. If the "Guy" or "Girl" is your lover, you want to see Him or Her without too much interruption, right? You can't understand because you know only selfish love. Phone up some friend who says that he wants to help you and dedicate his life to you. I really don't see how they could live *with* me, but they're the ones who asked for something, so I'll say. Exactly. You can't understand. So listen with sweet faith, and that will grow. Suddenly the causes will all become truer than your flesh-and-blood-smelling grandma and your tattooed friends, your constipated bowels.

Without a moment's notice
floods roared down the road.
We have them in Wicklow.

You have to think and act in
the catastrophic moment.
Or even in dead quality
refusing to get up and
thinking where could I go.
"Why all the mystery?
Is he quitting?"
"No! Are *you* quitting life?"

Don't ask stupid questions
of your spiritual master based
on two bits of rumor.

"You look good. We're getting older
and still selling panties, baseball
bats and drums to get us through."

They are so short on
money but what they really need is

not enough to fill the Bank of America.

He'd play well.
I fall down.
Stay out of jail. I *won't* let him
take my Prabhupāda. He's too much
mine and if he wants to bring him
to me, thanks, fine, but not to give away.

To escape prison they dug a tunnel. But they hit a main water pipe and water poured out. Oh Kṛṣṇa help us. Where is the Vaiṣṇava calendar? Something must have happened on this day maybe 500 years ago and we grieve and celebrate.

The water main erupted into the sheriff's office and the two convicts appeared there in their broad black-and-white-striped uniforms. They were obviously guilty of trying to escape, and they *did*—ran out the door while the water flooded waist high in the sheriff's office and the dignitaries from the French Ministry arrived in their limousine for an honorary tour of the little British jail.

I didn't see a chapel in the prison. The guests of honor should have inquired, "Do you have a chapel where a man can go alone (guarded by a machine-gun policeman) and speak to his God? Are there daily or weekly services and sermons for the various religions? No? Then how can you expect these men to reform while they are serving time—just by sitting on the bench?"

The two disguised "painters" walked out the door but very soon were spotted for their strange behavior, painting Halloween-like figures and finally smearing a paint brush on a woman's backside from top to bottom. They went back to jail for the second hundred years of their sentence.

15
CHAPTER FIFTEEN

He heard the bell. Someone was coming. The soldiers gathered at the gate ready to fight. But it was only a large pack of children begging at Halloween. No, no, that's October. He said, "Maybe I'm crazy." But we're all more or less crazy, the lawyer said in the testimony-story Prabhupāda told. I'm going back to taking pills and deep breaths. Why take deep consultation? You like me, you read my head, my mind. Don't throw this letter away, it's too valuable. I like it here. Come and be my nurse.

She offered the priests cake with Coke. It was a boring script. They finally went home but the script was a dud, nothing very good. Go to sleep tonight and you'll eventually find the golden bullet, maybe it enters your heart. Prabhupāda—bring the cat and Prabhupāda and if you had to choose one, then bring Prabhupāda.

Slugging always we went to lower altitude
to save the grunts
but planes have to stay high due to so much
          dust up there on the deck and the land.

I can explain. Extra should be disloyal
You just have two hours and his case
and I understand the American nuke,
how did you get so far away
from the bad places?

He forgot Kṛṣṇa. He was 26, bumbling, he was
turning to intimacy, chant young boy,
crop up enriching all the gents
who was playing with him? Christian.
You can travel. You can do what you want, grant
          your life, ask
someone to rub your arm and your neck
and say it's not raining it's okay it makes me feel better.

Justin didn't think so
Because God had won
that to meet you rather than me
Serve than me. Try you
Ouch I don't yet get the picture.

It doesn't matter, I'm an eagle. Or I am a tiny robin watching that eagle, absorbing its mercy. I'm so tiny I can't fly, but I can absorb the glory of the eagle.

I won't be so afraid. Even cheeky? I didn't do so wrong. He said, "My wife is smart. But for her everything is *feelings*. It's not the way in reality. There is the reality of the vow, and that's a feeling too. To do or to die. Even if they throw a pie in Swims' face and say, "You can no longer prepare papers for lectures at the lodge," that won't prevent some of us from going where he is and hearing from him. Maybe he'll be wearing Irish linen. Maybe he'll be humble and admit the whole thing. Let them laugh. Laurel and Hardy sank under the water in their car, along with the cop. All on laughing gas. Everyone was laughing.

Surrounded with people who don't condemn you. I don't forget you, I don't invite you. You can come if you want. I'm not so hot on your books, see you all as a bit silly with your sharing of secret feelings at all costs. I got a pajama party.

Ice storms slam. I'm ready for breakfast when they want to serve it. I've got two *daṇḍas* in Ireland and a cat whom I can try to get back here in New Hampshire. Haribol, you arrogant, aloof one. He said, "The kids will love him," but I know Haribol will disdain them. But I like some moments to be alone, cuddling, just like a little ball, my big-eyed pet, pulling on two years now.

Oh Holy Father, oh Holy Lord Nityānanda, forgive me and those who are cursing me. Let them get their claws off my back. No more James Bond. But 1920 funnies from the Hal Roach studio—cook it up for me. They want me to eat and sleep, even the writing is more important. Besides, you are tired.

Don't be tired, it's been hard
before but the rhythm is on,
continue in the Big Store the
Clock outside on
the fifteenth floor and Harold Lloyd is
hanging on hand three for dear life.

He wants to go to heaven, people seem
more intent on keeping the pipes in the organs
the blood, etc. Priests pray for their souls, saying
officially, "This is more important."

Where does the soul go after death?
To the daffodils of God or to the
springs of Spring.
I write, "I wish, I wish"
the prayers recite in unison
and there's one nodding
to himself
and doesn't even know what
heaven is.

All the lords and their consorts. "Consort" was an odd word when I first heard it. Are they married? Is it his mistress, his babe? I didn't want to be irreverent, but I basically wanted to know if they were married. I couldn't imagine another category except a shady one.

Now I know it's more glorious than marriage. It never grows old. No arguments about who's going to wash the dishes tonight or the wife wants more money. Even their disagreements are transcendental and for pleasure. Satyabhāmā wants the *pārijāta* tree, Kṛṣṇa in Dvārakā teases Rukmiṇī, saying she should leave Him, and that makes her faint. The best are Kṛṣṇa and the *gopīs*. The boys make a tollgate and block their way. Kṛṣṇa splashes milk from a cow's teat to Rādhā's eyes. The girls are better at word jugglery than the boys, and even out-wrestle them. It's mostly Kṛṣṇa trying to get the girls to please Him by some prank or other, or He appears to lose a wrestling match, or He appears to win, just to bring Her love to a higher pitch.

At first *rāgānuga* puzzled me, "Why do we worship Rādhā as better than Kṛṣṇa?" But it became clear that it's more pleasing to Kṛṣṇa.

See who you want and don't see who you don't want. It's a glass-enclosed, bulletproof wall. Just rest and take your medicine and don't let the psychologists bum you out: "You're still a little boy. You miss your mother's cuddling you, you were not constructed to be a *sannyāsī*." But he invited me. He thought I was good.

You have heard before—you're sick of
it? Someone's crying all day,
angry friend writes to you.
But listen, please, you can't, me in love.
Oh I did wrong, I did wrong, I did.
Angry friend wrote to you,
but listen, psych, you can't
force me to love. Oh I did
wrong I did wrong I did
I wanted to learn from Kṛṣṇa
I know that's who He is He
is crying for mother and father
whom He never knew.
He was trying to wrestle with Balarāma
to test Their strength
I think. Kṛṣṇa can outfight.

They fight with the *gopīs* out of conjugal delight—
let's capture from them
the flowers of Their garland.
Kick them out of "our" forest.
Out-logic Them and prove to Them
that it's Rādhā's forest. Take
Their clothes, threaten them with Kaṁsa.
Hah where?

We're not afraid
of Kaṁsa.

There's for Kṛṣṇa,
but if His mother gets really
angry and talks to Him, He's finished, He
can't say what He wants.

He's just a flip-flop, he has
so many choices in his mind.
"It's the mob"—in his dream,
there was a mob and that was *him*.

He has that confusion. Sleep it out.
Kṛṣṇa, you know I want sanity and
guru's kindness to others.
One and two is three
and not a nut who
depends on the accuracy of medicine
or too much sleep and lies, just
leave me alone in prayer. Please have mercy,
all my sins now
and at the hour of my death.

You don't even know what you're doing. I love you so much. You're picking your nose, your hose (stockings) are hanging but I don't criticize this because I love you. Don't dig deep with knives. A half-hour written, you can do it with yourself. I'm with you, friend, but I can't join you and help, and I can tell you why. I have flown to the sky with New Age wings and I'm going to be all right. You just *push yourself*, your shoulder and your counselors. Demand *step on it!* so it's like Harold Lloyd driving Babe Ruth to Yankee Stadium. Good!

"Gee Babe, this is the most thrilling moment in my life," taxi driver turns his head back to feast his eyes on Babe: "Yeah, if you don't watch where you're going, it's going to be the last moment of your life!" Angels of mercy, you confuse them all.

They thought you were a squirrel on a treetop. You thought they were an angry mob about to push you back away from their mosque. So you backed away from the mosque street. When the NBC reporter told his story, they fired him from the company: "We will never win this war." I got my little war. Love myself, get out of my madness; go to bed again. You don't know whether it's day or night. Peep peep, "Formerly I told you that you should love your neighbor as yourself, and now I tell the greatest law: you should love everyone as you would love yourself."

We can do what you can
do and are not afraid or on the
top of the skyscraper looking
the other way
worry— worry— worry—

I didn't do anything wrong.

There's nothing I want to say.
Just say it's a good wish when
you know Kṛṣṇa will forgive
you. You got tired of this

then came to know the man
we could trust, Prabhupāda,
but we could have obeyed him so very well.
As time went by, we got more
into trouble.

I guess I can understand one day
but I have to cure myself.
It has to come when the linoleum is
bright blue on the temple room floor
and it doesn't scare us even if the
soldiers marched down the street.
That was the biggest blowout. Didn't know
it was the sacred temple.
Dopes we are. Pray for me as I worked my share.

Poooooff f. The gas balloon started to descend. It had ascended in liquid serenity, our *śuci* bathtub dangling from the dirigible. They spoke only the very lightest conversation because General Carson mostly wanted to contemplate, get a break from military plans.

It was not good of me to peak around the corner, to pick corn from my teeth in public, to dislike you at the sound of your name, so ungracious. But most of all my various forms of love of God are my fault. The five million TV audience were shocked to hear the President speak this way on Administrative Professionals Day (U.S.). Was it a political ploy? He went on to say how happy he'd been at Bill Clinton's downfall and the war's deaths, from which he'd benefited, and then winding up the phrases with, "But I'm especially ashamed that I'm a poor born-again Christian." (He usually didn't use that word "born-again" in public, although that was his religious affiliation.) Yes, it began to sound like a ploy, but he was giving some juicy confessions along the way. Sorry I plugged a criminal climbing over the White House fence, maybe I executed too many criminals when I was governor of Texas. Were they all necessarily proved guilty without doubt? Some tears spilled.

Coincidentally, Blooy Baloney, under investigation with four other *sannyāsīs* and brothers, waiting in jail, were trying to muster their inner resources. They sent philosophical things to each other, like, "que sera sera" and "I don't give a damn" and "Kṛṣṇa will be kind," "it will be purifying for us" and "There's no real justice in this world anyway." One by one they marched them to the guillotine.

Why are you talking on this topic, Freddy, an observer, asked his pseudo-mink-shawled wife. She said, "He was always prone to self-disclosure, this Baloney fellow. It's just coming out like sewage and he can't stop it."

Stop what? What did he do wrong?

Lost his berths in heated rooms in 500 houses, opened to a lot of guff for a thin skin. Maybe he should get some tattoos and defy.

Calm down. Be careful, he said.
You can publish it 40 years after
you're dead, "They do that."
I know that.

But you're in love with your lines.
Lots of guts didn't keep mum. It was
the truth, they faced it and explained
it better so people could understand
them. And the karma could come
on time.

See what it's like. The face of God
cannot be seen usually by

demigods. But sometimes they can see.
We want to overcome the terrible
mountain of dust.

Confessing in Papermate
can't hurt the soul.

16

CHAPTER SIXTEEN

I don't know what to say. You got only one warm day. Talk about the war. I haven't heard the latest. Where are all these beach boys, boys still confined to house because of ice? Where is the new type of book? I confessed to two in 24 hours. "Attack!" they say, they warned. But we've got some *men* on our side, too. We've got the croppies against the Redcoats. Bury our bodies on this hillside if it comes to that and the rye will grow next year. Oh, Fred said, I heard it was the first day of spring. When I sit in the jacuzzi, I want the thoughts to build up to a dream where I know what's happening to each of us at the time of death. Where the universal process is—I can't see it because I can't understand the words—but he wakes up for lunch interrupted like Coleridge[35] in *Kubla Khan*. I'd like to know but mainly you have to live like a nice man. I didn't do wrong because we were freshmen and didn't know the process. We couldn't get into trouble because our intentions were too undeveloped. Blah!

All he knew was that a guardian angel guided him over the missing plank in the bridge. You want to get through, I'm here to guide you, just listen to me submissively in Pittsburgh-tough streets and there's nothing to fear. We will get through this macabre. In this film Babe Ruth[36] is played by himself, and Harold Lloyd too.

I mean to stay on the strict *bhakti-śastra* path, but the windshield wipers are broken—bought the car just yesterday—it's unnerving on our trip to Vṛndāvana on the Agra road. Not so auspicious? Don't worry about that.

Thank God I don't know how I
made it but we did. Martini? No thanks,
just let me rest in this dream.
The cowherd boys are playing

Bill Evans[37] in heaven
some dope is coughing.
But I've friends I can
trust. Fixodent
won't fall out.

"My foolish heart"[38] is looking for Kṛṣṇa
and Rādhā all over this
Sony radio/CD

player but I'm too confused to
get it right. My path has some
rocks in its boot. The path
to love is never smooth
said Bill Shakespeare.
He meant
you'll get into fights.

I'm looking for love, faith in Kṛṣṇa
and everybody else but no one
particularly carnal. Men and women
in this mold are hard to find.

The hermit's looking for nurturing. Her black cubs are born on the rocky hills and nurtured, and she plays and protects them fiercely. But it's too cold for a spring. Will there suddenly be a summer? The saints always suffered. It's not an easy risk to be so happy. You're being tested to see your strength, your real identity, took a long seek. Go after your goal. If I went looking thus like what the reflection shows me, I might be a permanent teacher at the Vaiṣṇava Institute for Higher Education. Organize courses, pick good preachers and open the doors. Do they find it boring, too heavy? NOD for the tenth time? But although they're hearing, it's better organized, the teachers have been learned in the books, but this time they're hearing also from a better organizer. The teachers have learned. Don't be envious. Finger your green apple in your back pocket.

Yes, my friends, we shall stay in the room and beware of

falling on hot, slippery floors. We can oversleep for the time being, but try not to rest too full. Guilty! Guilty! Guilty! As they should be, as Franz Kafka? Dog, you feel guilty.

Those depressions you are being hit with say no anxiety for me. The wooden room, 12 feet by 10, is built without any window among the branches of the tree, and the devotees speak there in rather low tones, but openly, showing authorized poems around, answering literary questions to their best capacity, sharing, preaching what we are able to. Here as others are doing, not just for hurts and whines of your own proposition. They tested themselves to be a little strong.

There is this group of elderly, mostly white educated Hare Kṛṣṇas who want to write, direct, and produce theater in New York City. They asked Chimpy if he'd like to play a monkey in the show. He was a monkey and he was insulted at them even more. Then they asked the human fellow with the arthritis if he'd like to have his writings adapted by their writer for the stage. Sure, he said, I'd be honored. But I have to pick the jazz musicians. "Don't put yourself down for any work," Fingus warned. "They'll suck you to meetings with the troupe, fading female beauties that still turn you on, make you read the whole script, travel to New York City with them. I think you'd be bored and get a headache."

It's not going to hit Broadway or off-Broadway.

I've got no plot. If you don't want to tell the plot, it'll be pure. Better leave me out. It's not good. You'll be in danger. You're going to feel like falling off a narrow rowboat and see your face overboard. Tell of the sleep-crossed and you tipped over as you crowded your way over to your buddies. And looking at the girl at the bottom of the stairs until she dropped her eyes.

You make the supper, you remember the fears—scramble of the ASPCA dog-catcher. (No, he was not fierce.) And you saw us but when we came near him and we told him what Father Ted told us—assistance for a dead Bill. The cat will make me calmer, mystic, tender. You want a cat—that means you are unfortunate.

You know your way over to the spiritual side, "Chant Hare Kṛṣṇa."

These aren't genre-benders. May we adapt your journal? It's a journal? My, may we rewrite it as a play? Oh no, not me. No more work. But *you* can do it, and I'll just reread to see that you haven't used words I would not use—and I'll pick the musicians. It's a dreamy idea. Let's go for it!

Mommy, what's a bomb? What's a thief? What's a knife in your back? I thought there were only beautiful things. My dad says my silky blond hair is bouncy after a haircut. Like naming the babies who come into our family, like behaving well and being loved.

No Suzy it's not like that. Maybe it's mostly like that on this street, but the newspapers report of other outbreaks in centers. Some are good, bad, not so good. But all ending in death at the last moment...don't look so good.

Now that's nicer,
forget the rest
the Americans in the belly of the bomber,
it could be a nice family with a
monk living in the center of it
amusing himself with old-time
women and going out to the preacher
where he leaves for better
places like Somalia and Slovenia—I was there

and I was there because
I know something
special
so unreal line in my faith, *brāhmaṇas'* faith in me,
black caps, jacket,
flashing light cop car!
"Nigger! Put your hands
behind your back. I said

behind your back!"

The motorist succumbs and the city
is burned to the ground in rage.

Tell us a goodnight story. Something
happened with my books, they got accepted
somewhere and I got happy
back home with some old chums
out of the Depression, I'm in New York,
near Albany, but big buff
is snowing the most it ever did
in the history of the world—
or from the beginning of keeping records.

Birth of Christ child,
Viṣṇu's lotus bud.

What's an oxy? Oxymoron. A man with sledgehammer-like blows punching his boxing opponent in the sides. You don't know what. Feel sorry for yourself. Freely because you can't find anyone to come run and tell you if you've taken the wrong pills. Probably you've taken the right amount. No one to talk to. Can't be all alone. It was a mild, mild mistake. Will you burn him at the stake after all these years?

The concern (I must switch this concentration from forgetfulness to forgetfulness, although you've heard it a hundred times before: call for God, but on the "annoying" beads. Could I pray with a man who soothed me, Kṛṣṇa? Prabhupāda's lecture *in me*. His somewhat loud volume doesn't smooth the orb. He's the holy one, and I want to be connected to him, but comforted. Maybe I'm just feeling sorry for myself.

Switch to the fresh and sloshy snow. Nathaniel felt better right away. But he thought he should take his baby head pang inside again. He wasn't so strong yet. I think about arranging the counting out of the numbers in a different way.

Agari, when you have deep, moving dreams but you can't

remember them, is it still an important sign that churning's going on? But should I try harder to remember them?

Good: men on my side who don't condemn me.

Once a week he wore a cuckoo hat to mass.

But no, the crucial topic is I never knew love. The footsteps. At that Vyāsa pūjā altar, you said you never wanted ... I will leave the kittens behind in Wicklow. I will take a little pill. His name is not yet given...

I wish we had more time for coherence
and castles in Spain
but I've got anxiety again
rather can't eat, can't move and want love
my kitten is like a symbol for Kṛṣṇa.
If I can nurture
love for me in him.

Summit Sully, she can pick him
but I get him, he's for me.
Don't call him Corky but instead
some Vṛndāvana master name.
I pray to Corky what you know, Vraja clichīs
are not so good and I'll wait out
all my names.

It was mild what
I needed. I suffered. My gambol-footed
Deities coming tomorrow so wear
your *sannyāsa* clothes. He
looks like a *bābājī* and when you hear him
make millions of songs of offering
he will be indistinguishable from me.
I love myself. I was told to.

Mr. Lee, I'd like you to meet Mr. Robert E. Lee of the Western Railroad Board. Associate Hal Roach, predecessor of Mr. Max Roach, at least by family name, we'd like you to sit together, and let's talk and play over our trades, painting, writing, drumming, fist fighting, etc. The main thing is how to be active when you're over 50. Our problem is that we're too weak. I called this meeting to see if we could help each other. The cellist Peggy Lee, who is over 60, burst into the room rudely but trying to be helpful and said, "You think you can't act, but you can, even if you have a headache." "It's not that easy," said magazine specialist Dr. Duramad. True, we cannot leap into the air from the tightrope walk safely or go without all meds, but some daring combination of meds and therapy. After a talk with the therapist you may feel inspired, but then you've got to keep it up by regular practices.

There have been great writers and athletes and artists who performed even while they ached. Glories to their *vibhūti*. Tim's got a low pain threshold.

The children happily ran across the lawn. I eyed them and then did not look at their mothers but tried to rest deeply in my chair.

The angels persisted in rapping on the windows. I'm afraid to keep telling Saci about the noises at night because they might think I'm going insane. After all, I came here with a disease rooted in the mental. Damn, Henry, how can I get you off this dilemma?

"I'm in your prose." What at least if I don't do it chronologically and everyone thinks I'm just practicing? What do you do anyway? It's authentic. The scientist thinks not of himself but the "television" he's inventing (19th century). I want to be famous, "maybe he's thinking."

No, there are hoards of goodwill people thinking how to better the world, not themselves. That's not an excuse. How about "first person is simply the most alive form of writing and I don't stick to it anyway."

Well, you're sure hung up on talking about it and talking in general. Gracie Allen also had a problem with talking too much. And Lucille Ball. A quiet woman in a corner of the scholar's section of the 42nd St. library researched the Nobel Prize writer. She wanted to publish a book about him. When

Bill entered and surprised her, she was elated and broke out of the cobwebs.

The library party men tried to study but kept falling asleep. Swims' specialty was to bump his head against the desk.

How do they chant 64 rounds a day and stay awake? Tim introduced a *Bābājī* into the room. He chanted and did not answer any questions, showing his determination. Hour after hour he went on with clear enunciation until Mrs. G interrupted, "Sir, would you like a cup of tea?" That annoyed him, and he rose and began pacing back and forth, but did not stop his *harināma*. "Okay," he said, "with a little lemon in it." But his chanting continued and he even raised the volume. The audience was awed and influenced. "Let's all pledge to increase our *japa* by the next month." The meeting ended and the *Bābājī* bowed low and did not rise.

NAMES

Chipper, Frisky, Kaulini picks
out the names of the people born
here and animals too. I'll let her
get my cat's name but I will keep a secret
pet name. It will evolve.

Then he'll be quiet and love
me even more and be allowed
to go outside. But if he runs away…
he knows "my food
is back in that creep's house,

the one who doesn't chant
Hare Kṛṣṇa very coherently."
How kind Saci is to me despite my wooden leg.

At the time he chose me he didn't
know I was so inactive
and in pain or complaining

of it, suspected.

Ask him, "If you had
to do it over, would you?"
No, don't embarrass him.

He's got DD Swami and a lovely
family. Plus he likes
to lay out my pills.

Holy Mary. My wall's now decorated,
it has pictures of Mount Aspiring
and lots of pine trees and print
and a fire extinguisher
and I'm looking for God and
He's in my heart, but
also in the hearts of all and
the mice and cats of Vṛndāvana.

A day warm enough for the veranda. Have you been in a fight? No. I've been in *lots* of them. But I lost most and won a few. My wrists are very thin. Back out of it. Be very polite. We are getting sleepy again.

You wake up and don't feel much like living. Later it's okay. How can such a precious thing later seem like a throw-away? Just got a mood. I ripened. But you've got to fight for it with determination. Two-gun-belt, lots of bullets and more laser weapons, control of the mind. I lie down but not for too long. Don't make out to become "down." Don't be more uninhibited and hip for any reason. The search is taking me back, they are buying me presents. I'll receive graciously, humbly—hey, watch out! That trolley almost hit that taxicab! I have to want so bad, so when the kitten comes in to be born, I'll get to be its mother. Why do you want that? I'm lonely. I want to pet. I don't want to wake and think, "Why should I live?" The cat will be there; bought a petty nuisance. Have to see. See see, get me the phone numbers. Yes, my dear, please come to Stuyvesant Falls and spend four days with us and act in a perfect way. Then Fred of the Holy Rollers woke up. “Ow!” He’s tired of these pain attacks but sympathetic. Can’t tell me, “No pills at all, you’re in rebound.” Say, “Take it easy.” Don’t like to pass the doctor, but neither do I leave myself up to that person who says, “You’ll never get any better.” Or go back to the shepherding of Crowhee.

Not only friendly prayers, more lapse, more hopes.

Ninety-six times “My romance”
why not 108? He can have
108 billion if He wants. Yes,
please come out of my dream. I’d
like to see you and bring your notepads
so I can color again and not get a
police ticket.

One hundred and eight times and more keep…
but you say you can’t, “I got a lack.”
No, you can break that lack.
Give up a trip on the bad-trip lane
tell me my life.

“Learn it yourself.
Face your God. You chose Him.
Love your guru. I know you like him.”
You’ve got to give from your side
to the Indian man smiling, replied
I struck the feeble opinion and
the dilemma. Think you were a born writer.
My romance.

Oh “Waltz for Debbie,”
means she’s a *sakhī* junior.
What do they call them?
I’m so forgetful. Assistants,
they brush the *kunjas* and arrange

but don't want to make direct contact.
So one was Debbie, assistant
to the assistants a thousand times removed,
and I thought of her brave and picky
and juvenile and joyful, making
remnants for flowers to help you

and me talking nonchalant to disciples
as if I knew anything about it but lore
of Bhaktivinoda Ṭhākura and Viśvanātha Cakravartī and
Śrīla Prabhupāda, what they saw, *sakhī*,
sakhī, Rādhā Herself, the girls who
the boys challenge because Kṛṣṇa's on
their side as a ruffian—
never mind if you forget what they said.
You just keep calling out their names
and making yogurt and blocking
their way, taking a tollgate.

Why did you accept me
as your guru when you
hear I know so little, have
surrounded myself with
rumors of lower self?
I like you because you
love me and like to take my hand—
oh he's back,
firm Lord!

17

CHAPTER SEVENTEEN

Pulled down the statue. Here I go, so sleepy. Can they get pride? Strawberries blossoming. I remember many years ago. Good for rashes.

You want to come see me?
An old friend calls a new one
and says Freddy
is in New York. Would
you like to see him now?
The one who asked about Freddy
says yes he'd like to see him.
He had hit it off with him.
She's right. I'd like to see the new ones.
So we're arranging it.

Will you be able to come see me?
Only problem is my head starts
spinning. On Sunday the doctor's
coming also. Saci says he's going to
really question him until
we know which method works faster
and cures. How sure am I into this?
What has to be the goal? How
can I get out of that after that?
Okay that's fine, get out now.
That's how I get it over,
I'm getting a hangover,
please excuse me.

Pull down his statue. Here it comes,
I get so sleepy. Can't they see?
Show being joyful and remember
years ago, good for hang-ups.

After sitting down, the *bhaktins* and *bhaktas* ate to their satisfaction and then raised their arms and shouted, "Jaya Gurudeva! Jaya Govinda!" at the end of the meal. The children then bowed down and went to wash their hands and mouths. They each took a little cup of aperitif. A what? A little anisette. Then the men retired in a room and sat on bolster pillows. The prominent women went to the washroom and cleaned. It had been a fine meal, plenty of pastry, nice *sabjis* and *dhal* and gift-wrapped packages for friends.

How are your yoga lessons?

How was your history class?

A little dry. I wonder if we can teach history as taught in Kṛṣṇa consciousness?

Bill brought a lawyer who said now for a job that takes me 30 seconds to do I can charge the same as I would for a job that took me three days to do 30 years ago. "I can trust John," said Fritz. I was a little surprised at the ethics. But anyway, what do I know? Appoint a man who can say on your behalf, "Rush him to the hospital for an operation." He's got power of attorney. Apply surgery, resuscitate him. Try to preserve him so he can write more books. I am not a lawyer, I write Kṛṣṇa conscious books with illustrations.

Sometimes I feel—everyone in my life is gone, no mother, father, boyfriends, girlfriends, trustworthy guru, good Godbrother, no one left. I just bluff as if I am not lonely. Shake his hand softly. You've got a new lawyer to decide what happens to you before it happens. But did Johnny O'Day have a mood change, seeking back to the old sod?

Oh, what a pain, he says, eyeglasses,
I'm okay, what if one of your books
became a bestseller? It could
go to GN. What if you died before
your attorney? What if your mother
never breastfed you? Would it matter?

Personal history of Henry VIII.
We wanted to know how he got
so high on the chords. He told
us, "I just charge 10 times what
I did 10 years ago." I was confounded.
I am just a goofy duck looking for Govinda
on the back of my sweatshirt. It came
in the mail. The BBT, the
ones who sell his books, that's fine
with me.

He's a member for life unless he
misbehaves. He's got to be the genuine author.
I'm smarter than you. I saw Kṛṣṇa
in the little robin.
You can see in my face how
gentle and asinine I am
and the hazel gentle confusions
can't tell west coast from east.

The operation is to pray Hare
Kṛṣṇa before you fall asleep but
it never happens. Unable the
day of your liberation—
he looks aghast happy
like a lad just given a
vanilla cone.

Is it possible that a professional man of boxing in the ring becomes unenlivened about what he was doing and quits this and takes up some other line of work before he dies. Wrestling or grammar? This is the "land of God."

Priest in "Father Ted": "There is not a shred of evidence for religion...the idea that devils will poke hot pitchforks up your arse for eternity..." The old bishop became enlivened: "Yes," it seemed true. "Be cautious, Bishop," the other priest said.

The priests and bishops weren't going to leave, but this one bishop was. He grasped the shoulders of the other younger priest, the loony one, and thanked him. He changed his clothes to a bandana and hippy pants and a flute and packed off with three friends in a van. "We'll go to India for three years and see what happens."

You can be sure I won't do that. But you never know what will happen. Where is breakfast?

We have seen recently how people make sacred vows, secret pacts, and then change them when their lives present different needs. "I took a vow, but then I realized it didn't encompass my needs, my *feelings*." Does that mean the maker of the vows was imperfect for not including feelings?

Oye! When she cried, I cried. Or rather—the boys were gathered in the caboose for an evening get-together. It was wonderful to be able to talk openly with friends, "to name your God," to open your heart, to joke. One friend had Jackie Gleason's *The Honeymooner's* series all memorized—he was in great demand to perform it every night. Tim did his Chico Marx Italian accent, but he did not have any plot or fresh material. They were cronies of various ages, 23 to 76.

Yet more compassion was coming into his own life. So many people he knew were suffering, and also a larger number were judgmental and unforgiving.

"Did you ever read or hear of a book—they even made it into a musical— *Les Misérables*? I haven't read it myself but I hear it's about a man who committed a crime, did time in jail for it, and about how when he was freed, people treated him as an ex-convict."

Oye, oye, Giovanni, what does it matter what they do to me? And what does it matter how others judge me? Timo wasn't paying complete attention to *The Honeymooners* but dwelling on his own thoughts. Yet as soon as he saw a person being rigidly judged, it moved him emotionally, sometimes to tears. "What if?"

"Give me privacy or give me death," muttered ex-tugboat captain Druthers as he puffed on his pipe. He had seen a lot, mixed a lot, but now preferred to be alone except when he could be with his sympathetic friends. Timo especially related to privacy, but he was also beginning to appreciate the caboose cronies and the things he was learning from life and other people.

"Things are changing. They are getting better. The old hard days in our religion are going," said Tugboat Annie, one of the very few women allowed to attend the meetings. "People aren't judging so much anymore. You don't have to be so strict."

The air was pure. The night was...uh...black with a partial moon showing, and you could peek at it. When he was young (17), Tim dreamt and worked at being a great "fiction" writer. He didn't think of it as "fiction," but *writer*. That was his dream and religion, just as in his younger days he worshiped and followed the Brooklyn Dodgers. (Someday a longer story about this, with details, when it's Tim's turn in the caboose — it will start with the grief of 1951, which he could tell and retell with emotion, up until how he suddenly lost interest in the Bums after 1955.)

Eventually Tim took the speaker's role. "I lost interest, or rather I realized I didn't have what it takes to become another Great Writer. Thank God all of this has to do with being a member of the Hare Kṛṣṇa movement. One of my college friends wrote to me when — after being out of contact with him for 10 years — we found each other and I sent him a book of my poems. He said they were "fatally parochial." He certainly could turn a phrase well. My other close college writing friend and I then got in touch at the same time, and I sent him a book of my poems. He said, "The fault of your poems is at the end you always wrap it up in the canon," and he recommend that I read Rumi. So they'll speak like that, and it's true that our writing is "fatal." They say some devotees are starting to get their books into Barnes & Noble, but I doubt mine ever will. Too much reference to the inside action. But what I wanted to say is that dream of being a great writer like the ones I used to like — Thomas Wolfe, J.D. Salinger, and I kind of faked liking Jack

Kerouac — in fact, many of these loves were just pretentious because *I* wanted to be a great writer. My desire was sincere and pure. In fact, it was my true religion. I was so dedicated that I was more interested in writing than in living, if you can believe that. I would rather be able to write well than to have a girlfriend, or at least that's how it turned out. But then when I met Prabhupāda, he kind of turned me off from writing that way, and I came to think it was false ego. That was a mistake on my part, or maybe a period of sacrifice I had to make. I'm not sure. There might have been a real neat way I could have combined creative writing with being a strict devotee. Am I strict now? I don't know.

Oye, oye, Giovanni, he's a good man. I'm a'gonna go and see him again. Why don'na summa of you join me?

Yeah — O Jai-O.
Remember? He'd say "jai-o,"
we'd bow down. We were playing a game with our sacred
grandpa. Jai-ho.
See you in the morning.
Jai-ho, Swamiji. I am your
boy. Can't spell Caitanya
right. Don't know any
Sanskrit except
    aham brahmasmi
and the great mantra for the deliverance of the world.

Oh boy, things may get
better even through suffering.
Don't worry, whatever is
coming is worth it — it
is due to you.

Whoever carries it to you
(like Typhoid Mary or the Hong Kong flu)
is sent by Kṛṣṇa so don't begrudge.

Oye Jesus Giovanni.

We gather and pray. Wished I
could read a book like I used to *learn* from it
for the first time.

Old-time caboose club.
Tears for the fallen. It
could be worse. Couldn't?
Mercy, cry — be grateful
I says to them.
What a bluffer.

Did you ever send that
e-mail? Ever learn there's
no Santa Claus? Learn
Kṛṣṇa is real. But
you're not good enough
(no *adhikār*)to see Him.

Why insist? He's asking for
too much. He wants to
preach a series on
sewers and hear how he climbed
out. It's a great idea —
God is teaching
through the fallen.

I'm coming to a better stage myself
oh go lift those weights.
Build your body.
Eat the lemon pie. Hear
the drum and your bodily pains.

Be grateful! I told her

that it hurts. St.
Therese *was* grateful.
Be happy. I told her, me the schmo.

Shut your mouth and say
your prayers. I can't say more.
Buy it at the store.

The surreal world, how marvelous. The spiritual world, how sublime. The ghetto, how miserable. The ending of Laurel and Hardy's *Varoom!*, how funny! *They themselves* were laughing at it.

But where's my inner child chanting Hare Kṛṣṇa? Aha! I never had one. He never knew the mantras, never liked the Hail Mary's...who you talkin' about, man? Uncle Remus? You sure ain't talking about Coltrane's boys. They was singing gospel music to Jesus as soon as they were tots with their mamas, and *hearing* it even before then. So I'm repentant, Rufus.

No, you have not answered my question, who is this saying, "my inner child"? This is Operation Eagle, a make-believe radio show (in contrast to a real one). This is the psychological file. *This is Pepper Adams, lamenting he wasn't a devotee when he should be rejoicing that at least he is one now.*

Pah! You talks like a mental juggler. You think you can help someone?

Surreal's charm, I admit, blows your mind. But it ain't *real*. Charming illusion of the mad mind, which is, after all, *God-given*. But the spiritual world is actually, palpably real, although we can't see it now. And it's full of eternity, knowledge and bliss! Think about that! Śrīla Prabhupāda on a walk asked (paraphrased), I know they don't believe in it, but if there were a world of eternity, knowledge and bliss, wouldn't it be great, wouldn't they want to go there?

Oh yes, yes, Prabhupāda, but they don't believe there is such a place.

Aside from that (big aside for the eggheads and buffalo-brains), what if there were a place with those qualities? We cheered faithfully, "Yes!! We'd want to go! They'd want to go! Let's help them want to go." How glorious is the *ācārya* because he does believe, he's pure, he leads us there.

And then comes the thump of heart. You pretend to others

more than you can help them. But I can! Even my fallen act can help them. Oh, do you believe that? Believe in the feet of Kṛṣṇa. Hear the *ācāryas* speak of those feet *ad infinitum*. But my guru says, *"Just hear. Stay low, no presumptions."*

Just hear. How many rounds? What quality? "O, here is the guy who does the free-write," sneered the thin swami as he paused at the book table. FW? Gimme a little. Prasādam's soup, too much cake, a groovy soup, healthy for you. Swami boys with their long shorts. *Private Eye Pope*. Why do we like C.B. as a poet? Because he writes so well. Teaches the pious how to be more clear and honest and not hide a shred. What's so good about disclosing? Keep that buck's shut. Keep your mouf shut. Blow it out the horn in sad-aspiring litany. Bee motion, C-motion, baseball, a disgusting collection of statistics. Beem is ripe for the fallen (rotten apple).

Is FW meant to be understood? Yes, it touches the dark and light spots, the inner spots, tickles you and makes you flinch and leaves you not understanding like that one guy I know who keeps saying, "What? Are you deaf?" Some joke Prabhupāda made, "What, are you deaf?" We laugh with him. "We ain't softening them up, we're *killing* them." Deep bow. You can do better than that. FW meenie mo, the broken heart, the new nun, cheering from far away in the grandstands.

Don't hit me, man! He threw the baseball at his head. I's protecting myself, but you never can tell when a rose thorn will cause your death as it did with Rilke[39] (don't bother me with facts!) and with elderly Dr. Pineskin, who aspired to *die peacefully* (he tells Prabhupāda this) but wakes up as Godzilla. FW must be religious or as Bogey said (end of *Casablanca*), "Life ain't even worth a pile of beans."

I do believe. Give me my
First Communion. I's
fallen from purity no more.
Give me my Confirmation slap
in the face from the bishop.

It's tarnished after so long.
Betrayer! They's talkin about.
Sidewinder, they can't take
you away from me.

Yeah, but Sidewinder
is just a faint amusement. No it's not.
It's the pulse.

The *material* pulse (I got a
big one on the back of my hand).
Sidewinder can't save you. Don't
open your mind to the gaze of the Godzillas.

It's too early to worry yourself to death.
Eat that soup. Take it in
while you can and build up
your muscles. I'm lifting
the 5-pound bar now.
My flexes are developing.

"Don't push me away or I'll
break your nose." Teach
him a lesson. Go back
to Ireland for visits.

He was silent when he
heard it. The big house
would be taken away.

He resents his daddy who gives orders and
who is imperfect himself.
Oh ho surreal. Give me mo' of W.C.
Fields but take out that
Cab Calloway band, *heidy*
ho up your …

Just give me strength for 16

rounds a day. It'll
come naturally as my biceps grow.

This is a good place for me to be.
He's not welcome here. Come and see me
when you want. The mercy of the Lord
is deeper than the sea.

Suffer a little embarrassment
and ... resort to FW when
you can't disclose, skip
a stone over the water, admit
you are a yellow chicken (coward)

and always was.
She said I am strong. Nurture
yourself. No self-esteem...
love yourself. Give it to the others.
Protect the chickies
in the way you think best although
all that is up to the decision of fate.

Sidewinder, get it? Sidewinder. A punch
from the side.

Consistently cold feet. What is your worst scenario? Doesn't sound so bad. Live in fear it comes. Where's the caboose gang? You want multi-opinions again? It's not going to be so easy to stay in touch. I pray for you, here's a snake in the back. No smoking in public in America. The bouncer in the bar told the smoker to put it out. He said, "I ain't gonna." The bouncer threw him out and the smoker turned and stabbed him to death. A victory for smokers in the tobacco war.

But I would not try to disobey. It's not so important for me to be a rebel. *Who's talking?* The shadow behind the wall, the telltale heart. "There's not a shred of evidence for religion," said the bishop, and he changed his clothes to a hippie's, jumped into the van with other hippies — "we're going to India" — and puffed on the marijuana they handed him.

18

CHAPTER EIGHTEEN

No, you can't do that. They've got the privy (toilet). They've got the papers signed by the original *ācārya* and pressed by the notary public. You can't fight 'em. So take your options. Increase your options. I'll live in an army tank.

Give me another voice. What if people didn't look at his paintings? He said, "That's how I paint. I don't do it to show." A good way to get rid of the ego; I'm proud of you. Oh, wide prairie. My soul is protected but not by my death.

"Your own nurse and nurturer. Love your own self. I don't hate him. Blow the horn. What's the difference between loving yourself impurely, like a stage show performer, and loving yourself purely?"

I can't find anyone in here to talk to because they have all gone to the first feeding of grains to Lakṣmaṇa, April 17. All fall down. Old-timer's club. They didn't like it as much as I did ("Father Ted"). Funny routines. Words without plot: "It's an ecclesiastical matter."

Simple. I'm your boy. I will try to help others. Deliver newspapers early in the morning. Take what you can get. You wanted to be loved, you'd have at least a few friends to give you a room with a roof over your head. No devotee association? That's okay. I'd make it for myself. My own cries and Kṛṣṇa hearing makes devotee association.

You and *harināma*. What about all the others you allowed to honor you? The snake in horror curls himself around D's arms, but he's fearless because he knows they're not poisonous. I told you that before. All warmup and now go. Give me that old-time religion. All I want is loving You and music, music, music, sing the cowherd boys and girls.

And Stefan failed again to reach the holy *dhama*. Tell us why it's so special. Rescue me from America, I'm growing too old to be confused.

Vamp is going open his mouf'
for first gums. If they knew how
bad he was would they
remember how good he is?

All I want is to protect
my chicks and if I can't
I'll find a way. Just do it for its own sake.

Corporal ripped off
Master Sergeant Bilko's[40] stripes but
he predicted he'd have them
back in 6 hours. What if you're not as
smart as he?

Live in a tool shed. Make
more close friends. The best humor.
No more Lucky Strikes.[41] Smoke in your
toilet: allowed? What's public?

Open your private hell to God, Kṛṣṇa, the Father.
Call to Him and call to Him, Abba,
I want to be with Prabhupāda.

He was so disappointed but
what can you do when
you face the music of
his stern frown?

This is Bee Vamp.[42] But
they don't live old usually.
Rhythm and blues and then
into the casket or burned
on the riverside.

He blooped, she slooped, the
sloop looked lovely
in the sloping sea. "Somewhere

there's music...how high the sky."

You can't get it together or is this
common sense? Keep your
mouth shut. You remember what
I did? He told the world
his daffodil.

She wanted to be a nun
very saintly girl. But when she saw
a rat in her cell she applied
for office duty.

"In the name of Holy Obedience
I order you to get off the
floor and look decent," said the Prioress.
Do what we tell you, bring
your own visions, but
let's hear it. Let's get this
thing over as soon as possible.

Bee Vamp. Before Christ
Kṛṣṇa is the sparkling supreme
known to very few
so we're trying
to artificially understand so much before
it's your time to
automatically join the sacred *līlā*.

Understand? Not yet. God gave me
this pen. I use it to hide and seek.
When I get my kittens I'll be happy.
I've such friends.

I've got protection. I've got rights
and shit all over my
head. You cause the sobbing
of hundreds.

Back in jail, Stan? How many charges against you? They dug a tunnel under the cell but busted a water main...the funny world is not the real world. But we love Stan and would like to stay with him.

Kṛṣṇa is coming, Nṛsiṁha! Swamis in saffron, five folds. Stevie's still among them. Don't dare adjust your *dhotī*, it's fine as it is. Could I go and live on Mt. Ranier in any case? It takes bucks, man, bucks, and you can live wherever you want.

But will they forgive me on the top of Mt. Ranier? ...The white wolf will never forgive. You'll get a post card from the Royal Mounted Police: "Exit the mountain. We didn't know you were passing stool outdoors, and you have no permit and no papers." The little fellow slid down the snowhill. "Surely I'll find supporters somewhere." And he thought how different it was to actually suffer frostbite than to see Charlie Chaplin do it in the movie. Where are my pills? Where's my mama, who used to serve me tomato soup and Ritz crackers for lunch?I could speed on my Schwinn bike home from school in five minutes and sit to eat while darling Ma watched me and chatted. Good times. Pre-puberty. Pre-ISKCON. Pre-Navy. But afraid of bullies. Great Kills had no bad gangs. Pleasantville. They like new comics, the *Rāmāyaṇa*. You tell *your* story, Mary, the unexpurgated one. When did you start sniffing coke? At what age did you begin praying to Mother Mary and you were miraculously cured? When did you enter the convent and when did they kick you out as a lesbian pickpocket? He never went to school. The boy she fell in love with also never went to school. She met him in the opera house where they were selling "Yankees Suck" stickers. Police chased them and they ran together hand in hand down Second Ave.

The blonde, the man waiting for Fibercon or a rubber band to act. Take to the stand and tell us the best Rip Van Winkle stories you know. The 7-year-old girls fidget and walk out of the theater. When they are 20 they will be fidgeting for love. That's my useless preface. Now let's begin. The priest converted the bishop into an atheist hippie. The hippo wallowed on the bottom of the sea. My head ached for that and I wanted it back—the simple speed bike ride from P.S. 8 to Katan Avenue, where Mom was waiting with the tomato soup and I hadn't a care in the world, just to watch those sharp corners around Brower Court and then stick your left hand out at Gifford's Lane, weave past a car, brake slightly, then pump hard down Katan Avenue, dragging up pebbles in the driveway. Nothing to worry about. The world is Pleasantville, but don't ask me questions, "Did you steal the Dentine gum and car emblems we found in your room?"

You don't have to be afraid I'll
defend you said
Karṇa said to Duryo.

To have a big strong dad to
push away the ruffian and
cheaters and even when you
are small the monkeys and fish and cats and dogs.

Stay here and we'll take care of you. Bite it off.
We sat around talking of Vṛndāvana and I...
Joe opened his mouth full of sweet potatoes
and told the story how Rādhā-Dāmodara got stolen
from Dallas.

Mariner told how big her bust
was when she was born. John
leaned over and felt such sadness in his self-
centered mind.

We know he's strong but something
is covering him. He's looking like
a healthy cat.

You got it man. Jackying,
they call it, a game kids
play in Vṛndāvana. They want to move on.
How much money can I get for this

place? You gave it to me, now you want
to take it back? Yeah but you used
it for 5 years.

Eat your heart out. I've got jackying.
Lord Kṛṣṇa knows that best playing
outdoes even Balarāma and Śrīdama. Oh
boy these are good days if you'll
just look at it that way.

Oh oh Giovanni! How's the stars
tonight and what does it matter to a SANNYĀSĪ?
I ain't worried because I got
nothing in this world anyway but private
and public parts.

On top of a roof the man
shouted, "They's comin down the hill!"
and we began firing mortars at
them. Nothing takes away
the gloom like shooting
demons. And watching the sky
filled with devas dropping flowers.

No matter where they put me
I got me *harināmas* and me finally all right
no excuses now.

Exactly what it means I don't know, but you do. It's love and victory. I'll have to fight the options and wind up in jail with black and white stripes. With *japa* dig a tunnel out and run into town—even if they catch you and bring you back, they forget you have God in your heart. They don't know how to stop you from learning the way to *kṛṣṇa-prema*.

A man should act morally, not thinking what the masses think of him. Sure, he should take advantage from learned friends. A man named Aldous was about to buy a house and his businessman friend gave him valuable advice that the price was much too high. Good, the less learned man listened, and was rightly influenced. But on some matters we have to act for ourself. When? When it counts most. When is it the most important decision? I can't say. Someone told me that it makes sense; you shouldn't be like a ping pong ball going back and forth, but listen to others also.

Give an example: He decides to be a writer. He decides to stick with his spiritual master. He decides to *live. He goes on with his natural style, considering it God-given.*

Short and stocky Jody paused, tried remembering his rehearsed speech, coughed, and continued.

When a man makes a mistake, he should admit it and take the consequences in a brave way (influenced by supportive friends). There is no hurry in some things. My old man, under the blue cloud of cigar smoke, used to say, "Take time to smell the flowers." One or two cats? Make up your mind. You're not going to live *that* much longer anyway, and the next life is determined by your present deeds. Follow great wise men of the past who saw this world as fleeting and advised to concentrate on the eternal. If you do it despite obstacles and the opinions of others, you are acting for yourself. After polite applause, Jody sat down, having completed his little oration. He attended a private school and each student had to speak once a year.

escape...they were afraid of the
consequences and ran into the church.
Escape the prostitutes and *guṇḍās* on the corner.

Build a temple and escape *karma*
of capitalism. Escape the Holy
Ghost. There is no escape from
death. This is Jody's poem. He worked
on it for 9 minutes only because
he...didn't bother. Wasn't a good
student, put his energy into the oration.

Escape getting an "F."
The long arm of Bacchus
and the enchanting face of
women's teeth, eyes, set in
a beautiful head that can
be dented.

They caught the guy who
was mixed up. He was trying to escape
the truth. "See? I told you,"
said the woman next door,
she had always suspected he
was a drug-abuser.

Is there a place you can go
where there is no one you'll
see day or night except a
few friends who know that you
want to be alone with your God?

You failed miserably. You
don't even call on Him with
numerical strength, how will
you make your escape
from Gorki Park?

I heard it all before. That
crap. We're trapped. Like
Little and Big Goof who have
200 year sentences
in jail.

Don't even talk about it.
Hell on earth and after.

Oh my! Won't He be softer than
that on *me*? No Jody,
He wants to toughen you up,

He wants to reduce
you to sense so you'll cry to
Him "no other escape."

Don't teach me something
else except how to speed
up and get through Gorki Park
and to the position of pleasing
Swamiji, the *ācārya* of
the lucky ones. All theory — for now?
No I can do it if
you help. And I know you will.

He's not looking good. Too much shampoo on his bald head. When are they going to take out his last teeth? He can't even make up his mind whether to own kittens. "Loose lips sink ships." Landor overheard the gang's plan on the telephone, and he devised a plan to save the day.

Caboose talk. Sunken-faced Billy Chimes came by one night and couldn't remember what to say. He specifically made a long trip to get there just to say something, but when he arrived, he forgot it. Can you jog his memory? Something about preparing for the worst? No. You're just introducing new topics. Whether to get cats? Hmm, that's close. Why a man has bodily maladies? How to get through it? Oh, Billy, you just sit here and listen to some others and maybe you'll remember yours.

There should be outright religious talk in every presentation. We are going to get our old edition of *Śrīmad-Bhāgavatam* and devote some time to it every day. Just read a little bit and pray for attention. Pray to think freshly what he is saying and why it is important. Write a little comment on it. Fight the dreary, "Oh I've read this before." Gather the knowledge and regurgitate some of it onto your own page. Don't think you're writing's better. Okay, but I've got to get the right *Śrīmad-Bhāgavatam* in my hands or I'll fall into that, "Oh, I've read this before and lost the taste." No, you persist, and even confess — say what he says and then say, "I'm bored." Try another sentence.

Somehow it will be a reading session. I could do some myself — from the book *Śrīla Prabhupāda Ślokas* — and read what I wrote to you fellas. That's what Billy Chimes wanted to say. The fellas and Tugboat Annie agreed he could do it anytime, even though they might be bored stiff.

Well, what animates you? You've got to take the strict road. All right, next time.

Weight lifters are invited. Joe Schmo sits on the edge of the circle, feeling cold and lonely. Come on, Joe, move in closer, this is a compassionate club. We're not shoving anything down anyone's throat. Eat whatever you want, leave what you can't.

He's eating his plate bare. I'm a
happy man to join the family
circle, I've got none of my own.
Bee Wee puts me happy
cats instead of kids. Doesn't make sense.
He's got his heart
fixed on the tenor sax. Please
tell us the story of Kṛṣṇa in 4/4 time
and enliven my soul.

Clap hands for daddy and get
your first grains. If you don't like it at
first, you learn to. What am I doing
taking up so much space?

They'll hire a company that moves
all your stuff into one container and
ships it wherever you want to go.

Where will that be? Plant it on
California soil. Then you'll have to
go live there and work
out your insanities.

No one will bother you
day or night. Wear a T-shirt

as you like and do what
you want, not what others
tell you. Put his sign
on the wall.

Hare Kṛṣṇa should come
out your mouth. Just a few more
and you'll reach the quota. Going
up or coming down? He looks
better now that he's
a Kṛṣṇa. Where's the focus?
I think it will be a happy day
to see W.C. Fields in person
in a reformed, happy smile or
even bitchy, as long as I can
surmount and chant
Hare Kṛṣṇa "as I used to."

Oṁ ajñāna timirāndasya "Do you have faith in your spiritual master? Do you have doubts in him?," asked Bumby the college student who had started attending the caboose meetings. "This is the core issue," said the devotee in saffron, and then said, "Excuse me, I have to use the toilet." As he exited, he said, "Can we have faith and some rebellion both? Is it dualistic? Don't we all *have* that but we don't admit it?"

You mean we can never write again because we can't publish it? You mean no one can read it because it'll hurt their faith? Is the author such a blackjack? He thought so and spent the whole morning in a double bind in bed.

But a few words from a friend assured him. He said they wouldn't kick him out even if he were treated roughly by the Supreme Court by a unanimous decision.

Oh come on! You have to pay for these offenses.

I'm paying, baby, daily. The knot is getting tighter.

He can do it. Must be
humble and admit the truth

and keep going as long
as he has a little shelter
from loved ones.
This is the kind of music
I like. Yes you can bring
the Sufi healer here.

Now "the opener" is over. It's another
song I wrote too. I'll go up and
sing with the Vaiṣṇavas now.
They said they wouldn't kick me out

but I may go somewhere else.
Never know what Kṛṣṇa has in store.
He may want no more
writing and publishing, he may want
the perpetual right-eye and drag
you through the mud more and more.

I'll keep playing "the opener"
and learning how to pray to
God, Lord, Kṛṣṇa.

Kṛṣṇa begins with chanting ABC, it ends with XYZ, *kṛṣṇa-prema*. But what about the letters of the alphabet in between? It was not anxiety in your case, he told me, it was fear. When you're fighting in the foxholes, it's fear. So I am living like that, World War III. I will, however, carry on and not cower or consider myself unworthy to teach. Just afraid. So it was a bad year. I intend to remain reformed. Don't pull down my statue as they did Hussein's in Iraq. But who am I to say? God wills these things.

"Do you pray?," Bee asked me.

"I chant my rounds."

"But do you pray?"

"I don't know how." Just a nice guy at best.

Gallopy. I sit and can't eat much, but try to nibble on the

stuff that's good for you and hear his preaching. Silent table sitter. At least I got to talk to a sweet book distributor. Afraid. And hung up on a strange disease that seems to have no end. Tied up in the anxieties. These are the letters in the middle of the alphabet and we all have them. Don't pretend you don't.

Be at peace and no one will get you. I'm afraid, not guilty. Am I authentic? Being a phony and others thinking yourself a phony — there's a difference between the two. I'm going on with my life.

Be aware that storms come
and rock the boat and skies clear
and head rocks with pain
sometimes. I like the music

God has allowed to emit from
the horns and drums
of angels and strugglers.

Go fast. We always want
to be free of sadness and unmellow
grudge. Please give us the best.

Rādhā-Kṛṣṇa are the summit.
I'm a climber who believes the
blues bring us there, lift
us instantly and take
cry! I'm afraid but I know my
Lord and I know His
kind followers. You came to Kṛṣṇa
through the door at 26 2nd Ave.
because there was a little sign
pasted on the window

classes Monday, Wednesday, and Friday.
You checked it out. You
entered and met the Swami.

Now I'm scared. I've become distant. I am
desiring he drag
me back to him. Call
loudly to him — Swamiji!
I've done some wrong things but
they weren't that bad.
Don't...
  Do ... give me courage to face what
comes. You're in my blood
and soul. I *do* know You.

If you can just get through June ... that's when all the visitors come. Protect me in a bulletproof glass room. The cane-user is not available right now; he's in bed with a migraine. Have a short meeting. These are the fellows who are leading the charge. Be respectful. But wants solitary time. "Sickness is a trump card." Do not disturb. Do not ask me to lecture or attend a 4-hour lecture. He knows the original Alfred E. Neuman[43] but don't tell anyone. It's funny how many people are actually connected to or have contacted the Hare Kṛṣṇa movement. The big child abuse case. More scandals ahead. Poor Catholic Church with pedophile priests. Smash them with media missiles, throw them in jail.

The wheels of justice grind slowly. Kṛṣṇa operates it all through His energies and agents in sometimes strange ways. What looks really bad can turn out better for you. You want to reach humility, dependence on Prabhupāda.

Dullard. Writes uninspired. What do you do in those last hours of the day? If you can get through June. This one is coming. That one is coming. Yes, he is. No, he isn't. "If you feel well and enlivened, you can talk with him." For a little while. Wants to chew on his cud and keep his secrets. Then talk about your father. Wear the FDNY T-shirt to the dentist and tell them your father was a fire chief. You can't keep wearing the same clothes. You can keep the same dentures. They'll put some suction in.

All the memories jumble in a kaleidoscope. The beautiful

girl with the safari suit in the dental office. Her big, perfect teeth. (But so big they could remind you of a horse's.) I think I'm Stan Laurel looking on the scene, foolish but observant. Too foolish to seriously pray. I hate the waiting room and the magazines. Yellow ribbons and American flags: "God Bless Our Troops." All right, I'm glad the war is over and they're coming home. When's the next war? God bless America. We talked of how I could give long lectures and *kīrtanas* and meetings. But I'd have to pay sometime.

Moved out of Wicklow for the cause of money. And maybe he thought the tenant was going mad, less than a guru. Consider these things as you lean back peacefully and the big gun pulls the pain away. Surrendered to your doctor. Until He releases you, which He may never do in this lifetime. But a boy has to chant his *japa* or where can he expect to go next *loka*? Just to keep saying, "I was there in '66, I'm his eternal son," may not be enough. Waning. Waning. The Hare Kṛṣṇa *maha-kīrtana*, so much enjoyed by the holy folk and pious and even impious. Kill this cynic bug under your foot. Wear your orthopedic insert until it wears out. Hare Kṛṣṇa *mahāmantra*. Don't let them tear you apart like a monkey. You're true to your spiritual master. Go up tonight and put Rādhā-Govinda to bed. This is not a diary, it is an essay on higher economics.

(He's so happy when on the
ride to Happy Hill,
Cecil Payne is a religious
monk. All he wants to know is
"when's the next set?"

They improvise but according
to what they remember the master
said. Sit down but the lecture
is too long.

He's talking about the *gopīs*
but not by name. He got

too ecstatic so he says, "A
particular *gopī* waves Kṛṣṇa
with a fan, another serves cool water."

Other gurus name all the names
boldly and their followers read
the most intimate books.
And who's to stop them?

Let's behave well and follow
Śrīla Prabhupāda. Be kind
to each other. Give a break to
the fallen. Give respect
to the renounced leaders.
Don't break the rules.
Work out in the gyms.

Hey man, how come you don't wear
your *dhotī* every day?
I want to see you shaved up proper
and to bed and rise on time.

The opener card
is shard on an inedible salad.
I'm living here
until I live.

CHAPTER NINETEEN

19

Life is so hard. Who do you want to be? Who can you be? Back in the Navy and they don't give me room to sleep, my uniform all wet. I've neglected to get prepared to go back to the Navy for too long. I have not saved money to get myself a nice uniform. Absurd. I don't have to go back or save money. I'm a "self-employed monk," a member of the Hare Kṛṣṇa movement, a religious minister. I don't want to get married. But so blue and down and confused. I just don't want to go to the party because I have agoraphobia. Then they ask, "If you don't want to join the dance, or even talk with us, then why did you come to the party? Why don't you just stay home? You're insulting us and giving yourself more pain."

Good advice. Give me a reclusive choice. Be who you are. Yet how can you do it in a fishbowl? And why does the pain come anyway? Don't you like to see Vaiṣṇavas and speak on Vaiṣṇava topics? (That's an offense.) Do you fake enjoyment when you're with them? I want to retire. I want to be left alone. I can't do it and live in a clear-glass fishbowl. I want to be alone and be a devotee by self-expression, writing, and painting.

Cats want to go in and out, in and out. They lose their affection for you. Do you want to be a disciple of Prabhupāda? Yes, but in my own way. Not pressured to conform.

A friend assured me this place is not a fishbowl for me.

You'd be so nice to come home
to, Kṛṣṇa and the cowherd
boys and girls, no headache

my anxieties chained away
in a cellar or blown off the earth,
come home to a peaceful setting.
Done enough fighting. Even

Varuṇa said, "We have grown
too old to fight, go see Viṣṇu
and he'll bash you."

To come home and think of beads
in lovelight
of eternal peace
and joy, secure in shelter of
the Lord of my spiritual master.

He never gave in to public opinion,
played the way God told him in his heart.
Not millions of people
accepted but some thought
he was the best, and he had the
lucky satisfaction of non-
compromise.

This is for You, divine one.
It has come from You and I offer it back
as interpreted by my
individual free will—
You said surrender all and I
will please you.

I'm doing it this way and
it is natural.

They may resign because it's too
much work and they don't think
it's worth it to stay up late and
fashion a magazine for their spiritual master who
writes kind of zooky
and now they have a guru who speaks
more like a capable and learned *sādhu*.

So what if there is no more
Among Friends? We are all still

among friends and have our
EJW and our life breath

friends, and solitude and solace and
spark of attraction and duty-bound
to the Supreme.

So you pack up your belongings in those hard plastic milk cartons, shrink-wrap the totem poles and wait for the movers. Who could do it but B? I was laughing when I remembered the weightlifter in the Chaplin film. I excused myself for wearing sweats and khakis in the house when I'm supposed to be always a *sādhu*. I'm putting on a show. But still I'm a *sannyāsī*. Only the celibates qualify to go to Goloka *dhama*. And they have to be much more than celibate. They must be immersed in *kṛṣṇa-prema*, followers of the *gopīs*, whose chief is Rādhā. This can be done by chanting the Hare Kṛṣṇa mantra. It will *automatically* bring you to realization of the pastimes and qualities of the Lord. Anything else is bluffing.

You misplaced a manuscript as soon as it arrived. This doesn't speak well for your sanity. But an old man can still work out on the exercise machines, the rower, the arms-lifter, the legs-lifter, the heavy punching bag, and finally the hot tub. "Are you feeling all right?" Yes. I ate all my spinach and cheese cake but didn't like the *dhal*. Is this too ordinary, no prayers? We have prayers.

Breathe deeply. Punch the bag. Where did you misplace that manuscript? Hit the bag, ten more seconds. He imagines he's a real palooka in the boxing ring, with skinny wrists and arms.

Breathe deeply, report to the doctor, more sleep, less medicine. Titration continues. They know what they're doing. He'll crack your back, a visiting chiropractor. He'll fill you with acupuncture pins. Schedule it all and try to get better.

Where could it have gone? Surely you will find it. It must have been taken out of this room. Maybe it went with my enthusiastic youth. New people are coming to help me.

He knows what he's doing,
he'll be true rain or shine.
Don't interrupt me in the midst
of an attempt to reach sublime.

I can't start it up again. Why
don't you touch your nose
directly and *tell us* what you're
thinking? Because *I'm trying
to say* it. I don't know what
it is.

A little of this and that.
The down mood of twenty
years' illness. The up mood
of hope and gratitude that
you're alive.

I'd tell you if I didn't
think you'd cut my head off.
We have written the letters
so it's too late to take them back.

You may have to walk through
fire and then you'll be accredited.
But Goloka, Vraja, they seem
so far away and their outer
coverings dismay me. As one
girl said, "Just to be in
a material body is enough
austerity for me."

I think that too,
a pampered fella, who
wants his songs rated top ten
on the charts.

Write them anyway. "How
do you feel?" Where is the

Blessed Mary? Where is the
Lord in the heart? Where is
Sats who used to chant so ably?

The autumn leaves are gone, it's
springtime and they're happy over
that but for me it means
more visitors and I've lost
the Wicklow house forever
where no mice ever entered
and Haribol slept all day.

Okay, okay, where's the religion? Swims was chanting his *japa* and interrupted it to go seek 7-year-old Kaulini and ask her to show him their new cat. Where's the religion?

We (Swims and most of us) attended Public School 8, which was a secular school. On Wednesday, however, two hours were allowed in the afternoon for religion. It was called Released Time for Religious Education. The Catlicks walked down the block to St. Clare's, the protestants took a bus to their church, etc. Probably no Jews, Bahais, Mormons, Hare Kṛṣṇas in those days. We attended a class lecture given by a nun and learned "our" religion. That's religion. Also you attended church on Sunday and eventually received the rites (Catholic) First Communion, Holy Confirmation. But you and your family (Swims' and most others) *never talked about religion at home.*

How strange. Was it such an unimportant subject that the Bible was never read at home or the pastimes of the Lord never discussed? Certainly the Hare Kṛṣṇa movement is different. Yet in many homes it is also not discussed much unless a *sannyāsī* attends. Individual members are bound to spend about two and a half hours privately chanting Hare Kṛṣṇa mantra on beads, like the holy rosary. Some don't do it, many do. Some admit they do it mechanically. Some are more advanced and under their directors live in temples and do constant spiritual service with the Deities or going out to sell books, proselytize, etc. Some live in the holy *dhamas* in India and spend many hours contemplating the names or praying at the holy sites.

Some grow doubts and seek help from elders. Some break down. Some live, as Thoreau said, "in quiet desperation" (aspiring to revive their spirit for the spirit).

The way you look today,
dear shark, are you seeking
my blood? Dear Sonny, how
can I and why should I
proselytize on your account?
Although I love you with
Monk[44] playing "The Way You Look Tonight."

My mission is to recover.
This is costing. I can't do all
the things they want me to
do. I tell Saci I can't
make it to the temple opening
unless I take another medicine.
"Then take one."

When I finally get my
reclusive house, you'll be
content or at least not take
so much medicine for pain.

Pain is the bottom line
says Dr. Ravi Singh. Get rid
of it at all cost, it
is hurting your organs.

At least if I can sing one
of these songs of appreciation
of Lord Kṛṣṇa's devotees—
"unknown devotees" you
might call them.

"Do you like this kind of
music?" I want to ask so many people

but they don't.
"Where's the religion?"
Or "Where's the rock?"
Or "Where's the higher
classical?"

I'll pray from where I'm
at. You look
beautiful tonight.

"I am glad I'm a daddy with a little son," said Bobo as he held his tot up in the air. The *sannyāsī* who did not preach saw it through the window. Well, he didn't lecture. He preached by trying to avoid the police. He stood on the sideline as the parade passed by.

"Don't mind me," he said, "I'm just testing out my new cane. It can be used as a weapon also, so don't get too rough with me."

One man said, "What you need is seclusion."

Another disagreed and said, "No, what you need is to learn coping skills so you can deal with people."

Another said, "It probably doesn't matter either way. You're stuck with reactions to your past deeds."

Such a nice feast. Swami Swims couldn't attend the ceremony but got to eat the meal in peace while hearing the *Bṛhad-Bhāgavatāmṛta*, which he couldn't actually realize—"the glories of Goloka." How can there be such a place, Śrī Sanātana? How could one like me attain it? All the spiritual inhabitants are satisfied even though they have different varieties of spiritual engagements. The simplest lecture with many anecdotes about Śrīla Prabhupāda and everything you've learned from him. Surely that should be good enough, so don't be afraid to try it again.

"Hey," Swami Swims burst into the room where the subpersons were already in their pajamas and lining up their pills. "The Deities haven't been put to bed yet, you guys! How can you neglect this?" He roused them and they trudged upstairs to change Rādhā-Govinda's clothes into their night outfits and tuck them into bed.

Yes it's sweet and you shouldn't
complain. With friends like
this soft-heart, strong-arm
solid and intelligent.

They wanted to help because
I lost so much when my
big friend went away. Don't
inquire into why. Just
accept with loving arms

that your new people are helping
you construct the house
that Jack built.

I wanted to be one of those
devotees like in *Bṛhad-Bhāgavatāmṛta*
but I'll have to crawl
on the earth it seems.

At least be a lover, follow the
ways of these good Vaiṣṇavas.
See how they act toward
each other.

Yes be like them and you'll feel
better right away. You'll never
have problems you'll be
competent to meet without
a pursuant headache. I don't
know if that is possible.
Who agrees?

Let's go have a beer, I mean a Kṛṣṇa
conscious drink and sing

nonenviously, hear the
Swami talk a full hour
while you shut up
and think of Bill
Evans Trio. Be in best
of health and Kṛṣṇa consciousness,
yours truly, Stevie
turned Svarup dāsa.

Mommy I'm lost. You're lost too. It's raining hard now and the rich people are going into the restaurants. I'll have to get out if they spot me. I have no friends, nowhere to go. *Nowhere to go.*

No home. I know another guy who said, "I have no home now." I said, "Nowhere at all?" He said, "Well, I know some people I can hang out with here and then," but no place of his own. Another person said that at Tompkins Square Park, they used to let the hippies live in boxes, but now the police close the place up at 12:00 midnight and no one's allowed to stay. He used to sleep on a bench sometimes when he was at a concert and it got too late at night for him to get back to Jersey.

I used to have a home. In Wicklow. It had a thatched, peaked roof. They gave it to me, but then they took it away. Anyway, I said I was stagnant and didn't want to stay there, so I came to New York, but I don't have a home. But I'm a *sannyāsī* so it shouldn't be important. In old-time pictures, always on the wall of the home it says, "God Bless Our Home." When I was growing up, we had one corny, humorous one, "God Bless Our Mortgaged Home," or "God Bless Our Heavily Mortgaged Home."

They say a lot of homeless people gather at the Berkeley temple and that's no good. But they have to have somewhere to go. Charlie Chaplin in "The Kid" went into a dump hotel for one night when they had no home, and the kid was kidnapped from there. What do you mean? Your home is in the spiritual world. He asked me, "What part are you reading now in *Bṛhad-Bhāgavatāmṛta*? I said, "We're up to 'The Glories of Goloka.' That's supposed to be the home, but what good is it if no one can go there? They have to have these tremendous qualifications. Practically everyone in the world is disqualified. They call it *adhikār*, you have to have the *adhikār*. But nobody really wants to go there.

Prabhupāda used to say nobody really wants to go to the spiritual world. Only a few. So it's a matter of desire. But I keep having these dreams, and they're scary. Like I'm inside that rich hotel and more rich people are arriving, getting out of their cars. They have fancy raincoats, and they go into the restaurant. But I'll have to get out if the top men spot me in there, because I don't have any money for a meal and I didn't come from any home. None of them get rushed out into the street. It's really bad. So be grateful you've got a place where people are letting you stay. They said they'd even call it Rādhā-Govinda Barn after me, because the Rādhā-Govinda Deities that I brought are here.

You fake. You haven't even been walking with your cane lately. You're supposed to be an official cane user. "We've come to take the Deities," said the lady, and it was a somber moment because Saci had borrowed the Deities and he didn't want to give them back, but she came with her husband and another man, and as soon as she walked in she said, "Now we've come to take the Deities back."

I joked and said, "You'll have to pass an armed guard up there," but there was no armed guard. That's my hot air. Wicklow used to be like home. That was my home. I could get up in the morning and think, "There's nothing I have to do." That was a wonderful feeling. I don't have that feeling here. There's always something to do.

KR said, "That's good for you. You have to learn coping skills." But my counselor said, "No, let's try it for a year where you don't have anything to do except what you want." Of course, I'm not a blob. I want to write. I want to paint, if it was set up nice. But when you're incapacitated, then all you do is take naps, and you're just a boarder. It's not your place. Anyway, this world is not a home, and some people wander through it with this attitude—just tramps, just travelers. It's all fleeting, but some make nests. Even though they know they won't stay, they make it as nice as possible for a while. That's not a bad attitude, is it? Make it as nice as you can while you're here, and you can even make some contribution to people of the future. I think everyone wants a home, a place they can call their own. And they're really lucky when they can come there, put their feet up and relax.

A hospital is not a home. A place people give you but later kick you out of is not a home. A place where you're staying temporarily is not a home. If you're a guest, it's not your home. I don't know why I'm talking about this, it's just this word, and it's my condition, and it's this dream I had of having to step out into the slashing, pouring rain, and that restaurant—me like Charlie Chaplin. But some of them, the tramps, are really hardened to it. They say the chair can be pulled out from under them, but they'll go on finding another place to sit and do their work.

Take it as Kṛṣṇa's will. He doesn't want you to get attached here to crocheted doilies sitting on the arms of your chairs. Watching too many movies on the video, looking at your bed in almost adoration, waiting for the next time you can lie down there. Your neat divisions of books, your wife (or lack of one), and of course your laptop e-mail, your crapper, your CDs, your friends.

Your parish church. Your mate. Your own heart. The doctor who's coming is a friend and he said he thought that I would be embarrassed if he stuck his finger up my anus for the prostate gland check-up, so he could bring another doctor friend. I said, No, I never said that. I very much welcome the check-up and want to hear the good news that it hasn't blown up too much. Because I want to stay on this home called Earth a little longer. And when you leave...you get the notice from Death—"Get out." Prabhupāda says they may give you no notice at all. So don't get too comfy. The human curse, ultimately homeless. Feel like a guest. Take it easy and behave, but don't think it's yours.

If I could learn how to pray, not to attain a home but to

understand my plight, that I have no home but Govinda—why don't I understand? It's so obvious. The body's breaking down. Why don't I accept the teachings and pray, "Take me home"?

Lady Bag, Gloria's step all
varieties is the world of spirit and
material as well. I can't
talk long with anyone so leave
me alone.

How well he can live in his
own house constructed by a
friend on a California hill,
where no one will see you.

You *will* get lonely but you
can work that out in paint.
"Oh it's strenuous,"
I told him, and keep the dogs
and even exalted Vaiṣṇavas
away from my door.

My borrowed room
they say they'll call it Govinda's Barn.
The inhabitant
plays checkers and likes to bring people
together for an old-time comedy.
That's his idea of time well-spent.

Obviously fallen. I was not taught
at any university to overcome
anxieties or stop pinches in the
right eye or cope with society. I
like a simple meal like
Mother Kaulini's baby food.

Six minutes is all you're given
and then the next reciter takes

his turn. You are nervous and egoistic,
you're kidding about weakness.

I told him the roto-tiller
noise won't bother me and
it doesn't. But if you knock on the
door, it will. Don't need a
snack yet.

He'll catch the commas,
he said, just blow from
the bridge. So I did.
Such a hip, encouraging
editor. Won't people like
it when you're laid to
rest and all these quirky religious poems are left?
Some will reject but
some like Dat will understand
and I better not make the
slightest claim, don't expect
the slightest reward, but just
pray it's not all in vain,
it can uplift
bring peace
make you think of Kṛṣṇa
right in the face and in
the way He likes best,
indirectly.

"Bebop furniture" said the sign and I knew I must be crazy. I have memorized the question and answer for *Among Friends*, and when Saci comes back from work I'll ask him to put it onto the e-mail. That doesn't mean I'll be able to pray better. I'll ask the readers to send in their understandings of how to do it.

Pray for the world, pray for help, pray to get off your butt. Perspiration and prayer. Guts. Not just pretty words. But recognizing the Supreme Lord. The Christian solitaries do it, and I was criticized for putting it into *Entering the Life of Prayer.* But I was right to imbibe their spirit and happy to find that Prabhupāda also told us that we should pray individually.

Holy moly. Holy Ghost, they've changed that now to Holy Spirit. Is there a ghost in the house? Downing your medicine, doubting if the process is true. D Swami laughed philosophically and said, "No matter what you do it looks like the headaches are your fate." So look for those little crevices in between headaches and come out with your words of prayer. Oh dear, Lord Nitai, please help me to reform my life so that I can get rid of these headaches and serve you better. But I seem to have crawled backward like an animal down into its hole. I don't want to give lectures anymore. Pray by painting, pray by talking to people individually, but I think you can't avoid the lectures too. Who is this talking?

It's Swims McGrarty. Swims the red-haired rookie from San Francisco. His mother was born of Irish parents. She had a statue of the Little King, Jesus, in the bedroom. One day her daughter expressed disgust in front of the statue, thinking that it was an idol, because she had now become a sophisticated atheist at Hunter College. Mother got very upset. Her daughter said, "I'm not laughing at the statue, I'm just looking in the mirror and not liking the way my hair looks."

I also joined the atheist ranks, me, Swims McGrarty. I don't know who's talking. Is there a mouse in the room talking? Saci said he'd be back from work soon. I will attend the *kīrtana*, said Swims. He sits in the rocker, doesn't know the Sanskrit songs but knows the simple Hare Kṛṣṇa mantra. Then they go down and sit around the dinner table and talk. The med has calmed the latest headache, but he wrote in his chart, "Feeling alarmed that headaches come so frequently and don't seem to be caused by any anxious events or meetings. Doubt in this process but can't think of radical change, such as different doctor or process. Someone recommends—two triptans a week and suffer. *Am I on medication-induced headache syndrome now?*

Ring around the rosie. Be happy and blow on the bridge, as Dat advised. Let it come out however it does, but look for that cry and that wittiness, as various favorite artists have told you in their own sounds. Coltrane[45] has the cry, and Sonny, the wittiness, the inventiveness. They say he's the most inventive of all the sax players. Give him a break. He doesn't want to make clichīs so let him rest. Don't demand more encores.

The Groucho films are too long for the people here. And I can't seem to take time out for it either. They say they have a jumpsuit for me if I want to paint. Swami Swims took a visit today to see Swami D, who's just down the block. Swami Swims said, "I admire your spirit of jolliness and I think I know where it comes from. You love to lecture on Kṛṣṇa, you're like a jazz musician whose only question is, 'When's the next date?'" I was thinking of 76-year-old Cecil Payne,[46] who lugs around the baritone sax and is joyous and gives joy and asks, "When's the next date?" D Swami is also like that and gets many chances to lecture. That's why he's so happy.

Swami D ignored all that and said, "Bhurijana once said that some people need some pill or something to keep them up, but I need something to keep me down." He proceeded to happily show us a painting on the wall, a new book that had arrived, his desk, his bed, and invited us to come any time we wanted.

Even that was too much for me. Walking back through the grass. This is a crevice I'm sneaking in. Blow from the bridge, look out at the city. Call for your own heart and call for faith and remembrance of the one who saved you. He definitely did or I'd be with Murray and Kowit[47] now, complete cynics talking about language, afraid of God.

Don't claim I'm any better. Lost the technique for subpersons. At least I've got one voice. One-at-a-time voice. Step up and say what you can. Try to help those people in need. Sam Snead, Ben Hogan.[48] The golf scores remain the same over the decades. They can't improve it as they do improve the scores in other sports.

Weightlifters lift more and more, but the golf scores remain the same. So what? I just thought I'd tell you what I heard in the marketplace, *grāmya-kathā*. You mix it in a little sometimes when you get tired of religious catechism. I'm not really tired, it's just that the words play like kittens and you don't like to refuse them. They must all come from God. You like to tickle the ticklebones of readers. She said, "Do you know where I tickle?" and he was supposed to find out. Do I know where you tickle? Why should I tickle you anyway? Because it's part of life, and even Vaiṣṇavas enjoy a tickle.

It's not a sad religion—the boys and girls of Vṛndāvana are decorating turbans, dancing and mock fighting, and there's no crucifixion. Their suffering is when Kṛṣṇa goes away, but that suffering is so deep and unfathomable that it's actually the greatest joy known. This is my prayer. To recover or at least to retain and to keep in touch with dear friends, to seek their protection and to help them if I can as I silently munch on my meal at their dinner table. Wear your *dhotī*, your disguise.

"Hey!" said Shorty, "I found a crevasse. Is there going to be a *kīrtana* tonight?"

Is this loud enough? I want you
to be aware that I have black
shoes and laugh at my mortality.
You can do that when you think
you're at a distance from death.

Now the happy time of life is for
babies? All blond around here and
honoring *prasādam* with great gusto.

I don't want too many visitors. I'm
on medical leave. Oh shoot you
are. You're just a fakir. You
want the ayatollah to rule the
country or you'll revolt.

There's no democracy or anarchy
in the spiritual world. Everyone is
happy with their love of Kṛṣṇa,

as mother or friend or paramour
even though the paramours are highest
and the servants of Rādhā the apex.

It's right there in the book.
He knew well enough not to
spoil his appetite. He ate his
way to almost empty the plate.

What do you want? He says
the little child's great ambition
is to take the cow off the altar
so they take it off and
let him hold it and then put it back
and say, "No touch."

I must take part one way
or another. Send them
some pictures.

Who is the man with the
beard, who is the shaven?
They're all in the book
Pariṣads..

This book is written with a perfect, exciting, seamless plot and is 100% Kṛṣṇa conscious. But you have to be tutored to understand the code. And it takes a lifetime. I realize this makes it almost inaccessible to some, so I made it in such a way that it's more enjoyable to read without knowing the code, but don't think it doesn't have a code. It's like Kafka said, his books are like the secret mystic Jewish book the Kabbala, which must be studied with an understanding of the code. Just think how long it took for that genius Jean Francois Champollion[49] to crack the hieroglyphics. When he finally cracked them and understood them in French, he was so ecstatic he fell into a coma for five days. But now we can read hieroglyphics. We're probably not so fortunate to read this book, although we could benefit.

In the present anecdote, Bob is trying to catch the Staten Island transit, but he had fallen off the train platform. There was a guy up on the platform whom he asked to reach down and help him up. The guy was very surly, and Bob thought that he was either a pervert or some kind of mugger bully. He refused to lend a hand, and even insinuated that if he did grab Bob, he'd steal his wallet. So Bob moved down a little further and struggled on his own, with great strenuousness for such a weak fellow, to finally make it up to the top, but the train was coming in his direction, and he would probably miss it.

The train was very organized, and they announced its stop and how long it would stop there. They also kept a very orderly queue of people, so that people couldn't rush on. I can't tell you what an exhausting attempt it was for Bob to shimmy up the wooden platform, but he finally made it. But with great disappointment he saw the people standing in queue so patiently. He had thought everyone would be able to get on the train, but it looked like you had to stand in queue, and if the train left on time (which of course it would), you'd have to stay in your place until the next train came. The story ends with Bob finding his place as the last one in queue.

You see how this connects to the previous episode and how it's Kṛṣṇa conscious? The *ācāryas* don't like to reveal the topmost secrets of Kṛṣṇa consciousness very openly to unqualified people. Only in the eighth chapter of the *Bṛhad-Bhāgavatāmṛta* do we learn that the very topmost devotees are the worshipers of Rādhā. It should not be given out cheaply, and we're told the method of attaining Rādhā worship—to chant Hare Kṛṣṇa in devotion. It could be told very simply at the beginning, but you might not appreciate it or you might become a *sahajiyā* and think you had already attained it within five minutes. Anyway, I'm just a pint-sized Vyāsa and I may not even know this story myself in terms of the code. But I feel relieved as a reader that Bob made it to the platform in one piece and that another train will probably come along if he misses this one. Now he'll have time to gather his wits and start his chanting again, and he can communicate.

20
CHAPTER TWENTY

Your indirect Kṛṣṇa consciousness ain't because of higher purity to please the Lord, as if you know His inner desire. Your indirectness is because it's mixed with the modes, like in a nightmare, like those big demons described in *Śrīmad-Bhāgavatam*, black giants with copper hair and copper eyes, and you jigging with them in rhythm and making up ditties, and they're appreciating your ditties, your sexual ditties, and you dance and fill up the whole car on the SIRT (Staten Island Rapid Transit), but you're too late to reach your class at Brooklyn College. So you think what the hell. I'll study the book instead of going to class, and that'll be just as good, instead of being in the classroom with pretty girls who are smarter than you. And anyway, you can't stop it. So it continues with hairy, ugly creatures, and you go up to the different groups of them, and they're appreciating you. Is this what you're indirectness is?

It's true, my indirectness is not like that of Viśvanātha Cakravartī's. Now I just want to get out of this train. I'm wearing the last civilized clothes I ever wore before becoming a devotee—a brown tweedish sports jacket and no pants. Moving back and forth with these uncivilized people in the train that never stops and that is sealed off at one end.

I asked, "Is this the SIRT?" He said yeah, but it doesn't seem like it to me. It doesn't seem like I'll get either to St. George, which leads to the Staten Island ferry to Manhattan, or just the opposite, coming home and getting off at Great Kills. It's just this nonstop sent to hell national lower religion of the demons.

And how could you become so talented at mixing with them and transforming and making the ditties? I don't want to come out and say it. But it could be what you think. It could be I'm transforming into a different kind of creature and I'm not good association for you. I don't want to scare you into putting down this book. I don't intend to contaminate you. I've got good association, actually, people who are trying to help me. But I'm feeding in some unconsciousness, or rather it's coming back to me in a mixture that's most devilish and sexual and rhythmic. In a way, I can't get out.

That was a putdown of my love
and I don't like it. It's sweet and
inventive each one. And keeps
me alive.

It's my church. My Gaura-Nitai,
best friend. Doesn't bore me like
some accomplished preacher telling
all the places he's gone.

It's fresh and creative and lifts
you. For a fellow like me that's
saying a lot. It's not like that
nightmare with the horrible creatures.
To say so is right wing propaganda.

Race is not the issue,
"religion" is not either.
Kṛṣṇa consciousness exists
separately? No it's flowing through
me in this way, maybe I cultivated it but that's the
way it is.

The cowherd boys stand
with this flute and dress
their hair and turbans as
Śrīmad-Bhāgavatam says. I'm just trying
to taste it within my perception
and I've found the joy here so admit
it happily to you.

Kṛṣṇa *is* a dancer and player
sweet, isn't He?
You don't think so?
Well I do, and you're not with me
but I'm praying to the Lord in
this form of devotional service.

This book has so many characters that you really need a glossary, like in the nineteenth century Russian novels, to know all the characters. I couldn't even pronounce their names in Dostoevsky. In my book, the name pronunciation is not the issue but it's to describe who they are and what they do, since they come and go like fleeting ghosts. Oh, to have your book called a novel—how I would aspire for that! But it's a genre-bender, and that's the freedom, to have fleeting characters who you hardly get to know before they're gone. One reason there's so many of them is that I can't get to know them very long, doctor's orders to have only short meetings. Another reason is they're all evasive subpersons beating around the bush.

Today an All-American hero is visiting this community and will speak in two different places. But our kind, protective host has got it lined up that I'll mostly be hiding—just as I am now, under an umbrella on the veranda—and they've got him limited to a 20-minute talk with me. My editor described this person as the All-American hero and me as the All-American antihero. At first she thought I was insulted because I didn't say anything about it in my next letter. But then I did and said I chuckled at the description, the comparison. When I see the All-American hero when I talk with him, I hesitate to bring up this comparison because he might take it wrong. He is genuinely heroic, one of the most traveling, daring and outreaching of all Prabhupāda's disciples, and very goodhearted toward everyone he meets. In fact, I even heard that someone mentioned my name to him recently when he was in Florida and he said, "Oh, he's my hero, he writes so many books." He's charitable and a nice guy. But would he understand the reference properly?

By All-American hero he might think I was teasing him, comparing him to a John Wayne macho type who boasts and exaggerates his heroics. And what's an antihero? I might tell him that in the books and movies of the twentieth century, the image of the antihero developed and people began to admire this person who broke pretensions and was cynical toward institutions, etc. That doesn't describe me either, but in the ISKCON fight against *māyā* I'm now a laid-back observer who does poke fun, sometimes even at those who would like to appear heroic. Since this man is genuinely heroic, I don't want to muddle it up with my joke.

But I prefer to hide under this umbrella and chant the bare minimum. Oh, how antiheroic can you get? Not something to be proud of at all. Not something to even talk about. "He gets so many headaches he can't chant his quota." Break the hearts, break the faith, tears from the corners of their eyes, anger. Why can't the son of a bitch chant his rounds? When *Japa Reform Notebook* came out, some leaders used to say, "What the hell is the matter with him? He's having trouble chanting his rounds?" And yet that book proved to be the most popular because so many people agree it is a struggle. One great Christian teacher said, "To enter a life of prayer is to enter struggle." Well now I know what that means.

Choose a few minutes when you have a clear head and write instead of chant? Sometimes I do it because the writing, I must admit, is as valuable as the recitation of my mechanical rounds. Well, that's a lot of straight confessing. Better get back to looking at the mosquitoes on the boards out here and holding my position while I can. I *will* have to meet the hero today, and I'll depend on my recently learned life skills to be self-assertive, decent, humble, and so on, and to be confident that he wishes me no ill. Hare Kṛṣṇa.

Mentioning names, Antihero Swami is actually Wannabe Stan Laurel Swami, and the All-American hero is Ex-U.S. Marines Swami. Both of them have been divested of their former names and impurities by surrender to Śrīla Prabhupāda, although they may maintain streaks of their former characteristics, usable now in the service of the Lord.

The author or scribe is merry and the editor is high. It's a wonderful world, this penmanship. Will you, will you, will you, will you join the dance?

Tell me what happened when
they met. We are anxious
to hear. Anxious to
meet. Avoid the meeting you
can't.

Stan is anxious. Did they
tell a Swami Prabhupāda story?
Embrace, of course.

The main thing is I'm eager
to get this down, it doesn't
matter what.

Stan is waiting. He's heard
the hero is so popular
he's being stopped along the way
at various cities and demanded to
appear to speak. "He's fun."
He has an expert musician with him.

The main thing is to get this done.
What *about* Prabhupāda?
Is he the center of your
heart? We know so much
of your advertised headaches and forgive
you but expect you to
love and serve the master in
your own invalid way writing.
But we've heard sick people
become very self-centered.
Your Prabhupāda is being carried from Ireland.

He can sit on the altar
here. Can that improve things?

Ah, the lines are filling in.
I'll get this in before they
interrupt and say, "They're here,
they want to see you briefly."
I haven't got the uniform
on exactly right, maybe
I should change it and wear a *kurtā*.
It's getting warmer.

Lord, Lord, the universe is running
under His command yet He plays in
the forest and at the same time sees
you're filling these lines from your
insect head with your non-
assertive worries and agoraphobia
and now you're even exaggerating it.

The wound is opening but
"Bemsha Swing"[50] is my
solace more than a hot tub
bath. Glory.

Is there a way to see things other than from the Vaiṣṇava world? Not for us devotees. No? Not psychology, more humane, more true love? Sing *bhajanas*, not other music. Follow the rules, the rules, the damned rules. But what if they are not authentic in their application? What if they ruined your life? Leave you waking up mornings thinking, "It's not worth it"? They have to be applied according to time and place. As the crow flies, he said, you are five minutes apart, but by car, it would be 25 minutes. Do you want to live that close to another *sannyāsī's āśrama*? Keep to yourself. He said you can read my books, order them on the Net. Tell them I don't read anymore.

Conjugate the verb. The burning of the eyes will calm down

but then it will rise again. In the in-between time, write an eloquent letter. Do your disciples love you? They go about their own struggle. Why should you want them to love you? Because that way they'll love Prabhupāda and God? You really think so?

I couldn't read a stack of mail. I couldn't bale a bunch of hay. He said the guru gets perks but in return must have unimpeachable behavior and nothing private.

I have some private stuff. What is the world without privacy? He's preaching to me that the "*ācārya*, spiritual master" must not do anything his disciples don't know. Otherwise he should retire, step down. He sits on a high seat and throws the bull. As long as it's from the *śastra* and he's a stiff-ass, they think he's good. He should never be out of uniform. He's not allowed a single serious mistake. Pop fly, Pee Wee Reese[51] gets under it. It's an important game. He muffs it! Red Barber[52] says, "Now don't be too hard on Pee Wee. I've seen him play for 10 years and I never saw him drop a pop fly." Give the guy a break. Ground ball right through his legs. He's no longer so learned.

By Kṛṣṇa's grace, we'll let you go this time. Seabiscuit[4] lost the race by a nose; second place is no good. Do you get any money for it?

What are you willing to do to give up the headaches? Try everything and only then we'll give up and say, "I guess it has to be." That was his advice today. What would I be willing to do? Not just lie down and suffer without meds, what's the use of that? The little children act bad and annoyed the day after a "program" (*sannyāsī* giving lecture in home). I don't blame them. They're schedule is upset. Too many people, noise, and a long lecture they can't understand and their mother taking them out of the room howling. The day *of* the program is also a scramble.

Are you capable of giving a *darśana*? Answering questions? They ask and you say, "I don't know," emanate holy humbleness but don't know any answers. I can't teach. Guru is one. The *dīkṣā* guru introduces and *śikṣā* reinforces (implies he's better). *Dīkṣā* isn't around anyway, on his bed in the dark.

I'm getting used to the noise of the basketball being bounced right outside my window, and the dog barking. But too many guests. "I want to get you on medical leave of absence" and see if that stops the headaches. If not, we'll know that nothing works, until you try the next thing.

You're happy and opening the
door. How long can it last?
His pain calmed down.
Confessions of an Opium Eater, *Anatomy of*
Melancholy, such strange
books written by men of the past.

None of Joe's books made the
bookstores. They were too
parochial. Who's going to read
a fellow's dreams, schemes
and indirect confessions?

All this Hare Kṛṣṇa stuff.
Does he want to be one or not?
How strict do you have to be?

I told him, "I joined the Green Berets"
and we were trained that way.
"We are not softening them up, we're
killing them!" He had to laugh.

Got a tattoo up my ass, says Mary Lou.
How far can you get from
the palatable truth? "We can talk about
Prabhupāda," he said, when he
visits. When Mrs. Mahajana visits
I'll get indigestion and
her husband Dr. S will examine my cough
while holding the scrotum
listen to the heart,
the good old loyal heart.

Lay me down to rest in some nice
place where there's grass and put
the body 6 feet down so that
gophers can't reach it until
6 months. In one instant
after you're dead your soul real self
flies to the next mundane destination.

You read this book of Goloka
but you remain in the New York barn.
You ain't going anywhere.

God wants to know the essence
bhāva-grāhī janārdana—but
He looks for whatever good
you did. Finds a speck and
promotes you.

That's how I've heard it goes:
"When I fall in love it
will be forever," let's give
Wayne Shorter[53] a round of
applause, it's all temporary.

Me and my counselor agreed
on Charles Mingus.[54]
"Do you know *Blues and Roots*[55]?"
Of course! He has a picture of
him. Reminds him of Prabhupāda
he said.

No, it's all right to say it.
Why shouldn't Prabhupāda
look like others and you're
thinking of him so much
that's why it happens.

Just give me a short meeting,

no more than 15 minutes. I've rehearsed
what to say: If I fall in love
with Rādhā and Kṛṣṇa it will be
forever or I'll never fall in
love." No persiflage. But I'll
pray something poignant I read
in his diary.

In some ways we are different.
And the moment that you say
that you feel that way too,
then I'll fall in love with you.

Going over the same things in her mind, Clare couldn't decide whether to join the band of Hare Kṛṣṇas. "Why are you serving these dogs?" the resident-guru told her when she said she was a waitress. So heavy. He seemed true. She went back to the restaurant and said she was taking the day off. Then she returned to the temple and they handed her a *sari*, "Put this on and live here." At the last moment she panicked and ran back to her job at the restaurant. Maybe she was "serving the dogs," but it was too shocking and premature for her to join them and that heavy guru. It would actually be years later that she joined the movement and in her own way, not wearing *saris*, but marrying a devotee who didn't wear *tilaka*. But they *were* devotees, and very lovable ones at that. They found a spiritual master they liked, they continued living in their own home, and he often visited. Sometimes they had "programs," and many people came. But the day after the programs, young children would be "bad" because of upset schedules and noise and too many people.

Swami Swims had been through a lot and made many mistakes. He was persevering, but his oaken boat was weathered and even leaky. He was attached to reputation and not disappointing others. He liked the new brand of devotees who moved along at their own pace, ran a business, and hired other devotees who bought homes nearby and also rarely appeared in *dhotīs* and *saris*. They blended in with the countrified upstate neighborhood yet were distinctive in their own way.

Green Beret, he called himself, and the hearer laughed. He meant I don't need a girlfriend. I'm ready to go into the mountains of Afghanistan. Well, not exactly. But I know what Frank Sinatra meant when he sang, "Love isn't what it seems, mostly other peoples' dreams." He would live in his anxiety world even if there was no solution for it, but he was planning for a medical leave of absence, as his advisor called it. We will wait a year until your little monastery there is built and we'll place you there, unplug the communications as far as possible and see if such disentanglement helps subdue headaches. If not, at least we will have tried it.

All those wonderful books he has written, Swami Prabhupāda, and this huge reading block that has formed for you. Try to read again and tell us about it, Swami Swims. You've still got miles to go, Swami, so don't quit yet. This was the article as it appeared in the local newspaper: "Wounded swami comes to live in sanatorium setting at the home of popular family." He hunched in his rocking chair and the *japa* increased.

No softie, but he's got a heart.

This is the demand of the
Foreign Legion. It's a cult
within a cult. They are gutsy
and don't allow members to
step out of line.

They threaten each other
love is not the priority.

So let it go, the deep sharing,
the most tender moments,
the tenderness brought out from
you...We are meant to

learn the *śastra* and give lectures. Our joy in
living in the covering of the holy dhamas.

And clicking *japa*.

He told me not to rush ahead
and agree to do it. But I did. To save my
neck, and remain reluctant
father to a family I
rarely see.

Do they read those books?
He's cut the cord.
May they both make it back to Godhead.

You don't have to worry about this book (writing now in a crevasse between headaches). It's guaranteed to succeed. I read it and Dat has read it and we approve. I'm not puffed up to say so. I'm saying it to increase my spirits, which sometimes sag. It's a good one. Never mind it has no plot and the Kṛṣṇa consciousness comes through material layers. It's honest, readable, lucid (for those who can see *Alice in Wonderland* and *Through the Looking Glass*), and a lively trot around the race track.

I'm eating breakfast. That critic referred to these as the "perks" of being a *sannyāsī*. That really made me mad. Make a nice breakfast for this wounded boarder. Saci is reading to me from BB. I'm trying to soak it in. The comment says the previous reference to Maharaja Parīkṣit being afraid of death (and this prompting his renunciation) was just "poetic." He's actually not afraid. Oh. I had taken it seriously and thought it was a good thing—fear prompts renunciation. In my case it's probably good. He wasn't afraid because he knew he was in Lord Kṛṣṇa's control and was going back to Godhead. I keep eating. Toast, milk ... He says when *Śrīmad-Bhāgavatam* ends, Maharaja Parīkṣit is almost dead from the bite of the snakebird but "there was some delay." So within this time he spoke to his mother Uttarā, who was so eager a devotee, whatever he had heard from Śukadeva Gosvāmī. But it appears to be higher subject matter than *Śrīmad-Bhāgavatam*. We stay tuned in during these last moments, this delay.

What will you do in yours? Can't expect to be speaking that poetry as Maharaja Parīkṣit does. Just hanging on to some rem-nant of Prabhupāda's *dhotī* in your mind, and begging forgiveness.

Now don't wear yourself out. Soon swamis are coming and you'll have to chirp up like a wheelchair veteran and show them your spirit is true to the red, white, and blue and you're proud of the troops and you'd be out there with them if you could.

I think he'll like this, he's a
special connoisseur like me.
They say a guru has no
private mind. Everyone is
supposed to know what
he does or he should quit.
What BS. Prabhupāda
had a private mind, things
we didn't know.

They don't know the human spirit
is also spirit and Trane had a
profound religious experience.

You can hear it on "India."[56]
But it's a bit repetitious and
it might be wrong to share.

Private, Sergeant, Colonel.
Private no entry.
Not for everyone.
Qualified personnel only.
You must be at least 15 years
old to see this video.

You can receive first Holy
Communion only after training and
permission from the nuns. I
remember a kid ran up to the altar and
received a wafer before he was qualified!
The nun ran after him but she was too
late. The holy Eucharist landed
on his dirty tongue by his own desire.

What's really in your heart,
in your pockets?
If it's not good enough—*especially if
you have no money*—out you
go with the tramp.

And as for spiritual merits, they
get measured by the Almighty
and it could be a big surprise
to the ecclesiastics who measure
these things while we're alive.
The tramp could go to heaven
and the big *sādhu* to hell.
The lady with good manners
to a lower *loka*, and the sassy
one higher.

Is it time to quit? The
sannyāsīs are here? All right
I'm ready to end. I don't
think I'll share this one.
It's too esoteric. India. Go back
there and see.

You owe me prose. But there's little time left. The hero asked me, "How much time do you write a day?" I said, "I call them writing sessions. They last 45 minutes. With my headaches I get to do about one a day, but sometimes I sneak in a second."

He said, "You receive Mahāprabhu's mercy when you're in the field." I told him the anecdote I like from his book. He had just finished his tour, going from town to town despite all opposition, presenting the big festival. When it was all over, he went to Hungary to celebrate Janmāṣṭamī with the devotees. Although the devotee festival was a very gala affair, his mind kept going back to the Polish people standing in their Sunday best looking up at the stage at the devotee festival. He loved them, he lived for them, he lived for giving them Kṛṣṇa. Then a pause with nothing to say.

It is true. "Goodbye, vet," said his companion. "Keep writing." Oh yes I do. I take it from the scriptures. Uttarā and Parīkṣit. I don't remember what he read at lunch.

The movement is increasing by "home programs," and devotees acting normal and mixing with their neighbors and obliging them to attend a program to which a swami comes. Hope he doesn't talk too long or over their heads. I would start like this. Our teachings come from the *Bhagavad-gītā*, which is the ABC's of Kṛṣṇa conscious knowledge. There are many books of higher knowledge. But most people in the world don't even know what's contained in the second chapter of the *Bhagavad-gītā*. Then I might go dumb. Talk some Prabhupāda stories. Half an hour is enough, ask for questions. Nowadays they love long *kīrtanas*. I can't take it. Get up and leave, lie down on a bed.

Johnny Williams and his family were clients of Rasa Prabhu, so they attended the program when he asked. They liked the sweet rice and the children until the children started screaming and were asked to leave.

The philosophy makes common sense. The preachers are well-trained and exercised. They eat a lot in between lectures and then move on to another lecture. Always ready to sing and speak. It makes sense. *Bhagavad-gītā* written five thousand years ago. If someone objects or asks about the place of women, he's ready because he's heard all the questions before, deft and evasive if need be. Humorous, friendly, authoritative. It's all in the scriptures, by the method of hearing from authority, the highest proof.

He plays it better, the poor
ignorant *brāhmaṇa* Gopal
was at Prayag and he didn't
even know the loud *kīrtanas*
were pure praise of God.
He said, "What's this racket?
Why don't you stop and do some
useful work?" Some *sādhakas* told
him to get lost, some just laughed,
but a few compassionate ones took
the time to explain to him the
meaning of the loud *saṅkīrtana*.

Swami Swims needs an explanation
too, why it's so long and so loud
and the same mantra repeated.
He doesn't speak up to get
chastised. He *thinks*
though, like Gopal did, why all this ruckus
for so long

when I could be quiet or
hearing a preferred sound?
He spoke up, please tell
me so I can get the ecstasy too
and be willing to travel miles
carrying my little baby just to
hear more *kīrtana* and authoritative
speech of Kṛṣṇa.

I don't know much
about it so I hang on until it's
over and ask some kind
person on the side, "Does
it have to be so loud,
does it have to be so—so?"

That ignorant was Gopal
that he didn't even know
and yet he chanted always
the Gopāla mantra and it
worked—stupid or mechanical
it works and thus I
Swami Swims am benefiting
even in my stupor.

Sergeant Joe dreamt that he walked into a shady gypsy place. He consulted a woman who was a representative of a so-called mystic gypsy named Grammas. This representative changed the appearance of Sergeant Joe, making him a little taller, better looking, and she cured his headaches! But at the same time she changed the appearance of Joe's sister, who suddenly appeared in the store, and his sister's two children disappeared! Joe's parents heard about this and were very angry and got on Joe's case. Then a message appeared from the sky saying that Grammas was a bona fide and very powerful personality who could change peoples' sexes, bring the dead back to life, cure any disease, and many other wonderful things by her powers inherited from higher beings. She explained that the two children had been taken away from the sister because they were mistreated and in a state of malnutrition. They would be returned in six weeks in healthy condition. And it was true, six weeks later the children returned looking healthy and hearty.

But the Hare Kṛṣṇa people got on Sergeant Joe's case and asked him why he was messing around with a goddess named Grammas. Why did he go into the gypsy shop? Joe listened submissively to their chastisements, which weren't followed with any punitive measures, but he thought to himself, who is this Grammas and what does she have to do with Kṛṣṇa? Will I actually be cured of the headache at some time? Should I pursue some kind of "worship" or seek contact with Grammas? The people in the gypsy shop seemed like low-down cheaters in a way, and there was even some suggestion of sex. Money was in the air. So he didn't want to go back there. But he had certainly tasted some power of Grammas, especially in her defensive letter, which appeared from the sky. Grammas... Grammas... was she anything like Giovanni, the common man he met in the market who spoke some common wisdom? Makes you think of gramophone. An odd combination of letters which may in the future be unwound and revealed as more connected to Kṛṣṇa consciousness. Wait for the bright light. I certainly don't want to go to Grammas. By hearing the readings of *Bṛhad-Bhāgavatāmṛta* Sergeant Joe knew the highest goal was the spiritual world of Goloka. There was no mention of any Grammas. We know from Vedic literature there are so many gods and demigods and price tags connected to them and their worship. They can give you benedictions but not eternal life. We want to hear the name Kṛṣṇa.

I promised my friend today that I would try to improve my *sādhana*, chant 16 rounds. That's the important step up.

We may meet persons in our dreams who are combinations of persons in our past and present lives, coincidences or actual persons of minor powers. Don't go with them. Go with Prabhupāda.

He ate his snack. Never feels well enough. No guts to go into the gym. "I don't do anything." The waves come and go, not solid and clear. No inspiration to put on a jumpsuit and paint. I'll change as Kṛṣṇa desires, I seek no boons from Grammas. I do not know our Lord except from the confident quotings and arguings, the utter convictions of Śrīla Prabhupāda and the deep, unfathomable light of his eyes. That's enough to go on. And his successful campaign.

Sitting in the park with Mary Lou/you'll never be blue, until it's over. A big groundhog in the clover, too massive for the kitten. In his questions and answers, the Swami is a master. In the feasts the ladies prepare, there is more than enough to give you indigestion, in the running around of their children, there is joy and annoyance until their parents finally carry them out. The veteran rocks in his rattan straw chair and waits for it to be over. He has almost no knowledge of how to pray. Rain in May. The material world was created by God, and

Bhaktivinoda Ṭhākura says it's amazing, although in another sense it's nothing but an illusory castle in the woods.

The wise one led us to
understanding the soul,
first step. The body can't
move without the soul.

And the soul is commanded by
the Supersoul. Join our movement.
Then everyone will take to it,
the wise one said. But if
just a small percent of
leading persons take, the
Kali world can be saved.

Saved me. Institution grew
in strange and tumultuous
ways, even the wise one
was challenged and criticized
by the evil force of the age,

even by his own disciples.
It always happens.

He's always peaceful because
in direct shelter of the Lord,
sweet Kṛṣṇa.

He knows the ultimate conclusion of Vedanta.

You should listen to
him. Follow his ways.
And stay closer.

You have to work for it
and be tested. You'll slip
and fall. Get up, you'll be
forgiven. The wise one
will lend a hand. Extend your own.

21

CHAPTER TWENTY-ONE

What do you want to be when you grow up? A fireman. She told me, "Pick up your *sādhana* and we may meet in the spiritual world." "What's it like there?" They are released from quotas. I hear they naturally love Kṛṣṇa, *crazy* about Him. Disdain the impersonal void and even the formal worship of Vaikuṇṭha, ask yourself, honestly, how could a fallen person like me make it in one jump after this patched, faulty lifetime? A friend said he realized it can and *likely will* happen because Śrīla Prabhupāda will be there at our death and take us. I believe he could do it. Maybe, though, he'll consider we need some intermediate *loka* for further purification in devotional service. He may want us to help with the preaching in the material worlds. We should accept that gratefully.

The soul is in the body and it doesn't die but flies off to its next destination perfectly arranged by one's deeds, reactions and mercy of guru and Kṛṣṇa.

The preceding paragraph was written by Junior Barks, an offspring of Hare Kṛṣṇa devotees, and an 8-year-old student at the Rudolf Steiner[57]–inspired Waldorf School. I showed him the manuscript of this book and he was appalled by its lack of straight *śastra* and orderliness. I tried to convey to him the impression Swami Swims was trying to make in his writing, but Junior couldn't comprehend. Too young and straight. He didn't understand why I "jumped like a frog" and said it's not directly Kṛṣṇa conscious. I told him how Kṛṣṇa likes indirect Kṛṣṇa consciousness, but he'd never heard of that and guessed it wouldn't apply to what I was doing. So I accepted his sentence because he's right, a book of sober theology is required. But I like it the way I do it, and there are plenty of straight theological students and teachers to fill that need. Perhaps I'll let Junior Barks add some more here and there when I get overcome with digression, laughing gas, attachment to the "truth" of what my senses perceive, and other disorders. It's too late for me to go back in time and get the right parents and attend the right school. If you could, would you?

All the things you are
a mixture of granola and
bread and rice cakes with
spreads, too heavy a breakfast
for me. But I eats it.

Junior Barks' critique on the brain?
Not really, regard him as a square.
Pray to my Lord as all-encompassing
and taking my offering too. Know it
comes from joy of being alive,
gratitude of His allowing me
to do anything at all.

Somehow it comes out this way
whales and porpoises, Iraq war
for nothing, an ayatollah in charge,
Muslims, Hindus, Christians,
Prabhupāda said they're just nominal.
Kṛṣṇa consciousness teaches the science of God.
Whoever lives with uninterrupted devotion is a lover
of the one God Allah, Christ, Kṛṣṇa, Buddha.
All the things you are,
revisited, seen anew, the actual objects,
the real people with their flaws.

Come to see this man and see
how bad he is physically by examination,
inquire of each member of the family
how they are doing,
downside reported by me, upside reported
by Saci to Dr. Ravi Singh.

I say they're consistent, chronic, several-a-day,
Saci says "but we're not using the more powerful meds,
a head bath often works."

This is cable TV, the smallest
world for a family who are interested.

Junior Barks phoned Swami Sam. Junior said he was talking to a representative of Torchlight Press. He showed them one of his little essays. They said if he gathered a manuscript, they would print a book for him. So he would not write for Swami Swims anymore, and he wanted back the one paragraph he'd written.

"That's okay," said the Swami, "I wish you luck in your career." He hung up the phone thinking, "But I won't give up that one paragraph he gave me. I never signed a contract or anything. Besides, I can write like that too. It's just my memory. And I don't have any books here except *Śrīla Prabhupāda's Ślokas.*"

The invocation praises the spiritual master. You can't attain spiritual advancement without him. He's the direct representative of God and should be treated as good as God. He never makes mistakes or eats ice cream cones or looks at pretty women or goes to non-ISKCON movies. Even if his complexion isn't perfect or he has a broken nose from his previous life, or if he's ill now, these shouldn't be seen as disqualifications. His disciples shouldn't attempt to instruct him, neither should anyone else attempt to instruct him. He's humble as pie and always wears his *tilaka* and brahminical thread. Go to him and inquire from him, "What is cloning?" "Was the U.S. right in bombing Iraq?," and be willing to serve him. The critical student of the spiritual master becomes the next spiritual master. Ecumenical red tape is involved in the institution, but you can't have an institution without the laws and cops. This applies too for making spiritual masters. The invocation is called '*maṅgalācaraṇa*' when you pray to the gurus generically, then your own guru, then Śrīla Prabhupāda and the gurus in the Gaudiya *sampradāya*, and then the Vaiṣṇavas, Lord Gaurāṅga, the Pañca-tattva, and Śrī Kṛṣṇa Himself:

he kṛṣṇa karuṇā-sindho
dīna-bandho jagat-pate
gopeśa gopikā-kānta
rādhā-kānta namo 'stu te

"Oh my dear Kṛṣṇa, oh ocean of mercy, oh friend of the distressed and the source of the creation, oh master of the cowherd men and the lover of the *gopīs*, especially Rādhārani, I offer my respectful obeisances unto You."

Swami Sam thought, "I wish I had a better, more *rasikā* name. But Sam is Śyāma, right? Okay, don't complain. Whatever name the guru gave. I can remember if I have a book and read a few verses." It's like drinking whisky, as Father Jack does. Once you get a few shots, you get warmed up. Get going with a few verses, be confident the memory will open and connect to other subjects spiritual and to personal anecdotes. Gun the accelerator, know you've only got to go 30 minutes. Are you actually convinced, and do you want the people in the audience to become Kṛṣṇa conscious? Pray for that, just do it and it will come. If Junior Barks and Well Studied, much blessed heroes, can do it, I can too, even though I've been out of practice for so long. It's something you never forget. You're unique, although simple ABC. The soul, a bright shining star, an actual person one ten thousandth the tip of the hair, resides in the heart. When he's liberated he assumes his spiritual body. Don't bother me with technical terms. Be confident in what you first learned and admit you never heard the rest. Come to our house and speak, they ask. You promise you will. You have no home, which is proper for a *sannyāsī*.

He said, "There are mice in the shed."

"Which shed?"

"The art shed."

"What? Do you think I'm going in there dancing around mice while I paint?"

What then? Kill them? Don't paint? Just get in ecstasy and imagine you don't see them skitter by? That's the world. I wonder if Torchlight would take me on. I could write on the "I" in Walt Whitman's *Song of Myself*, and how we Kṛṣṇa conscious people don't believe what he's saying, that he's the locomotive and the mother and the elm tree and the mice in the art shed. Literary view from the Hare Kṛṣṇa viewpoint. Write them and see what they think.

Dear old Stockholm, I was
there where midnight is
sunny, the chiropractor is
not coming tonight, you are
free to relax and count up your
beads, *just hear.*

Let the subpersons relax.
My favorite songs in an album
offered to Lord Kṛṣṇa.
Don't be disappointed, Prabhupāda
says. Get up and try again.
The Lord will accept your
sincere effort. I'm not
forgetting and neither is He
the attempts in Boston,
to overcome your timidity and cowardice.

The artist in me is the
best devotee because he's
most joyous. They didn't
give him enough time to stretch
out. Cut him down. Didn't understand his approach,
"too long and inept"—what rubbish. He's our man.

Swami Prabhupāda is the
founder-*ācārya* and that's it.
Anything else is distasteful.

Now I have to go, they'll be in
to administer pills and
crack your back. Test
your blood and genitals.
"Are you sexually active?"
"No sir, I'm celibate,
don't you know what saffron means?"

All these fools don't know
God rules, they want to enjoy
forever and make money—
we want the songs and praise
of God but they don't sell.

I asked a traveling preacher what he lectures on, since he doesn't use consecutive verses of *Śrīmad-Bhāgavatam* as they do in the temple. He said he speaks from whatever he's personally studying. That seemed to be a sensible, inspiring and non–labor-intensive way.

Swami Swims then thought, "What do I study?" Nothing. Yeah, I'm talking about the invalids in the New York sanatorium. They wave their ISKCON flags when the preachers go by. They climb the stairs slowly (and out of duty only) to attend the evening lecture. They say things they don't mean just to get along. "Yes, I thought the *kīrtana* was great." But they don't study because they can't read due to some malady or other. It hurts too much to read, their arthritis prevents it, or poor eyesight, the volunteer who agreed to read to them had to run out to do errands. And most of the day they are—valiantly let's say—licking their wounds and surviving.

They study the chiropractor's beard. The stunning smile of a worker at the dentist's office, even when she smiles with her mouth closed. Of course, none are saints, so with self-absorbtion they study their pain's intensity. They think about the visitors in anxiety. So you can't lecture on that stuff. They think, "Lecturing is Prabhupāda's mood. So if I get well again I can do it and speak on what I'm studying."

The fat groundhog, big as a large cat. The kitten is afraid to go outdoors. The children get really upset, run indoors crying. What happened? Pushes her father aside hysterically and runs to her mother. Study the schedule the host gives them. Remember to be grateful. Looking for a good night's sleep. They are not so eager to go into the gymnasium to build their muscles because it may exacerbate their pain, and they are lazy too, but the doctor says no, go to exercise even if you are reluctant. The caretakers encourage them. They're doing much better, but if that's true, it's by baby steps.

He said do it your way.
Reclusive or meeting people,
but what you want,
who you are.

I've got to stay close to the meds
and the bed and a caretaker as
sweet as Saci. As sweet as
you are, he imitates the birds,
what's wrong with that?

I'm starting to tell you about
the subpersons in this sanatorium
and what they lack and how
they're growing up and becoming more alert.

They're chanting their prescribed *japa*.
Melancholic? I wouldn't say so but
a touch of that in the horn
of the fated Booker Little[58]
was prophetic. If he could
have lived much longer, Eric[59] too,
to celebrate the Lord as they strongly desired.
I've been given some time
so don't waste in "poor quality
of life," lying around on couches

in beds, watching the time go by.

Don't die premature. Study
Bṛhad-Bhāgavatāmṛta. Hear your
master's lectures. "Everything is
in Prabhupāda's books because
he teaches humility and humility
is everything."

Take me on a ride with You.
Even if I'm reluctant, I'll
go out and exercise. But if
it hurts too much I'll have
to back out. I am not made
of sterner stuff.

Dependent. Whoa. Joy in
words. And seeing friends.
Be grateful for every mouthful,
an opportunity to be kind
and render service. The
bonesetter wouldn't
take a fee. "Pass it on," he
said. So here is my payment
Dr. Michael, tall bearded man,

although you may not understand
my language. Don't go too long or
you'll be unwanted, the babies will
cry, and boredom will pervade the
hall. You can come back
tomorrow or even this evening.
Go now and drink your
two quarts of H_2O and remember
Kṛṣṇa is the taste of water.

The inmates are in beds early after a rough day. It's an open dorm with a few private rooms. How long will this go on?

Even when lights go out they talk and listen to noises in the walls. Some stay up completing their *japa* quotas. No more visitors, at last. Darkness. Will the *siṁhāsana* arrive without cracks in it from transit? I don't want to write goofy so I won't order a new book by a poet they said was goofy. War on pain. Be religious and meet you in the spiritual world.

Humorous description of Gopal in Prayag. He's dumb, yet he goes on chanting his Gopāla mantra, given by Kāmyaka. Therefore he makes advancement. Other forms of God don't attract him. He needs a guru and better association, however, to attain the lotus feet of the object of the sixteen-syllable mantra. I like hearing how he is dumb and even offensive, yet he makes advancement because he's so determined to chant—until he much enjoys chanting—this highest mantra. What a lucky fellow. If he just persists he'll make it.

Take that as a lesson, my friends. Monitor comes through dorm and asks the *japa* chanter and the chatterers to cease all sound. It's time for needed sleep so the body can serve Kṛṣṇa. Let's get to know the individuals. An all-male ward. They'll play and pray in the morning. Some have special friends. But in the eating times, all hear about Gopāla. That's their study. This scribe is too wounded to do more this evening. Shouldn't have written a certain letter, should write other letters. Oh Lord, help me to persevere and take whatever comes. And may I remove all blockages in devotion to my master, understand his love for me and accept his individuality.

Take it easy. I'll sneak in a
lullaby. Hurt eye he's telling
his friend. Shouldn't write
then. People aren't quiet as
they should be. It's too late
to meet. I'll see you tomorrow.

Rest in Kṛṣṇa's arms
figuratively and real someday. Eons away but your
spiritual master is for this lifetime.
Don't throw it away. Make it grow.

Your strategies. He told me
not to be so risky, because I
live in an institution. We
know what they did but
some are still hiding out.

The secret police can wreak havoc.

So many friends are coming and I
try to meet them. They sit
by your bed in the ward (have you a private room?)
and talk only an hour.

Tell some laidback tales
but try not to forget you are
bhaktas and should chant
and hear. Run out of gas, why push it?
Tomorrow is another day. A day
of up and down. I can't
take any more tonight.

Each subperson on his own now,
own dreams and troubles,
but one God and that's why we are
in the Prabhupāda ward.
Don't kick us out even if we
never recover. We are grateful.

Up early in the morning and saying their *japa*. Some sitting up in bed, some sitting in their chairs, some walking back and forth. Some were allowed to use clickers because their minds couldn't concentrate using the beads and they didn't know which way they were going to count properly. But most had beads in the *japamala*. The monitor didn't allow the chanting to get too loud because some inmates were disturbed. Lucky ones in the private rooms. And how the minds went all over the universe. Picking up trivia, dwelling on troubles, going blank and falling asleep. And those small periods of yearning to actually hear, to actually understand that this was the most important thing in the day. Not embarrassed in front of the others because we all know it's a struggle. If someone was actually advanced and tuned into the value of the Holy Name, well good for him, we're not envious. We want his association. Hare Kṛṣṇa Hare Kṛṣṇa Kṛṣṇa Kṛṣṇa Hare Hare/Hare Rāma Hare Rāma Rāma Rāma Hare Hare. That's all there is to it, the simple repetition of those names. Lord Caitanya made it as easy as can be, so a fool can do it, can handle the precious gem and get benefit. What to speak of a learned *brāhmaṇa*?

An hour goes by. Some have chanted more than others. All are encouraged. And then they take a break.

Spaced out. Reviewing a Laurel and Hardy plot. Faces float by. Something someone said. Drink water and pee. Just hear, just hear. Look over at another inmate and see how he's doing. He has allergy and the pollen count is record high; he's scratching his eye, which makes it worse. "I can't help it." One nods out and becomes aware others are looking at him so he picks up his head and chants loudly and distinctively for awhile. Where is the inner experience of the mantra? Gopal sometimes *saw* the Deity of his mantra. We mostly just see heads and feet, some have decorative bead bags, ink-stained, and the clickers. Everyone is making at least some progress.

The Holy Name is absolute. Even if you chant mockingly or by accident or the sounds aren't spaced—words like "ramada"— still, it has the effect of chanting the Holy Name. The inmates knew this and so they chanted, knowing even a poor recitation was the most important thing to accomplish in a day. The numerical strength is also important. So don't excuse yourself. Meet you in the spiritual world. Don't fall behind.

The sun began to pour through the window blinds. Another day had begun. They filed into the temple room to watch a few *brāhmaṇas* undress and bathe and redress Rādhā-Govinda. Then they went down for breakfast. There was an early-morning guest so they got prepared to see him and embrace him, half-regretful that it would take away some *japa* time. But they tried for it later. Hare Kṛṣṇa Hare Kṛṣṇa Kṛṣṇa Kṛṣṇa Hare Hare/Hare Rāma Hare Rāma Rāma Rāma Hare Hare.

Inmates recover in this way. They live in harmony under the shelter of the Holy Name.

Light blue, chipped teeth,
mashed hand, my good friend
brings an unbroken *siṁhāsan*
across the sea and now
Rādhā-Govinda and Prabhupāda
are joined happily on the little
altar in Rādhā's barn.

We can climb the stairs and
sit on our rockers and
listen to Swami sing a half
hour and join in the chorus.

We can bathe them in the morning.
No time to do Prabhupāda in
weakened condition. Pray to him
early in the morning even
if it takes a walk upstairs,
you can do it. Hare Kṛṣṇa
music and art.

Light blue means
he's not outgoing but he's happy
he gets to go near the
japa quota and he's so
dependent on dear friends
who don't mind taking care of
him even though he's
a grownup man.

He's making it up, he
never loved and read
like he said in his
younger days. He's making up
everything as he goes along
praying to keep a decent reputation.

He's keeping to the outskirts but
meeting famous people as they
come through. They lecture to
crowds and give him a little
private time in his private
room of the sanatorium.

Keep the tune. To a friend
who does not mind he plays
"Coming on the Hudson"[60] and
says "I just like it always
even though now I'm an
enrolled renunciate for
my whole life."

I dig it says A
and they don't let the others hear
because they couldn't understand a monk
loving God in his own
way each one, and God accepts them all.

"I got an astrology reading," said Bhakta Tim on his bed, "and it said if I could handle it, a pilgrimage would be good for me for a few weeks in October and November this year. But I'd have to have someone help me administer my medicines and so on."

Some of the other subpersons gave their different opinions that he probably wasn't up to it but some said it was an excellent idea and he ought to get off his duff and go and get the mercy.

One of them quoted from the *Bṛhad-Bhāgavatāmṛta* which had just been read to them at lunchtime where it said that the highest goal can be attained by chanting the Holy Names of God *and* visiting holy places.

Another remarked, "But it's such a strain to go to India, so austere for a weak fellow like you, Bhakta Tim. You have to take astrology with a grain of salt. It could turn out to be a nightmare. You know you'd meet up with all kinds of people you don't like. And your regulated life like we have in the sanatorium wouldn't be possible. But what do I know? There's great benefit in going to the *dhama* they say, and that's an absolute truth."

"Maybe if some of you guys went with me," Tim said, "you could help me get through it."

"I ain't going nowhere," said Anuttama dāsa. "We have a very good deal right here for being with good people, being taken care of, and there's no shortage of hearing and chanting. We're in the best circumstances. So don't throw that away in a premature trip to wild India."

"But it's not 'India,'" said another. "That's just the covering. If Bhakta Tim goes, he'll have to suffer the covering to get to the inside. He'll have to be prepared for that. Good things don't come so easily."

"You're getting your pains every day right here, in the best situation for an invalid. How can you fly off and act like a rigorous renunciate? And look, you have a cane, and you have to wear those orthopedic shoes. You wouldn't even be allowed in the temple."

"Don't put him down. Encourage the idea. If not this year, then the next."

There was an important statement for me when Gopa-kumāra was about to tell his own life story to the *brāhmaṇa*, when they were together in Vṛndāvana. One might think to talk about oneself is not bona fide. Gopa-kumāra didn't want to appear puffed up talking about himself. But he knew talking about what he had gone through to reach the goal of perfection was the best way to instruct the *brāhmaṇa*. So he was confident and went ahead. The commentator says, "Experience is the best form of proof." There may be other statements about the best form of proof, but there it is in *Bṛhad-Bhāgavatāmṛta*, and I rejoiced to see it and present it to you now. Even if your experience is not the experience of one who has reached the goal of truth, describing it is the best way of instructing someone or telling them what is real, what is true. Mary Oliver entitles her latest poetry book, *What Do We Know?* We know what we have experienced, that's for sure. It may be faulty knowledge, but we know it happened. The person who hears from us will get authentic stuff. Even if it is a tale of woe, an uncouth tale, a tale of what we should *not* do. Of course, the experience of a perfect person is perfect proof in the very best sense. But I have taken it to mean that the experience of a struggler is also the best way to get a particular kind of truth. He's not bluffing, and you can learn from him. In other words, one form of teaching by experience means, "Do as I did," and the other is, "Don't do as I did," and both are instructive and even inspiring.

Bhakta Tim had so many worries, and now a new one to add to the others. He was in the sanatorium—and not on the front lines in the battle against *māyā*—because he was a Worrier and it caused him diabetes and arthritis and other diseases. He was thinking he'd let a friend run a horoscope on him, and the news came back that Rāhu, the dark, evil planet that covers the sun, would often visit him. If he could live past age 71, lots of good things would manifest, but it was unlikely he'd live that long because of something about Jupiter mixing with another planet at a bad time and Rāhu moving in again. Tim worried like anything. His pro-astrology friend said, "Ask the astrologer if there's something you can do to offset this shortened longevity."

"It's just bullshit," said Swami Swims. "If you start listening to those guys, you won't be able to make a bowel movement unless they tell you it's okay. You already have a guru in Prabhupāda. Chant Hare Kṛṣṇa and all the palm lines in your hands will change. And if you're going to die at 70, so what? Get on the move and chant your beads and step up your advancement. Anyone of us may go at any moment, regardless of the stars' prediction. Remember from Shakespeare,

"The fault, dear Brutus, is not in our stars,
But in ourselves that we are thus or thus." (from *Julius Caesar*)

When is snack time? When is rest time? When do the babies play in the backyard? A friend writes and says, "It was in Hawaii (ISKCON) that I found I was Prabhupāda's son (after depression from a divorce) but in Māyāpura I found my heart," cried tears there everyday and wants to make yearly visits. But you can't enter the temple with shoes on. You are expected to stand a lot and hear the class. He could do it and he loved it. Don't exile yourself. The sanatorium is also a sacred place, and they're getting a bigger altar for Prabhupāda and Rādhā-Govinda, with drawers for all their clothes. Go up there and chant. Discursive prayer, mantra meditation with an unsteady mind. Humble and grateful. Stay out of the firing line.

Why don't you visit our house? Why don't you look forward to the next dentist's visit? The subpersons get the call from the monitor. They have to go to the gym and exercise, like it or not. Drill time, visitors' time. Don't take a pill unless you absolutely need it. Left, right, left, right, left, right, oblique march, about face, left, right...

They just had a little difference,
and it spoiled their performance.
You've got to play as lovers and
good humble friends to
discover the best in the group.

Looking for Kṛṣṇa. He's everywhere.
Some place is concentrated. Make your
own temple in the heart. I
don't have time to read a
Christian book, *Difficulties in*
Mental Prayer, sent
in the mail, but they said you can
talk to God even at awkward times
when you can't sleep
or you're in the
doctor's waiting room.

All those magazines in waiting
rooms. All the fits you can
get from worries and threats.
Take it to God. A friend advises
you often write in your books
use everything for Kṛṣṇa so
why not try psychic path
and pray to the Lord
"Could you please relieve me
from these pains?" Remember
Rūpa Gosvāmī said material things
unused in the Lord's service
are *phalgu-vairāgya*.
Higher is to use everything for the Lord.

I'll write to him and tell him I
am, to a limit. Except I don't
know how to pray. But I do
talk to a counselor and we
hash it out and he's very good.

I blew it again. Should have
let the authorities enjoy
having the upper hand. I
wrote back pushing the envelope,
reminding them of their own
wrongs and stating that compassion
is best.

Counselor said it was a mistake.
"But that's you. You take risks
you're innovative." Just be
careful it doesn't get you hanged
at the gallows.

Be more legalistic and cool and
that you have just been

given the "Get Out of
Jail Free"[61] card. There's no more
to say then. Not like Sgt. Bilko.
When he's defeated, he touches
his authority on the shoulder and
says, "Two for flinching."

I'm okay I think but I must learn
to seek legal advice before
I move so fast into blabbing
about compassion to those
who seem more concerned
with judgment and fines.

Under dark stars, said Bhakta Tim, I've been under dark stars and dangerous planets for a year and a half. I made it through by the skin of my teeth, the astrologer said. Death was in the sky. Does that mean bright skies and starry nights are ahead? I sure hope so. So much anxiety, worry, wrong on my part. Wondering how it would manifest in this material world. Because I want to be a good boy. "How I want to be loved!" said Charles Lamb,[62] "And what I will do to be loved!" Only two more years to become a senior citizen and get social security. But if Rāhu passes, a worse scenario…no, I shall not worry myself to death. Everything is under control of the Lord.

A life of peace
you can't have all the time.
Bumps in the road

they point you to the Lord,
even if you're unseated.
"Mahāprabhu's mercy is to
those in the field." What
about those in the sanatorium?

Those who are moms busy
with their kids? The *sannyāsīs*
have a special role to play.

He's calming us, assuring us,
but the sharp edge is warning us,
you live in an institution and
there are rules. Tote them.

Peace is something deep.
Lord Rāma had it even when he was
exiled, Yudhiṣṭhira too and
Haridāsa Ṭhākura while being
whipped. They were under the
control of Kṛṣṇa and did not
care for the influences
of demons or in the case of a *sādhaka*,
reactions to their own wrongs. "This was
coming to me. I am not suffering as an
orphan but under the protection
of my Father, who is righting me."

PEACE

So don't complain.
Cry. I don't deserve...but
now I see a light of dawning
Prabhupāda's son,
heart found in Nadia.

Kṛṣṇa is a living being and wants you back,
you are transcendental
to the influence of those
malefic planets. If you
just call out *hari-nāma*
and see the holy *dhama* at
least in your mind's eye,
tomorrow?

NOTES

CHAPTER ONE

1 Joe Louis (1914–1981). Joe Louis—"The Brown Bomber"—held the world heavyweight boxing title from 1937 to 1950, a longer period than any man in history. He successfully defended his world championship title 25 times. His overall professional record was 69 victories and 3 defeats; of his 69 wins, 55 were by knockout.

2 John William Coltrane (September 23, 1926 – July 17, 1967) was an American jazz saxophonist and composer. Starting in bebop and hard bop, Coltrane later pioneered free jazz. He influenced generations of other musicians, and remains one of the most significant tenor saxophonists in jazz history. He was astonishingly prolific: he made about fifty recordings as a leader in his twelve-yearlong recording career, and appeared as a sideman on many other albums, notably with trumpeter Miles Davis. As his career progressed, Coltrane's music took on an increasingly spiritual dimension.

His second wife was pianist Alice Coltrane, and their son Ravi Coltrane is also a saxophonist. He received a posthumous Special Citation from the Pulitzer Prize Board in 2007 for his "masterful improvisation, supreme musicianship and iconic centrality to the history of jazz.".

CHAPTER TWO

3 Sgt. Bilko is a character played by actor and comedian Phil Silvers (1912–1985) in the situation comedy, *You'll Never Get Rich*. The program aired from 1955 to 1956 and satirized life in the U. S. Army.

4 Charlie "Bird" Parker (1920–1955). Alto saxophonist who is generally accredited with being the creator of bebop jazz, the first truly modern jazz style (prior to the rise of bebop, jazz was a form of dance music). In the summer of 1937, Parker played an extended engagement in a band led by Tommy Douglas and George E. Lee at a resort in Eldon, Missouri. During this time, Charlie did a great deal of woodshedding and greatly improved his technical proficiency on the saxophone. Also during this period he became addicted to heroin. In 1939, Bird headed for New York, where he joined the great Earl Hines band and emerged as one of the foremost creative forces in

modern jazz. From 1945 to 1946, Bird traveled to California with the Dizzy Gillespie band, but the California crowds were hostile to the bebop style. In 1946, while in California, Bird attempted suicide. This led to a 6-month stay at the Camarillo State Hospital. In 1949, Bird was again in New York, playing at the newly opened Birdland. In 1955, at the age of 34, Bird succumbed to heart failure, pneumonia, and cirrhosis of the liver.

Charlie Parker's importance to the history of jazz cannot be overstated. Saxophonist Phil Woods, who has performed with Dizzy Gillespie, Thelonious Monk, Oliver Nelson, and others, relates his impressions upon first hearing a recording of Charlie Parker when Woods was 15 years old:

"I brought my first copy of *Koko* to the rehearsal of the kid band I was with: Carmen Ravosa and His Rhythm Aires. (My father always called us Carmen Ravosa and His Riveters.) They laughed like hell when I put it on the turntable in the living room, where all the aunts and uncles would sit and watch us rehearse. I cried as I told them that it was the greatest music ever. I quit the band and went home and listened to Bird for hours on end. I went through three copies of *Koko* that year. It was the first Bird solo I ever transcribed.

"I read in *Down Beat* that Bird liked Stravinsky's *Firebird Suite* and Schoenberg's *Pierrot Lunaire*. I dutifully checked out both items from our well-stocked city library and listened to this music. My parents thought I had completely "wigged out," to use the argot of the day. Jazz was one thing, but 12-tone caterwauling of a contralto was something else.

"As I sit and write today, I can look over my computer and see the inscribed photo: 'To Phil, "Charlie Parker."' The only problem is that the handwriting is mine. Yes, I was so smitten by Bird I forged his autograph! My morals are neither better nor worse than most mortals, but this strange act has always amazed and confounded me. I used to get autographs and had an extensive collection. Woody Herman's trumpet section signed phony names: Neal Hefti wrote 'Bunk Johnson,' Sonny Berman wrote 'Max Kaminsky,' and I forget what Pete Candoli signed. So I was an honorable autograph collector; I always had a pen and a neat book. I was shy but not that shy—and I had seen Bird play on 52nd Street, so I could have gotten it. The photo shows a young, handsome Charles Christopher Parker, Jr. The eyes are clear and focused, and the fingers caress the horn, resting just off the keys, like a well-trained classical saxophonist. Bird sports a double-breasted pinstripe suit with a jaunty (natty?) polka-dot tie. It is a photo of a man who is about to change the world. And I love the quotation marks: 'Charlie.'

5 *Father Ted* is an award-winning British television comedy that aired in the U.K. from 1995 to 1998. The show recounts the misadventures of three nearly-defrocked Irish Catholic priests exiled on remote Craggy Island (well-known as having the most consistently awful weather in the world). Father Ted Crilly, played by the late Dermot Morgan, was sent to the remote parish after going on holiday to Las Vegas with money intended for a sick child (as Ted explains, "The money was just resting in my account.") Assisting Father Ted is the junior priest Father Dougal, a dim, blindingly optimistic lad who has no apparent knowledge or understanding of Catholicism. Then there is aged, intrepid (and arguably demented) Father Jack, whose propensity is to sit in a chair shouting, "Girls! Drink! Arse! Feck!" Rounding out the team is Mrs. Doyle, a housekeeper who keeps a vigilant eye on the Parochial House and its guests and who cannot stop making tea. The irreverent comedy is today enjoyed by television audiences in the U.K., Canada, and the United States.

6 Sarah Vaughan (1924–1990). Storied jazz vocalist who by the age of 20 had become a well-established figure in the jazz world for her bebop jazz stylings. *The Penguin Guide to Jazz* relates the following about Sarah Vaughan: "Never as popular as Holiday or Fitzgerald—and some would say, better than either."

CHAPTER THREE

7 Milton H. Erickson, M.D. (1901–1980) is widely acknowledged as having been the world's leading practitioner of and authority on hypnotherapy, and he is one of the world's greatest clinical psychotherapists. His influence in psychology and psychotherapy extends to solution-focused therapy, systemic family therapy, child psychology, so-called brief therapy, and sports performance.

8 Wayne Shorter (b. 1933). Composer and tenor saxophonist Wayne Shorter is one of the most prolific jazz recording artists of all time. He was a member of Art Blakey's Jazz Messengers and the Miles Davis Quintet. In 1970, he and Joe Zawinul founded Weather Report. In a brief period in 1964 he recorded Night Dreamer, Ju Ju, and Speak No Evil, three albums that are considered masterpieces. Wayne Shorter continues to perform to audiences throughout the United States.

CHAPTER FOUR

9 Archie Bunker is a character played by Carroll O'Connor on the television program *All in the Family*, which aired from 1971 to 1979. Archie was a cigar-smoking, conservatively patriotic, bigoted New Yorker who worked as a loading dock foreman. Archie Bunker is the role for which actor Carroll O'Connor is best known; Carroll O'Connor died in 2001 at the age of 76.

10 Crazy Horse (1849–1877). Lakota Sioux war chief who, along with Chief Sitting Bull, led a combined force of 2,500 warriors to victory at the Battle of the Little Bighorn (Custer's Last Stand) in 1876.

CHAPTER SIX

11 SK refers to Søren Kierkegaard (1813–1855), Danish philosopher and theologian.

I first found out about Søren Kierkegaard from a philosophy professor in whose class I lectured. After my lecture, he congratulated me. He recommended that I read Søren Kierkegaard because he was a theistic philosopher and gave good arguments for the existence of God. I was intrigued and set about it. I can't remember which books I read first. Kirkegaard is hard reading—even the scholars admit it. His style is not easily accessible, and he sometimes writes in a roundabout way. He's also very intellectual. I got a lot out of reading his two-volume biography. I also read many books about Kirkegaard and got to understand the man as well as his thinking. He was very appealing to me as a devotee of Kṛṣṇa. His classic spiritual book, *Purity of Heart Is to Will One Thing*, is a tour de force of defining pure devotional service without any taints, just as in Rūpa Gosvāmī's verse, *anyābhilāṣitā-śūnyaṁ*—pure devotional service can contain no *karma* or *jñāna*. Kierkegaard shows very systematically that if you have anything else in your approach to God except the pure desire to love Him, then yours is not pure devotion. I sent the book to Bhurijana Prabhu, who liked it very much. He said Kierkegaard was incredibly intelligent, but that he thought his devotion was more from the head than from the heart.

After all, Kirkegaard is a world-class philosopher, and so we can't expect him to be anything less than intellectual. And that's part of his strength for us as devotees. He can fight off all the intellectual atheist philosophers, not only of his time but up to the present time and in the future. He writes so strongly in favor of the existence of God, and he writes very strongly against merely nominal religionists.

What I liked about Kierkegaard was his emphasis on the individual as subjectivity. A philosophical historian once said that before Kierkegaard, philosophers studied God in an objective way—His existence, His omnipotence, His omniscience, etc. But Kierkegaard said the more important thing is to study one's individual relationship with God, since these "objective" qualities are inconceivable anyway. How pure is your relationship with God? How honest? These are the real important questions of theology.

One of my favorite examples that Kierkegaard gave is about how you can't enter the spiritual Kingdom of God by belonging to a nominal religion, nor can you enter en masse, just by belonging to a church. The example was that thousands of people are trying to storm the gates of the king to get his audience. They think that if they can burst open the gates, they can all get in and there will not be individual examination. They will be pushed in by the forward movement of the crowd, unexamined. But the gatekeeper is actually very strict and does not allow this mob entrance. Each person is examined individually as to his qualification for getting to see the king. At the time of Kierkegaard, Lutheranism was the official state religion of Denmark. Kierkegaard believed in the dogmas of Lutheranism, but he said there was actually not a single Christian in the state of Denmark, because all were taking it superficially and not giving up their material *anarthas*. He said it would be preferable if people were honest and admitted their faults, that this would be more pleasing to God, rather than claiming in a puffed-up way that they were ideal Christians. *He had a passion for truth*.

Kierkegaard lived only until he was 42. They used to call him "little Kierkegaard," and he had a slight bend to his shoulder, making him stoop-shouldered. He got into an argument with a popular satirical magazine, and they used to mercilessly mock him issue after issue, pointing to trivial things such as the fact that he wore his trousers slightly short. This mockery caught on, and the people of Denmark used to tease him wherever he went. Kierkegaard used to love to walk in Copenhagen and talk to ordinary people as part of his daily routine. But after this mockery began, he could not even go out for his beloved walks. He did not have to work because his father left him a sizable inheritance. So he worked at home every day at his desk, writing and publishing some 30 books and a journal that was twice as big as all of the books. He was leaving the bank with the last of his legacy when he collapsed in the street and had to be taken home to bed, where he died.

In his will, he asked that his tombstone simply say, The Individual. But his conservative relatives would not allow this and had his tombstone inscribed with his name and the dates of his birth and death. College students who were in favor of Kierkegaard protested this, and there was almost a riot in the cemetery when the tombstone was put in place.

Bhurijana Prabhu is probably right to say that Kierkegaard wrote more from the head than the heart. But powerful intellect was the *śakti* that God had given him. He did not write simple songs like Francis of Assisi. However, by his dedication to God consciousness and his exposure of hypocrisy in religion, he certainly proved himself a man of heart who hungered for love of Kṛṣṇa and for the distribution of His glories all over the world.

12 Lester "Prez" Young (1909–1959). Pioneer jazz tenor saxophonist Lester Young is particularly known for his work with the Count Basie Orchestra during the 1930s and 1940s and for his recordings with Billie Holiday, with whom he shared a lifelong friendship and from whom he received the nickname "Prez." There are two accounts as to the origins of this nickname. In one account, the name was short for "President of Jazz" or "President of Saxophonists"; in another account, the name was short for "President of the Viper's Club" (in the 1930s, "viper" was hipster jargon for a person who smoked marijuana). Young had a colorful way of speaking — he tended to call everyone (including Count Basie) "Lady"; it was he who gave Billie Holiday the nickname "Lady Day," and he referred to Ella Fitzgerald as "Lady Time." He has been attributed with having introduced the word "bread" as slang for "money."

CHAPTER EIGHT

13 Sonny Rollins (b. 1930). Widely considered to be the greatest living jazz saxophonist, Sonny Rollins rose to prominence in the golden age of jazz improvisation in the 1950s and 1960s, collaborating with Charlie Parker, Lester Young, Dizzy Gillespie, Miles Davis, Clifford Brown, Max Roach, Thelonious Monk, John Coltrane, Coleman Hawkins, and others. In 1956, Rollins, who is a self-taught musician, suffered from anxiety related to his feeling that he could not live up to the reputation he had achieved. He subsequently took a 2-year sabbatical from recording and performing. During this period, he lived on Manhattan's Lower East Side. To escape his cramped apartment and to avoid disturbing his neighbors, Rollins would practice his saxophone on a catwalk high atop the Williamsburg Bridge, overlooking the

East River and the New York City skyline. These practice sessions became legendary. Says Rollins, "I was just looking for a place to blow my horn." His album *The Bridge* was released in 1962. Through the influence of John Coltrane, Rollins became interested in yoga and Zen Buddhism. From 1966 to 1972, Rollins took yet another sabbatical, during which he traveled to India, where he studied in a yoga *āśrama*. Sonny Rollins continues to record, to perform, and to practice daily.

14 Ornette Coleman (b. 1930). Revolutionary saxophonist who initiated free jazz, characterized by a disregard of conventions of harmonic, rhythmic, and melodic structure. Coleman has been heralded by composers Leonard Bernstein and Virgil Thompson for his innovations in jazz. In addition to his contributions to jazz, Coleman has composed string quartets, woodwind quintets, and symphonic works, and he has influenced composers Harry Partch, Charles Ives, and John Cage.

15 Cecil Taylor (b. 1933). Recognition came late to classically trained, innovative pianist/composer Cecil Taylor, who in the late 1960s and early 1970s held jobs as a record salesman, cook, and dishwasher. Virtually all the music Taylor produced from 1967 to 1977 was recorded in Europe. In 1973 Taylor started his own record label, Unit Core. Determinably avant-garde, Taylor is one of the most originally innovative figures in jazz and was one of the founders of the free jazz movement in the 1950s. He was elected by *Down Beat* magazine's Critics' Poll to the Down Beat Hall of Fame in 1975.

16 Anthony Braxton (b. 1945). Composer, multi-instrumentalist, teacher, and conductor, Anthony Braxton has recorded widely and performed throughout the world. In 1970, he and Chick Corea studied scores by Stockhausen, Boulez, Xenakis, and Schoenberg together, and he joined Corea's Circle. He made his bandleader debut in 1972 and played solo at Carnegie Hall. Braxton's extraordinary output makes him one of the leaders of the avant-garde.

17 Harold Lloyd (1893–1971). "The King of Daredevil Comedy, " Harold Lloyd is best remembered as the young man dangling precipitously from the face of a clock tower in the 1923 silent-film classic Safety Last. Harold Lloyd was one of the most popular and highly-paid stars of his time. Bright-faced, bespectacled and sporting a skimmer, Harold Lloyd's multidimensional film persona — which he referred to as the "Glass Character" — is both funny and moving.

18 Ralph Branca (b. 1926). Right-handed pitcher for the Brooklyn Dodgers (1944–1953, 1956), Branca is famous for throwing the pitch that New York Giants' Bobby Thomson hit for a three-run, ninth-inning homer to cap the Giant's historic comeback win of the National League pennant in 1951. Thomson's homer, the "shot heard round the world," is regarded by many to be the most famous home run in baseball history.

CHAPTER NINE

19 Harry Langdon (1884–1944). After spending 20 years traveling with minstrel shows, circuses, burlesque, and vaudeville, Harry Langdon joined Mack Sennett's film company in 1923 at the age of 39 and attained stardom. His film persona was juvenile in appearance, clumsy, wide-eyed, and all together trusting in the world's goodness.

CHAPTER TEN

20 "Oleo," a jazz composition by saxophonist Sonny Rollins. "Oleo" was originally released in early 1963 on *Sonny Rollins: Our Man in Jazz*, a live recording of a much-heralded performance at the Village Gate in New York's Greenwich Village during the summer of 1962. "Oleo" has been recorded by many jazz artists, including John Coltrane and Miles Davis.

21 William Carlos Williams (1883–1963). Arguably the greatest American poet of the twentieth century, Williams experimented with meter and lineation while taking as his subject matter the everyday circumstances of life and of the experiences of common people. He had a major influence on the poetry of Allen Ginsberg and the Beats; he wrote the introduction for Ginsberg's first book of poetry, *Howl and Other Poems*, published in 1955.

22 Alice B. Toklas (1877–1967). Born in San Francisco, Alice B. Toklas was a close associate and intimate confidante of Gertrude Stein in Paris.

23 Gertrude Stein (1874–1946). Avant-garde American writer, Stein's home in Paris became a salon for leading European artists and writers in the period between the world wars. She was well respected for her literary and artistic judgments. Stein and her brother, the art critic Leo Stein, were among the first collectors of the paintings of Pablo Picasso, who painted her portrait, and the Cubists. She attempted to apply the aesthetic theories of Cubism in her writings. The only book of hers to reach a wide public was the memoir *The Autobiography of Alice B. Toklas*, published in 1933.

24 Miles Davis (1926–1991). Trumpeter Miles Davis was the most consistently innovative musician in jazz from the late 1940s throughout the

1960s. He is considered to be one of the all-time great melodic soloists and a master of restraint. Davis, together with saxophonist John Coltrane, is an important figure in the development of modal jazz, in which composition is based on a small number of modes, or scales, rather than chord changes. In 1982, at the age of 56, Davis suffered a stroke that left his left hand partially paralyzed and that forced him to retire from performing. He took up painting as a form of physical therapy and quickly established himself as a serious artist. His artwork has been well reviewed and has been exhibited in cities around the world.

25 Frederick "Fritz" Perls (1893–1970). Originator, in collaboration with Paul Goodman, of Gestalt psychotherapy.

26 Donald Hall (b. 1928). Prize-winning American poet and author.

27 George Herman "Babe" Ruth (1895–1948). Baseball player Babe Ruth, the "sultan of swat," led the American League in slugging average 13 times; home runs, 12 times; runs batted in, 6 times; and batting, once (in 1920, with a .378 average). In 1927, Ruth hit 60 home runs—a record that was not surpassed until 1961, when Roger Maris hit 61. Ruth remains the all-time leader in slugging percentage (.690).

CHAPTER ELEVEN

28 "The Wreck of the Hesperus," one of Henry Wadsworth Longfellow's best-known poems, was published in 1842. It portrays the loss of the schooner Hesperus in a snowstorm off Gloucester, Massachusetts. The poem was inspired by a series of storms—the so-called triple hurricanes of 1839—that struck the northeastern United States in December of that year. Over 1,000 vessels and 40,000 lives were lost during these storms.

29 Trumpeter Dizzy Gillespie's oft-recorded jazz standard "Night in Tunisia" is regarded by some jazz historians as having ushered in the bebop style. Gillespie wrote "Night in Tunisia" in 1942 while a member of Earl Hines' band. Gillespie's close friend Charlie Parker was also a member of the Hines band at that time.

30 George Herman "Babe" Ruth *see*: note 27 Chapter 10.

31 Gilbert Ray "Gil" Hodges (1924–1972) was first baseman for the Brooklyn Dodgers from 1943 to 1957. During his career Hodges won three Golden Glove awards (1957–1959), drove in 100 runs in seven consecutive seasons (1949–1955), hit 370 home runs, and was an eight-time All-Star. On August 31, 1950, Hodges tied the major league record by hitting four home runs in one game. In the 1952 World Series between the New York Yankees

and the Brooklyn Dodgers, Hodges was hitless in 21 at-bats; during this slump, prayers were said for the first baseman in churches throughout Brooklyn.

32 Roy "Campy" Campanella (1921–1993) was catcher for the Brooklyn Dodgers from 1948 to 1957. Campy caught in five World Series, won the National League's Most Valuable Player award in 1951, 1953, and 1955, and was the first black catcher in Major League Baseball. He was inducted into the Hall of Fame in 1969.

CHAPTER TWELVE

33 Jonathan Winters (b. 1925). A top-name American comedian whose career became established through television appearances on the Jack Paar Show, the Steve Allen Show, and the Tonight Show in the 1950s and 1960s.

CHAPTER FOURTEEN

34 Billy the Kid aka Henry McCarty (November 23, 1859—July 14, 1881). Best known as Billy the Kid, but also known by the aliases Henry Antrim and William H. Bonney, was a 19th-century American frontier outlaw and gunman who participated in the so-called Lincoln County War. According to legend, he killed 21 men, one for each year of his life, but he most likely participated in the killing of fewer than half that number.0.

CHAPTER SIXTEEN

35 Poet Samuel Taylor Coleridge (1772–1834).

36 George Herman "Babe" Ruth *see*: note 27 Chapter 10.

37 Bill Evans (1929–1980). Shy, modest, articulate pianist Bill Evans' reputation became solidified in the jazz world through his work on Miles Davis' classic album *Kind of Blue*, recorded in 1958. In the course of his career, Evans recorded with some of the top names in jazz, including John Coltrane, Charles Mingus, Art Farmer, Stan Getz, and Oliver Nelson. His playing had a significant influence on the pianists Herbie Hancock, Chick Corea, Keith Jarrett, Marc Copland, and others. Evans was a prolific and profoundly creative artist and a genuinely compassionate, gentle person.

38 "My Foolish Heart" is a standard written by Ned Washington and Victor Young in 1949 and recorded by Bill Evans on his classic album *Waltz for Debbie*, released in 1961.

CHAPTER SEVENTEEN

39 Rainer Maria Rilke (1875–1926). German writer and poet who died of an infection he contracted after pricking himself on a rose thorn.

CHAPTER EIGHTEEN

40 Sgt. Bilko *see*: note 3 Chapter 2.

41 Brand of cigarettes.

42 "Bee Vamp." Jazz composition by trumpet player Booker Little. "Bee Vamp" was recorded live at the Five Spot, in New York City's Cooper Square, on July 16, 1961, by a storied quintet consisting of Booker Little, Eric Dolphy, Mal Waldron, Richard Davis, and Ed Blackwell.

43 With a gap in his teeth and a crooked grin — and the byline, "What? Me worry?" — Alfred E. Neumann has graced the cover of every issue of Mad magazine since 1955. The young boy who posed for the caricature of Alfred E. Neumann is now a senior member of the Hare Kṛṣṇa movement.

CHAPTER NINETEEN

44 Thelonious Monk (1917–1982). Master jazz pianist and composer whose collaborations with Dizzy Gillespie, Charlie Parker, and Kenny Clarke helped establish bebop.

45 John Coltrane *see*: note 2 Chapter 1.

46 Cecil Payne (1922-2007). Although he is one of the finest baritone saxophonists to emerge in the bebop era, Brooklyn-born Cecil Payne has been underrated and overlooked throughout his long career. He was a key member of Dizzy Gillespie's big band (1946–1949) and has worked with numerous artists, including Woody Herman, Count Basie, John Coltrane, Machito, and Lionel Hampton. Payne was a high-school classmate of the great jazz drummer Max Roach.

47 Murray and Kowit. Friends of Satsvarūpa dāsa Goswami while he was living on the Lower East Side in New York City in 1965 and 1966, before meeting Śrīla Prabhupāda.

48 Golf professionals.

49 Jean Francois Champollion (1790–1832). French linguist Champollion is regarded as the Father of Egyptology for his having deciphered hieroglyphics from the Rosetta Stone. He research in hieroglyphics began in 1808 and culminated in 1824.

CHAPTER TWENTY

50 "Bemsha Swing" is a track from Thelonious Monk's album Brilliant Corners.

51 Pee Wee Reese (1918-1999) was the captain of the dominating Brooklyn and Los Angeles Dodgers teams of the 1940s and 50s. He was an outstanding

defensive player and never missed an inning of the seven World Series in which he participated. He was elected to the Hall of Fame in 1984.

52 Red Barber (1908-1992) From 1939 through 1953 Barber served as the voice of the Brooklyn Dodgers. During his 33-year career Barber became the recognized master of baseball play-by-play, impressing listeners as a down-to-earth man who not only informed but also entertained with folksy colloquialisms such as "in the catbird seat," "pea patch," and "rhubarb" which gave his broadcasts a distinctive flavor.

53 Wayne Shorter (b. 1933). Composer and tenor saxophonist Wayne Shorter is one of the most prolific jazz recording artists of all time. He was a member of Art Blakey's Jazz Messengers and the Miles Davis Quintet. In 1970, he and Joe Zawinul founded Weather Report. In a brief period in 1964 he recorded *Night Dreamer*, *Ju Ju*, and *Speak No Evil*, three albums that are considered masterpieces. Wayne Shorter continues to perform to audiences throughout the United States.

54 Charles Mingus (1922–1979). Master bassist and brilliant composer who worked with Louis Armstrong, Kid Ory, Lionel Hampton, and Red Norvo from 1941 to 1953. In the 1950s, Mingus recorded with Charlie Parker, Miles Davis, Bud Powell, Art Tatum, and Duke Ellington. In the mid-1950s, Mingus formed his own recording and publishing companies, and founded the Jazz Workshop, a group that enabled young composers to have their works performed and recorded. Mingus recorded over a hundred albums and wrote over three hundred scores.

55 *Blues and Roots*. Released in 1959, *Blues and Roots* is a masterpiece of original compositions and is one of Charles Mingus' greatest albums.

56 "India," a song from John Coltrane's album *Impressions*, released in 1961.

CHAPTER TWENTY ONE

57 Rudolf Steiner (1861–1925). German philosopher and clairvoyant who endorsed a mystical philosophy involving imagination, defined as a higher seeing of the spiritual world in revealing images; inspiration, defined as a higher hearing of the spiritual world through which the creative forces and creative order of the spiritual world are revealed; and intuition, by which penetration into the sphere of spiritual beings becomes possible. Steiner's books include *Truth and Knowledge*, *The Philosophy of Freedom*, and *Mysticism and Modern Thought*. He was one of the editors of the Standard Edition

(Sophien Ausgabe) of Goethe's Complete Works.

58 Booker Little (1938–1961). Memphis-born trumpet player and composer Booker Little had become a well-established jazz trumpet virtuoso before his untimely death from kidney failure at the age of 23. Booker's virtuosity complimented that of Eric Dolphy, and their collaborations constitute Booker Little's best-known work. His sister, Vera, is an accomplished opera singer who has recorded with the London Opera.

59 Eric Dolphy (1928–1964). Jazz virtuoso on saxophone, bass clarinet, and flute and brilliant composer who died at the age of 36 from complications of undiagnosed diabetes. His album *Out to Lunch!*, recorded in February 1964, is one of the most important jazz albums of the 1960s.

60 "Coming on the Hudson," a jazz composition by Thelonious Monk recorded live at the Five Spot Cafī in August, 1958, and released on the album *Thelonious in Action*. Accompanying Monk were Johnny Griffin, Ahmed Abdul, and Roy Haynes.

61 In the board game "Monopoly," a "Get Out of Jail Free" card enables a player to get out of jail without paying the usual $200 fine.

62 Charles Lamb (1775–1834). English critic, essayist, and the lifelong friend of poet Samuel Taylor Coleridge. In 1796, his sister, Mary Ann Lamb (1764–1847), in a fit of temporary insanity, attacked and wounded their father and killed their mother with a knife. To save her from a life in an asylum, Charles had himself declared her guardian, and after 1799 they lived together. They collaborated on several books for children.

GLOSSARY

Glossary of Sanskrit Terms

Spelling used in this book (shown in brackets) complies with ISO 15919;2001 an international standard for "Transliteration of Devanagari and related Indic scripts into Latin characters"

A

Acharya (ācārya)—a spiritual master who teaches by his personal behavior.

Anartha (anartha)—unwanted thing; material desire.

Aparadha (aparādha)—offense.

Arjuna (arjuna)—one of the five Pāṇḍavas. Kṛṣṇa spoke the Bhagavad-gītā to him on the Battlefield of Kurukṣetra.

Ashram (āśrama)—a spiritual order: *brahmacārī* (celibate student), *gṛ*hastha (householder), v*ā*naprastha (retired), sannyāsī (renunciate); living quarters for those engaged in spiritual practices.

B

Babaji (bābājī)—one who devotes the major portion of his life to solitary devotional practices, especially chanting the Lord's names.

Bhagavad-gita (bhagavad-gītā)—lit., "song of God." The discourse between Lord Kṛṣṇa and His devotee Arjuna, expounding devotional service as both the principal means and the ultimate end of spiritual perfection.

Bhakti (bhakti)—devotional service to the Supreme Lord.

Bhaktisiddhanta Saraswati Thakur (bhaktisiddhānta sarasvatī ṭhākura)—the spiritual master of His Divine Grace A.C. Bhaktivedanta Swami Prabhupāda; an ācārya in the Gaudiya Vaiṣṇava sampradāya.

Bhakti-vaibhava (bhakti-vaibhava)—understanding Kṛṣṇa's manifestations by devotional service; secondary devotional degree awarded by Vaiṣṇava institutions.

Bhaktivinoda Thakur (bhaktivinoda ṭhākura)—an ācārya in the Gaudiya Vaiṣṇava disciplic succession; the father of Bhaktisiddhānta Sarasvatī Ṭhākura.

Brahmin (brāhmaṇa)—one wise in the Vedas who can guide society; the first Vedic social order.

D

Dandavats (daṇḍavats)—lit., "like a stick." To offer prostrated obeisances, extending one's limbs in a straight line.

Darshan (darśana)—vision; audience; philosophical system.

Dasa (dāsa)—lit., "servant" (masculine). An appellation that, along with a name of Kṛṣṇa or one of His devotees, is given to a devotee at the time of initiation.

Dhama (dhāma)—abode; the Lord's place of residence.

Dharma (dharma)—the duties prescribed by one's nature and social position; ultimately, dharma means devotional service to the Supreme Lord.

Dhoti (dhotī)—a garment wrapped on the lower body of men, commonly worn in India.

Diksha-guru (dīkṣā-guru)—the spiritual master (guru) who initiates (dīkṣā) the disciple into the chanting of the Hare Kṛṣṇa mantra.

G

Gaudiya Vaishnava (gauḍīya vaiṣṇava)—a follower of Lord Caitanya Mahāprabhu.

Gayatri (gāyatrī)—a prayer chanted silently by brāhmaṇas at sunrise, noon, and sunset.

Gopa (gopa)—a cowherd boy; one of Kṛṣṇa's eternal associates.

Gopi (gopī)—a cowherd girl; one of Kṛṣṇa's most confidential servitors.

Gurudeva (gurudeva)—one of many titles that may be used in addressing one's own spiritual master.

H

Haribol (haribol)—"Chant the holy name."

Haridas Thakur (haridāsa ṭhākura)—a great devotee

of Lord Caitanya Mahāprabhu; known as the *nāmācārya*, the master who taught the chanting of the holy names by his own example.

Hari-nama (hari-nāma)—lit., "the name of the Lord."

Harinam (harināma)—public chanting of the Hare Kṛṣṇa *mahā-mantra*.

I

Ishopanishad (īśopaniṣad)—one of the principal Vedic scriptures known as the Upaniṣads.

J

Japa (japa)—individual chanting of the Hare Kṛṣṇa mantra while counting on beads.

Jaya (jaya)—an acclamation meaning, "Victory!" or, "All glories!"

Jiva Goswami (jīva gosvāmī)—one of the Six Gosvāmīs of Vṛndāvana.

Jiva (jīva)—the individual, eternal soul or living entity; part of the Supreme Lord.

K

Kali-yuga (kali-yuga)—the present age, which is characterized by quarrel and hypocrisy.

Karmi (karmī)—one engaged in karma (fruitive activity); a materialist.

L

Lila (līlā)—pastimes.

Loka (loka)—planet; celestial plane or destination.

M

Maha-mantra (mahā-mantra)—the great chant for deliverance: Hare Kṛṣṇa, Hare Kṛṣṇa, Kṛṣṇa Kṛṣṇa, Hare Hare/ Hare Rāma, Hare Rāma, Rāma Rāma, Hare Hare.

Maharaja (mahārāja)—great king. Also used as a title of respect for a sannyāsī.

Maya (māyā)—the external, illusory energy of the Lord, comprising this material world; forgetfulness of one's relationship with Kṛṣṇa.

Murti (mūrti)—a form, usually referring to a deity.

N

Nama (nāma)—the holy name.

Nrisimha (nṛsiṁha)—the half-man, half-lion incarnation of Lord Kṛṣṇa who appeared to save Prahlāda Mahārāja from Hiraṇyakaśipu.

P

Pancha-tattva (pañca-tattva)—Kṛṣṇa as manifested in five different features in the pastimes of Lord Caitanya: The Lord—Śrī Kṛṣṇa Caitanya; His plenary portion—Śrī Nityānanda Prabhu; His incarnation—Śrī Advaita Ācārya; His energy—Śrī Gadādhara Prabhu; and His devotee—Śrīvāsa Prabhu.

Param padam (paraṁ padam)—the supreme situation. May refer either to the spiritual world or the impersonal brahmajyoti effulgence.

Parampara (paramparā)—the disciplic succession of bona fide spiritual masters.

Prabhu (prabhu)—lit., "master." Added to a devotee's name to show respect.

Prabhupada, A.C. Bhaktivedanta Swami (prabhupāda)—founder-ācārya of ISKCON and foremost preacher of Kṛṣṇa consciousness in the Western world.

Prahlada (prahlāda)—a great devotee who was persecuted by his demoniac father, but who was protected and saved by Lord Narasiṁha.

Prajalpa (prajalpa)—foolish, idle, or mundane speech. Talks unrelated to Kṛṣṇa consciousness.

Prasadam (prasadām)—lit., "mercy." Food that

has been spiritualized by offering it to Kṛṣṇa and that helps purify the living entity.

Prema (prema)—love of Kṛṣṇa as in kṛṣṇa-prema.

Pujari (pūjārī)—a priest, specifically one engaged in temple Deity worship.

Purnima (pūrṇimā)—the full moon day. Gaura-pūrṇimā is the festival of apearance of Lord Caitanya.

R

Radha(rani) (rādhā-rāṇī)—the eternal consort and spiritual potency of Lord Kṛṣṇa.

Radhika (rādhikā) —(see: Rādhārani)

Raganuga (rāgānuga)—devotional service fol-lowing the spontaneous loving service of the inhabitants of Vṛndāvana.

Ratha-yatra (ratha-yātrā)—an annual chariot festival in which the Deity of Lord Jagannatha is pulled in procession on a ratha (chariot).

Rupa Goswami (rūpa gosvāmī)—one of the Six Gosvāmīs of Vṛndāvana.

S

Sabda (brahma) (śabda)—transcendental sound, considered by Vedic philosophy to be self-evident proof of knowledge.

Sabji (sabji)—lit., "vegetables."

Sadhaka (sādhaka)—one who practices regulated devotional service.

Sadhu (sādhu)—saintly person.

Sahajiya (sahajiyā)—a class of pseudo-devotees who take the conjugal pastimes of Kṛṣṇa and the gopīs cheaply and who do not follow the proper regulations of vaidhī-bhakti.

Sankirtan (saṅkīrtana)—the congregational chanting of the holy name, fame, and pastimes of the Lord; preaching.

Sannyasa (sannyāsa)—renounced life; the fourth order of Vedic spiritual life.

Sannyasi (sannyāsī)—one in the renounced order of life.
Shastra (śāstra)—revealed scripture.Shyama (śyāma)—a name of Kṛṣṇa, meaning "blackish".
Siddhanta (siddhānta)—the perfect scriptural conclusion according to Vedic tradition.
Siksha (śikṣā)—instruction.
Sloka (śloka)—a stanza of Sanskrit verse.
Sravanam (śravaṇam)—hearing about Kṛṣṇa.
Sri (śrī)—a prefix used as an honorific.
Srila (śrīla)—a term of respect given to a spiritual master.
Srimad-Bhagavatam (śrīmad-bhāgavatam)—the Bhāgavata Purāṇa, written by Śrīla Vyāsadeva, which specifically points to the path of devotional love of God.
Sukadeva (śukadeva gosvāmī)—the sage who originally spoke the Śrīmad-Bhāgavatam to King Parīkṣit just prior to the king's death.
Swamiji (svāmījī)—lit., "great master." A common term of respect addressed to sannyāsīs. *Also*: Swami

T

Tilak (tilaka)—auspicious clay markings that sanctify a devotee's body as a temple of the Lord.
Tirtha (tīrtha)—holy place of pilgrimage.

V

Vaishnava (vaiṣṇava)—one who is a devotee of Viṣṇu or Kṛṣṇa.
Vishnu (viṣṇu)—a fully empowered expansion of Kṛṣṇa.
Vraja (vraja)—Vṛndāvana.
Vrata (vratā)—vow.

Y

Yajna (yajña)—sacrifice or a ceremony of a fire sacrifice.